Japanese Tourism and Travel Culture

This book examines Japanese tourism and travel, both today and in the past, showing how over hundreds of years a distinct culture of travel developed, and exploring how this has permeated the perceptions and traditions of Japanese society. It considers the diverse dimensions of modern tourism including appropriation and consumption of history, nostalgia, identity, domesticated foreignness, and the search for authenticity and invention of tradition. Japanese people are one of the most widely travelling peoples in the world both historically and in contemporary times. What may be understood as incipient mass tourism started around the seventeenth century in various forms (including religious pilgrimages) long before it became a prevalent cultural phenomenon in the West. Within Asia, Japan has been the main tourist-sending society since the beginning of the twentieth century, when it started colonizing Asian countries. In 2005, some 17.8 million Japanese travelled overseas across Europe, Asia, the South Pacific and America. In recent times, however, tourist demands are fast growing in other Asian countries such as Korea and China. Japan is not only consuming other Asian societies and cultures, it is also being consumed by them in tourist contexts. This book considers the patterns of travelling of the Japanese, examining travel inside and outside the Japanese archipelago and how tourist demands inside influence and shape patterns of travel outside the country. Overall, this book offers important insights for understanding the phenomenon of tourism on the one hand and the nature of Japanese society and culture on the other.

Sylvie Guichard-Anguis is a researcher at the French National Centre of Scientific Research (CNRS) and works as a member of the research group 'Spaces, Nature and Culture' in the Department of Geography, Paris-Sorbonne (Paris IV). She is co-editor of *Globalizing Japan* (Routledge, 2001); *Crossed Gazes at Cultural Heritage in the World* (in French and English, 2003) with the collaboration of UNESCO; and co-author of *Grand Hotels in Asia, Modernity, Urban Dynamic and Sociability* (in French 2003, Korean translation 2007).

Okpyo Moon is Professor of Anthropology at the Academy of Korean Studies, Korea. She is the author of *From Paddy Field to Ski Slope: Revitalisation of Tradition in Japanese Village Life* (Manchester University Press, 1989) and the editor of *Consumption and Leisure Life in Contemporary Korea* (1997); *New Women: Images of Modern Women in Japan and Korea* (2003); and *Understanding Japanese Culture through Travel and Tourism* (2006).

Japan Anthropology Workshop Series

Series editor:
Joy Hendry, Oxford Brookes University

Editorial Board:
Pamela Asquith, University of Alberta
Eyal Ben Ari, Hebrew University of Jerusalem
Hirochika Nakamaki, National Museum of Ethnology, Osaka
Kirsten Refsing, University of Copenhagen
Wendy Smith, Monash University

Founder Member of the Editorial Board:
Jan van Bremen, University of Leiden

Japanese Tourism and Travel Culture

Edited by Sylvie Guichard-Anguis and Okpyo Moon

Routledge
Taylor & Francis Group

LONDON AND NEW YORK

First published 2009 by Routledge
2 Park Square, Milton Park, Abingdon, Oxon OX14 4RN

Simultaneously published in the USA and Canada
by Routledge
270 Madison Avenue, New York, NY 10016

*Routledge is an imprint of the Taylor & Francis Group,
an informa business*

© 2009 Editorial selection and matter, Sylvie Guichard-Anguis and
Okpyo Moon; individual chapters, the contributors

Typeset in Times New Roman by
Swales & Willis Ltd, Exeter, Devon
Printed and bound in Great Britain by
MPG Books Ltd, Bodmin

British Library Cataloguing in Publication Data
A catalogue record for this book is available from the British Library

Library of Congress Cataloging in Publication Data
   Japanese tourism and travel culture / edited by Sylvie
Guichard-Anguis and Okpyo Moon.
      p. cm.—(Japan anthropology workshop series)
   Includes bibliographical references and index.
   1. Travelers—Japan.   2. Tourism—Japan.   3. National
characteristics, Japanese.   I. Guichard-Anguis, Sylvie, 1951–
II. Moon, Okpyo, 1950–
   G330.J35 2008
   306.4'819089956—dc22   2008023494

ISBN13: 978–0–415–47001–8 (hbk)
ISBN13: 978–0–203–88667–0 (ebk)

ISBN10: 0–415–47001–3 (hbk)
ISBN10: 0–203–88667–4 (ebk)

Contents

Figures

Tables

Notes on contributors

Millie Creighton is a Japan specialist and Associate Professor of Anthropology in the Department of Anthropology at the University of British Columbia, where she serves as a faculty member of the Institute for Asian Studies, and on the executive management boards of both the Centre for Japanese Research and the Centre for Korean Research. She has done extensive research in Japan on department stores, consumerism, tourism, popular culture, minorities, ethnicity, work and leisure, place, nostalgia and identity. She was awarded the Canon Prize for her analysis of contemporary Japanese identity and nostalgia as reflected through department store retailing and other forms of consumerism. She has conducted and published research on contemporary tourism campaigns invoking a modern Japanese desire to reinvigorate icons of Japanese identity, such as taiko drumming, or past way of life, such as heritage silkworm cultivation and silk weaving.

Nelson Graburn was born in London and educated in natural sciences and anthropology at Cambridge University, McGill University and the University of Chicago (1963). He has been employed as a research anthropologist by the Government of Canada, the University of Chicago and Northwestern University. He has taught at the University of California, Berkeley, from 1964 to the present, and has served as Curator of North American Ethnology at the Hearst Museum of Anthropology since 1974, and as Co-Chair of the Canadian Studies Program since 1986. He has also served as a visiting professor and researcher at the National Museum of Ethnology, Japan, 1979, 1989–90; at the Centre des Hautes Etudes Touristiques, Aix-en-Provence, 1980; at the National Museum of Canada, Ottawa, 1982; and at the Research Center for Korean Studies, Kyushu University, Fukuoka, in 2005. His teaching and research interests include: kinship, social structure and the history of anthropology and ethnographic methods; Canada, Inuit, circumpolar peoples; visual anthropology, art and social change; Japan, Korea, China, Ainu tourism and cultural conservation; heritage, museums, material culture, symbols and nationalism. He has curated five major exhibitions at the Hearst

Museum, published or edited 21 books, and written over 200 articles, chapters and reviews. He is now working on a volume on contemporary Japanese multiculturalism, and is continuing his work with Canadian Inuit culture, history and heritage.

Sylvie Guichard-Anguis as a researcher at the French National Centre of Scientific Research (CNRS) is a member of the research group 'Spaces, Nature and Culture' in the Department of Geography, Paris-Sorbonne (Paris IV). She is also an administrator of the Centre of Research on Asia, Paris-Sorbonne (Paris IV) (CREOPS). Her research interests include cultural heritage, tourism, tea culture and children's illustrated books in Japan. She co-edited *Crossed Gazes at Cultural Heritage in the World* (in French and English) with the collaboration of UNESCO (PUPS, 2003) and co-wrote *Grand Hotels in Asia, Modernity, Urban Dynamic and Sociability* (in French, Publications de la Sorbonne, 2003; Korean translation, Humanitas, 2007).

Joy Hendry is Professor of Social Anthropology at Oxford Brookes University, Director of the Europe Japan Research Centre, and a Senior Member of St Antony's College, Oxford University. She has carried out fieldwork in various parts of Japan, but principally in the Yame-shi tea-producing area of Kyushu (Fukuoka-ken) and in the fishing community and holiday resort of Tateyama-shi in Chiba-ken. She has also travelled widely within Japan and in several other countries, where she always tries to put her Japanese research in a global context. Her most recent work attempts to place the situation of the Ainu people of northern Japan in the context of other indigenous peoples. Her publications include *Wrapping Culture: Politeness, Presentation and Power in Japan and Other Societies* (Oxford University Press, 1993) and *The Orient Strikes Back: A Global View of Cultural Display* (Berg, 2000).

Okpyo Moon is Professor of Anthropology at the Academy of Korean Studies, Korea, and has been Edwin O. Reischauer Visiting Professor of Anthropology at Harvard University (2000–01) and a Visiting Professor at the National Museum of Ethnology, Osaka, Japan. She has carried out extensive research on both Japan and Korea focusing upon family and gender, urban and rural community making, ethnic minorities, tourism, popular culture and heritage maintenance policies, etc. Her major publications include *From Paddy Field to Ski Slope: Revitalisation of Tradition in Japanese Village Life* (Manchester University Press, 1989); *Consumption and Leisure Life in Contemporary Korea* (Academy of Korean Studies, 1997, editor and co-author); *New Women: Images of Modern Women in Japan and Korea* (Cheongnyeonsa, 2003, editor and co-author); and *Understanding Japanese Culture through Travel and Tourism* (Sohwa, 2006, editor and co-author). She is currently working on comparative research on 'generational shifts in lifestyles among the Japanese and

Korean urban middle class' and 'the work and life of silk weavers in Nishijin, Kyoto'.

Markus Oedewald was educated at Helsinki University. He has lived in Japan, and his studies in Japanese schools started in the senior high school Hanyu Dai Ichi Gôtôgakkô in Saitama-ken. His research interests include school excursions, tourism commodities, traditions and symbolism. He has carried out fieldwork in senior high schools in Saitama-ken and many school excursion attractions in various parts of Japan. He has worked for many years with Japanese tourists as a tour operator of a Japanese-owned company in Finland, and has taught and worked as a researcher in the multinational project 'Japan as the model of Asian modernization: the mechanics of cultural transition' at Helsinki University. He is now working as a programme director in the Business College Helsinki-Malmi and continuing his work with the meanings of learning during school excursions.

Bronwen Surman spent her childhood living and going to school in a number of diverse cultures from Croydon to Kiribati, and it is from these experiences that she developed a keen interest in anthropology. After studying education at Exeter University she moved to Japan to take up various teaching posts. Her four-year stay culminated in an extended home stay, living in rural Japan with a local family and working in the family business while studying certain martial arts and obtaining a black belt in karate. After returning to the UK she obtained her MA in the social anthropology of Japan at Oxford Brookes University, focusing on Japanese tourism to Britain. Subsequently she has worked in research for both academia and the media industry.

Merry I. White is Professor of Anthropology at Boston University. Her focus has been on Japan with particular reference to families, education and material culture. She has visited Japan regularly since 1963, and conducted fieldwork in Tokyo, Kyoto and many other parts of Japan. Her work has included studies of schools (*The Japanese Educational Challenge*, Free Press, 1985), studies of internationalization (*The Japanese Overseas*, Free Press, 1986), studies of adolescence (*The Material Child*, Free Press, 1993) and studies of families and social change (*Perfectly Japanese*, University of California Press, 2002). She has published many articles as well on various topics including foodways and tourism, culinary anthropology, young women and consumption and, most recently, critical factors in social change in Japan. Her current work is on urban social spaces in Japan, and she is writing a book on the social history of the café in Japan. She also is engaged in the development of coffee production in an agricultural cooperative in north-eastern Cambodia, where she also supports the construction of elementary schools.

Shinji Yamashita is Professor of Cultural Anthropology at the University of

Tokyo. His research focuses on the dynamics of culture in the process of globalization, especially with reference to international tourism and transnational migration. His recent books include *Globalization in Southeast Asia: Local, National, and Transnational Perspectives* (co-edited with J.S. Eades, Berghahn Books, 2003), *Bali and Beyond: Explorations in the Anthropology of Tourism* (translated by J.S. Eades, Berghahn Books, 2003) and *The Making of Anthropology in East and Southeast Asia* (co-edited with Joseph Bosco and J.S. Eades, Berghahn Books, 2004).

Preface

The present collection is another set of papers that has emerged from meetings of the Japan Anthropology Workshop, this time carefully forged over more than one gathering. The original panel was held at Yale in 2002, a session entitled *Tabi no Bunka*, where the idea of the collapsing of time and place in the contemporary Japanese experience of travel emerged as a common theme explored by the participants and now featuring in this book. In Hong Kong, in 2005, the editors met again with some of the original panellists to consolidate a more detailed plan for the volume and to propose other contributors who might make the volume more coherent and comprehensive. This is one of the best ways we have found to proceed for our series, for those who offer papers to a conference proposal come forward in a rather random fashion, and to build up a theme for a book requires a little extra consideration. This volume exhibits a good outcome to such a procedure, and the result will offer much to those working or teaching in many aspects of Japanese culture, as well as to those looking for broader theory on the subjects of travel and tourism.

The vision of the editors was to address the theme of *tabi*, with all the implications that the Japanese term evokes, and Sylvie Guichard-Anguis discusses these in the Introduction, where she lays out an ethnographically and historically informed Japanese context for the other materials that follow. The other original themes were time and space, and the early chapters indicate the extent to which Japanese *tabi* often override the distinction between past and present, and between home and away, as travellers set out to explore and understand their history and traditions. The later chapters turn to Japanese travel further afield, but the distinctions between time and space again become blurred, as many Japanese look to their own cultural heritage, even when quite far from home.

The contributors to the book range from quite big names who have specialised in the subjects of tourism and travel, through those who look at the themes in a broader context of understanding Japanese society, to younger scholars just making their way in the publishing world. There is also a variety of nationalities among the authors, and an even greater variety of present working locations, so the approaches are quite various too. The result is a refreshing collection of new and intriguing ideas about a subject with a long and oft-remembered history. Another great contribution to our series!

Joy Hendry
May 2008

Introduction

The culture of travel (*tabi no bunka*) and Japanese tourism

Sylvie Guichard-Anguis

At the turn of this new century the word *tabi* (moving, journey, trip) seems to enjoy a wide usage, in spite of being associated with famous historical journeys on foot through the Japanese archipelago, which will be examined later on. To put it in other words, those walks through a Japan of past eras seem still to play a part as icons of contemporaneous journeys. Although another word meaning travel (*ryokō*) does exist, the idea behind *tabi* seems to correspond to a need still prevailing in a world where the internet allows travellers to book their stay directly thousands of kilometres away from their destination. Two Chinese characters form the word *ryokō*: one which is the same as *tabi* and the other which means 'moving'. Before going further and in order to introduce the present context, we shall illustrate the popularity of the notion of *tabi* through a large variety of examples in today's Japan.

Close to Tokyo railway station, the Library of the Journey (*Tabi no toshokan*), opened and managed by the Japan Travel Bureau (JTB), Japan's largest travel agency, offers a vast array of documentation including magazines, guidebooks, academic works, etc. In this space created by an agency involved mainly in selling package tours, visitors plan their travel or journey carefully by themselves.

It is not only individuals who display a liking for the word *tabi*, but companies too, for example the Eastern Japanese Railways, whose monthly magazine is called *Tōran bueru* (from the French *Trains verts*, or 'Green railways' in English), with the subtitle '*Tabi* feelings or *tabi* thought' (*Kanjiru tabi, kangaeru tabi*). The use of the word *tabi* is not limited to the general title, but each different monthly issue seems to make a fair use of it, as with the April 2007 issue: 'Making *tabi* inside the food culture of Yamagata' (northeast Japan). In 2006 its April issue was titled 'Small *tabi*', with the subtitle 'Spring and early summer on the Tokiwa Road'. Highlighting a journey by foot, even for a railway company, underlies the importance of the association of the notion of *tabi* to the one of the road in Japan.

The very popular work of the novelist Shiba Ryōtarō (1923–96) *Going along the highway* (*Kaidō o yuku*) was published as a serial from January 1971 until March 1996 in *Asahi Weekly* (*Shuukan Asahi*). It was even turned into a TV series. In 2001 the four-hundredth anniversary of the establishment of the post stations on the Tokaidō Road, the highway from Edo (present-day Tokyo) to Kyoto, was celebrated by several events and even a symposium organized by the *Asahi* newspaper. In Europe roads might be much older, as testified by the large network of them dating back to the Roman Empire, but they do not enjoy the same attraction as the Japanese ones. The idea of walking along those roads and experiencing a kind of journey seems limited to the pilgrimage to Santiago de Compostela in Spain and largely along its Spanish branch called the 'French road' (*Camino Frances*). Old roads are not enough to be fond of *tabi*, so we may ask what else do we need?

The notion of *tabi* is not restricted to adults but seems to attract children too. Anno Mitsumasa (1926–), one of the most famous authors of illustrated books (*ehon*) in Japan, who received the Andersen prize, the most prestigious in this category, in 1984, issued in 1977 his first *Journey Illustrated Book* (*Tabi ehon*), which soon had foreign editions in most of the developed countries. This very first book introduced the reader (Anno admits to making no distinction between generations) to landscapes both rural and urban created from a kind of European fantasy, a mix of several periods and countries. A lonely horseman invariably crosses them. Full of small details but lacking any words, each page of the books bewitches the readers and attracts them to the world of dream and imagination. Unexpectedly, Japan seems totally absent from this series, which illustrates first Europe in general and then Italy, Britain, the USA, Spain and finally Denmark. Why does the author use the word *tabi* to describe these travels through foreign countries? We have to admit that the journey in the manner of *tabi* happens worldwide and not only in Japan. Dream forms part of the notion of *tabi*, but what else?

This contemporaneous meaning of *tabi* found one of its greatest illustrations in the historical evolution of the magazine *Tabi*, issued by the Japan Travel Bureau from 1924 to January 2004, number 924 being its last issue. An enquiry into the content of this monthly magazine over the years (Guichard-Anguis 2004) gives a fair view of the topics selected. Most of the hundredth-issue numbers deal with railways, a topic addressed on a regular basis in this magazine, with the exception of the nine-hundredth issue in January 2002, which centred on Japanese inns (*ryokan*). The most popular third topic in this magazine is the spa (*onsen*). According to data from 2002, a large proportion of the readers are men in their forties or over who live in the three biggest urban regions of Japan (around Tokyo, Nagoya and Osaka, and Kyoto) and travel on an individual basis. During those years, targeting women was left to other magazines. This segmentation of the press comes from the notable tendency among Japanese people to travel exclusively with people of the same sex, either family or friends.

The magazine was sold and has been edited by Shinchosha since May 2004 (see the homepage: http://www.shinchosha.co.jp/tabi/top_fl.html); its editorial concept changed drastically with the issue of May 2005. With a new title, *Women's magazine called Tabi* (*Tabi to iu na no jōseishi*), it focuses on travel abroad, mainly to large cities in Western countries: Paris, London, New

York, Seville, Prague, Istanbul, etc.). It also dedicates a few pages to inside Japan in 'Small travels to a small town' (*Chisana machi he, chisana tabi*), introducing historical cities on a small scale: Hita in Oita prefecture (2005, November issue), Wajima, Suzu and Noto (2008, March). This evolution shows how deeply rooted the notion of *tabi* is in the Japanese perception of contemporaneous travels.

The use of the word *tabi* does not seem to be limited to the private sector but also has a lot of public currency. To give a brief example, in 2005 the general public was invited to submit travels plans entitled 'My journey', and among the 786 *tabi* plans received the Agency of Cultural Affairs selected the 'Best 100'. It considers that 'Japanese people will rediscover the vanishing history and culture of local areas' through these plans. The grand prix was given to a journey to visit various local producers of craft lacquer ware. Should we think that dream has to be associated with nostalgia and the local in order to be part of *tabi*?

In modern Japan people are still making *tabi*, but using trains, the internet, etc.; in other words, they do not ignore the most recent technology in making those journeys which follow famous ones in history, as we will consider later on. It goes without saying that the influence of *tabi* on Japanese tourism is tremendous and gives it some of its original aspects.

This volume comes from a research panel organized during the Japan Anthropology Workshop (JAWS) Conference at Yale University in May 2002, with the title 'The culture of moving' (*Tabi no bunka*). The collapsing of time and place in contemporary Japanese experience of travel was one of the common themes explored by the participants. Before going into each chapter, let us investigate more fully the notion of *tabi* as connected with literature, leisure and tourism.

Tabi: walking and searching for the meaning of life

In the Japanese archipelago for over a thousand years, people have not only travelled but written about it, either at the time or later. Since antiquity, the travelogue has played a significant part in Japanese literature. It goes without saying that, as we shall see, this literature offers historical evidence and documents how people living inside the Japanese islands used to move about. Compared to the very small number of works left by the pilgrims to Santiago de Compostela, this literature needs closer examination. Between the tenth century and the eighteenth century, only around 15 records were left by the millions of pilgrims who went to Santiago from every part of Christian Europe (Guichard-Anguis 2007b). Going further in this comparison, we notice that the experience of the European pilgrims had nothing to do with the notion of *tabi*, as it lacked the idea of playing (*asobi*). In the *Liber Sancti Jacobi*, also called the *Codex Calistinus*, the fifth book includes a guide for the pilgrims, written around 1139. It consists of several lists of the dangers which might be encountered on the road, classified by genre, for example good and bad rivers. It includes not a single allusion to the things which might please the pilgrim on his way to Santiago. Conversely, the Buddhist priest Saka wrote a diary during his pilgrimage to Ise in 1342 (Sadler 1940). Poems composed at the several spots enjoyed by Saka enhanced this pilgrimage, in which sightseeing and playing have a part. Although this work dates back to the fourteenth century, the Japanese reader has the strange feeling of having some familiarity with this kind of traveller, looking for acquaintances on his way and open to any kind of religion as far as it offers places to visit.

The richness of the present meanings of the word *tabi* has already been underlined by several examples, and we may ask whether literary works which directly try to deepen this notion offer the same image? Among such authors Okada Kishu focuses his work on this notion in several essays (1975, 1977, 1991, 1992). In the book *Discover on Tabi* (1977) Okada insists on the individual and human experience associated with that notion, which requires the five human senses (Okada 1977: 11). In that sense experiencing *tabi* gives the opportunity to discover oneself, as the whole human being is involved in it. According to this author, this is the main reason why the poet Matsuo Bashō (1644–94) remains so popular. Making a journey in the manner of *tabi* allows one to put one's feet behind Bashō and find the true meaning of life. Landscapes evolve and will change through time, but discovering oneself through walking along the road will always attract human beings. Only by leaving one's everyday life and environment does one have the chance to experience this encounter with oneself, as human beings are generally too busy to focus on themselves while conducting their everyday duties. Several poets like Saigyō (1118–90), Sōgi (1421–1502) and Bashō who have given a classical genre to this kind of literature tend to express the transformation of oneself through *tabi* using different poetic forms. All of them tend to express the same kind of feelings, through the beauty of impermanence, curiosity, loneliness and gratefulness.

In *About Tabi* (1975) Okada explains why walking among changing landscapes is so important. Descriptions of night time do not appear in those diaries because the authors are walking during the daytime. Unlike the journey of today's traveller, who can sleep or try to while on the train, for instance, the journey on foot allows the traveller to absorb all the sensations which follow one after the other along the way. Okada insists on that difference, noting that today people tend to move more as *passengers* (using the English word) rather than travellers. From the 1960s, driving a car has begun to prevent people from nourishing their sensitivity, as they used to do, by moving on foot. Time and space are needed to experience *tabi*, as the sorrow of parting with people and places should be part of *tabi*. Nostalgia for the past, of something which has been part of the present and has gone, is part of the emotions associated with *tabi*. Okada stresses that an unknown future does not create dream. Nostalgia for things disappearing, as for instance steam locomotives at the origin of a revival phenomenon in Japan (Guichard-Anguis 2002), plays a great part in the notion of *tabi*. Travelling on trains on local railways lines and enjoying the diversity of experiences are still very popular topics in Japanese travel magazines, as underlined before.

If Okada centres his discourse on the individual, others like Iwai (2002) focus on the fact of moving as synonymous with *tabi*. The meaning of accomplishing *tabi* is taken in a broader sense by this historian, and ultimately involves all those who make a living by moving. Hunters of wild animals in eastern Japan (*matagi*) are put on the same level as merchants, pilgrims, pedlars, medicine sellers, craftsmen and the like. Through descriptions of a great variety of ways of life, the author gives a lively picture of all those who while moving on the roads helped to connect places and to circulate information. If necessity was the main reason for not staying at home, even some of those people moving along the roads of the Edo period were seeking play, as emphasized by the pilgrimage to the Kotohiragu (familiar name: Konpira-san) in Kagawa prefecture, Shikoku, dedicated to a Buddhist–Shinto syncretic deity until the Meiji period (1868–1912).

Until the beginning of the Meiji period, as nearly everyone was walking, except for a small minority, moving meant going along the road on foot and could be assimilated with *tabi*. With modernization, trains came, and then public transport, and later on cars, etc., which changed those patterns completely. A new word came into use to name travelling using such methods: *ryokō* (travel). In the middle of the nineteenth century in Europe and especially in Britain the word 'tourism' came into use and meant travelling and enjoying oneself. In Japan this concept came into general use during the Taishō era (1912–26), but all the authors insist on the fact that moving for the purpose of play had already existed in Japan for centuries. Ishimori (1989b) underlined that one out of 30 Japanese was travelling on the Tokaidō per year, as testified by the German physician and historian Kaempfer (1651–1716) in his two-volume book *History of Japan* (1727–28), written back in Europe. According to him this huge proportion can be compared to today's Japanese travellers going abroad, as documents and budget required are roughly the same in comparison. If in Europe the aristocratic elite used to travel, this phenomenon was kept to a minority and had nothing to compare it with the Japanese one. In the Japanese archipelago there were two reasons for the granting of permission to move: pilgrimages and going to hot springs for healing. But, as will be analysed later on, they were merely excuses. At this point of the analysis we can notice that Japan distinguished itself from other countries by having experienced moving associated with playing in a popular way that was not so frequent in other countries, and that moving was done by walking.

For Shirahata (1996), alluding to Yanagita Kunio, *tabi* has a dark image, including suffering, compared to *ryokō*. To put it in other words, for all those famous writers such as Saigyō, Bashō and the like *tabi* was life and life was *tabi*. Today literary works centring on the perception of oneself while moving are put on different shelves in libraries compared to the books including the word *ryokō*, which comes to be more associated with the idea of leisure and fun. But we can ask with him if inside these *tabi* of bygone times, even among those famous works, the idea of something similar to *ryokō* was present already.

To sum up, a kind of opposition seems to exist in the perception of *tabi*. On one side some authors tend to focus on the *tabi* centred on oneself as illustrated by some major works of Japanese travelogue, and on the other on the moving activity accomplished by millions of Japanese, described for instance by the poet and writer of popular fiction Saikaku (1642–93) or today's historians, who associate it with looking for play.

Tabi in literary perspective: travellers who write

In 2006 a one-page advertisement in the *Asahi Shimbun* read: 'With a pencil the Narrow Road to the Deep North', and added: 'Discovering one's inner self as a Japanese'. This advertisement speaks about the continuing great popularity of one of the most famous literary works of Bashō, which is explained in the text in modern Japanese, and can also be copied by the reader with a pencil on the text itself. The feelings included in this work are nowadays associated with being Japanese. *Tabi* associated with travelogue seems to play a part in the definition of today's Japanese identity.

According to Okada, for a very long time records of travels could only be put in words (Okada 1977: 44). As far as the earliest ones are concerned, with the *Tosa Nikki*[1] considered as the ancestor of this literary genre or the *Ise Monogatari*,[2] they all retained the same pattern. First they offer a kind of geographical approach, then give details of the roads and finally propose considerations about the feelings of the author himself. And to illustrate those feelings, poems are added to the description. According to Fukuda and Plutschow (1975), travelogue is close to diaries because these authors too speak of their solitary relations with themselves and nature. In *Tōkan Kikō* (Anon. [1242] 1999) and *Izayoi Nikki*[3] from the Kamakura period (1185–1333), which are classics of the travelogue literature, landscapes are described, as they were yet unknown, but nothing of the way of life of the people in those unknown environments seems worth noting. Okada goes as far as to say that the anonymous writer of the *Tōkan Kikō* did nothing more than take pictures of the landscapes he had the opportunity to see. Those literary works begin and end with what eyes can see. Plutschow (2006: 321), after going through some of the famous works of travellers of the Edo period, says nothing more of those diaries:

> One may argue that, to the degree a traveller is confronted with unfamiliar 'reality', all travel is enlightening. If that criterion applies to our travellers, then one would have to consider the poet-travellers who sought out the *utamakura* and the poems that had been composed about them, as enlightened traditionalists who, for the sake of tradition, refuse to confront and describe the reality of travel. It is in contrast to such

traditional travellers, as there were many from, say, the tenth century until the nineteenth that we must consider our traveller as truly enlightened.

According to Fukuda and Plutschow (1975), whose book covers 69 travel itineraries between 934/35 and 1598, including maps and a detailed list of all the stops, most of the works depict only going or returning but not both, and in general the first is favoured. Authors and purposes vary according to the periods. During the Heian period (794–1185) the literary works came from nobles sent from the capital to the provinces or even exiled, or who undertook a pilgrimage. On the contrary, during the Middle Ages the authors tended to belong to one of three types: the first was travellers who undertook an elegant wandering, as personified by Saigyō (1118–90); the second was civil servants who had to make the trip between Kyoto and Kamakura, as illustrated in *Tōkan Kiko*; and the third was men of literature who moved for safety purposes. It goes without saying that those reasons could be combined. The main purpose of *tabi* seems to be writing a new piece which could be added to the travelogue that already existed, adorned by pillow words (*uta makura*).[4] In other words it came to be a genre in itself. *Michiyuki bungaku*, a poetic genre dealing with literary travels, which could even be imaginary travels (Pigeot 1982), is the form of the Middle Ages from the twelfth to the sixteenth century, and can even be found in theatre performances such as Kabuki or Joruri (dramatic narrative chanting associated with the puppet theatre). In more recent times these works take the form of novels, numerous records of famous places, or geographical studies and, later on in the Edo period, works like the *Tōkaidōchu hizakurige* (Jippenshā [1806] 1992), not to mention woodblocks from Hokusai or Hiroshige (Satō and Fujiwara 2000).

All the essayists dealing with these several kinds of literature dedicated to *tabi* try to answer the same key question: why go on *tabi*? For Fukuda, the country of Japan compels people to travel, because of its richness in diversity, enhanced by the passing of the seasons. Moving inside the Japanese archipelago offers the opportunity to satisfy a Japanese sentimental tendency, by leaving the everyday environment to go deeper into oneself. A great majority of those essayists, too, point to reasons which will be examined a little further on, mainly associated with belief and recreation. In their analysis they suggest that *tabi* again seems synonymous with insecurity and anxiety, compared to travel (*ryokō*), which means enjoying oneself. One of the main reasons why people undertake *tabi* is the satisfaction of successfully doing it, the required courage and will, in spite of the hardship it implies. In other words, it can be compared to today's pilgrimage to Santiago de Compostela or to the more sporting pursuit of climbing a mountain, as the feeling provided by its achievement is worth all the difficulties on the way.

As emphasized earlier, in the twentieth century the popularity of these writings did not decrease, and new names were even added to the already very well-known ones. The work of writers close to the classic image of the wandering monk poet, as shown by Taneda Santoka (1882–1940), the Soto Zen monk who travelled mainly through western Japan as a mendicant monk writing *haiku*, novels like the ones of Shimazaki Toson (1872–1943) or Kawabata Yasunari (1899–1972), and the huge volume of travel diaries written about experiences abroad tell how much writing while travelling is still taken for granted.

Tabi in historical perspective: travellers who pray and play

As we mentioned earlier, all those different kinds of works, whether they are writings or illustrations, provide a great deal of information on travels and are today important sources for research. The association between moving, playing and praying has been underlined and points to a phenomenon that is not so widespread in other parts of the world (Graburn 1995). The origins of tourist activity in Japan, historically speaking, can be sought well before the word 'tourism' came into popular use in this part of the world.

During the Edo period (1603–1868), in order to get permission to leave one's own community, one could most conveniently use the excuse of visiting temples or shrines. Kanzaki (1995: 43) goes as far as saying that the *oshi*, who originally were missionaries spreading the faith of the big shrines of Ise, turned into what can be called the original travel agencies in Japan. As their relation with the shrines became loosened, the annual distribution of charms, providing local products from Ise and even providing accommodation to the groups of pilgrims organized in groups who wanted to worship at shrines or temples (*kō*), became their main sources of income. Among all kinds of pilgrimages, the one to Ise had the highest frequency, with peaks of millions of visitors during auspicious years. During those two and a half centuries nearly everyone could go on a pilgrimage, compared to more ancient periods when this activity was still limited to the aristocracy, monks and priests and later on opened to the warrior class.

All over Japan, pilgrimages also showed an extraordinary diversity which reflected Japanese relations with belief (Kitakawa 2002). Long before the Edo period, Shinto, Buddhism and syncretism had already created a great variety of forms of pilgrimages, whether they were circular including several stops, as for the most famous, the 88 stops of the Shikoku pilgrimage and the 33 holy places of Kannon in the Western Provinces, or had a single holy place, whether a shrine, as in Togakushi in Nagano prefecture, a place of mountain ascetics or a temple. The Japanese language even establishes a distinction between both types, speaking of *mairi* in the case of several stops or *mode* in the case of a single place. The natural environment with, for example, a single mountain, such as the Kiso Ontake in Gifu prefecture, a site of mountain worship, or mountainous regions such as the Kumano Sanzan (three mountains of Kumano), and conversely the urban environment, such as Nagano, with Zenkoji one of the most popular temples during the period, were religious places to which pilgrims headed.

Figure I.1 The post town of Narai (Nagano prefecture).

Photo by Sylvie Guichard-Anguis

Roads leading to such places and economical inns dedicated to the pilgrims at staging posts and near the holy places are parts of settlements which can be found all over Japan (Guichard-Anguis 2007a). A great number of urban centres inside the archipelago thrived during this period because of those visits, which involved several kinds of consuming: accommodation, food, buying souvenirs (Kanzaki 1997), visiting nearby interesting spots and last but not least playing. Urban landscapes in these religious cities today still retain some of the atmosphere of those bygone days, for example Kōyasan in Wakayama prefecture, around the Buddhist monastic complex of the Shingon sect, and form a fair proportion of Japanese national cultural heritage through several kinds of designation. The Kumano Mountains, for example, have been listed as a UNESCO world heritage site since 2004.

But pilgrimage does not represent the only reason to move and visit a shrine or a temple, as we have already noted. The reputation of the place as a famous one (*meisho*), or its attractiveness due to a particular event, can encourage visitors. *Meisho* was a concept associated with the pillow word (*uta makura*) mentioned before, until the place tended to become a real tourist destination during the Edo period. To the famous places celebrated by Japanese poetry, new places were little by little added, which were chosen for their own characteristics. All those places became listed in all kinds of

Figure I.2 Kumano Hongū Taisha (Wakayama prefecture).
Photo by Sylvie Guichard-Anguis

information books, illustrated (*meisho zue*) or not. The temporary exhibition of a famous statue or image belonging to a temple or a shrine (*kaichō*) or to another religious place (*dekaichō*) could offer opportunities to mingle with a crowd eager to see all the attractions and nearby shops, synonymous with pleasure (Ishimori 1995). And last but not least, some of the most famous pleasure districts of the Edo period were close to the religious destinations; to name just one, Furuichi in Ise was part of the attraction of the holy place.

In consequence we have to be very careful not to categorize all the pilgrims of the Edo period as very religious persons, accomplishing their duties carefully and avoiding everything unrelated with the main purpose of their travel. From reading the works of Saikaku (1642–93) it is obvious that pilgrimage could be a mere excuse for looking for fun, away from the daily environment. Compared to the situation in Europe, moving associated with playing was already well developed in Japan some time before the industrial revolution and the opening of railway lines (Ishimori 1989a). In fact a second important reason can be added for the development of pilgrimage, as going to hot springs (*onsen*) also developed considerably during the period. The origin of this activity can be traced to antiquity, as Japan is blessed by thousands of hot springs all over the country. During the Edo period hundreds of them turned into groups of small villages or hamlets, where long stays during the cold season could be undertaken in different kinds of lodgings according to one's budget. These hot springs come in a variety, which reminds one of the pilgrimages, as their scale goes from one building to small cities. Their location shows the same diversity, as they can be found in the mountains, along the seashore, close to large cities and in remote places. To these two main purposes for leaving one's daily environment, a lot of other reasons can be added which could enhance the enjoyment of travelling to and from one's destination.

Cities and well-known landscapes were also sought-after destinations (Kitakawa 2002). Theatres, famous foods, festivals, souvenirs associated with well-known local handicrafts, etc. were part of the attraction of cities. Mountains such as Mount Fuji, or series of landscapes such as the three famous ones of Japan or the eight landscapes of Omi around the Biwa lake, saw their reputation growing and became places one has to see once in one's life. The

Figure I.3 Kinosaki hot spring (Hyōgo prefecture).
Photo by Sylvie Guichard-Anguis

passing of seasons, and especially spring with the cherry trees blossoming around some famous place such as a shrine or a temple, the banks of a river or even a particular area such as Yoshino in Wakayama prefecture, offers opportunities to set out on foot and see the flowers blossoming (*hanami*). It is not only famous places and handicrafts that can become souvenirs that attract those travelling, but among well-known things (*meibutsu*) local sweets are not the least mentioned in a lot of travelogues. Their number is such that one of the most famous sweet trades in Japan recently organized an exhibition dedicated to this topic (Toraya Bunko 2006). Even those compelled to travel for political reasons, such as the *daimyō* with their escort accomplishing alternate attendance in the city of Edo (Yamamoto 1998), could not help but enjoy what the cities of that time afforded (Vaporis 1994).

It is also during this period that we saw a gradual institutionalization of the organizational aspects of a distinctively Japanese culture of travel, such as *senbetsu* (farewell money), *omiyage* (return gift) and the tendency to group travelling. As long-distance travel to such places as the Ise shrine or Kumano mountains involved physical danger and considerable economic expenses, people often travelled as a group. The expenses for such travel were provided by the members of the group to which the traveller belonged, such as specific religious groups (*kō*) or a village. Members of the group provided the expenses for the journey or a pilgrimage, and the person who travelled in the name of the group was obliged to bring back a small gift for those who remained in return from the places he or she visited (Kanzaki 1990, 1997).

Japanese tourism and *tabi* inside Japan and overseas

Within Asia, Japan has been the main tourist-sending society since the beginning of the twentieth century. It goes without saying that this situation is mainly due to economic factors. Yamashita underlines in his chapter that Japan in 2006 ranked as the fifth biggest tourist spender in the world, so the tremendous importance of Japanese tourism not only in Asia but in the rest of the world should not be overlooked. This volume does not focus on Japanese tourism per se, but on the culture of travel (*tabi no bunka*) inside Japanese tourism. It assumes that a large percentage of Japanese tourists have their perception of travel still deeply rooted in the culture of travel (*tabi no bunka*). It is an attempt to analyse why some peculiar forms of tourist expectations became established among Japanese tourists. Those expectations compel some foreign destinations to give some sort of answer to the unexpected demands from these Asian visitors. This volume does not assume that Japanese tourists are the only kind of visitors who have special demands, but it focuses on them. Generally speaking the tourist development of destinations adapts to markets which usually show some diversity. For instance, Europeans tend to be fascinated by the past, history and authenticity, which they are looking for wherever they visit, be it Rajasthan in India or the historic cities of Uzbekistan.

For a more concrete image let us consider two well-known examples: Jean-Henri Casimir Fabre and Anne of Green Gables. The first one, a famous French entomologist (1823–1915), seemed so popular among Japanese visitors that it prompted the creation of a cultural and educational centre in the former home and garden of this author, located in Sérignan du Comtat in the *département* of Vaucluse. The novel *Anne of Green Gables* by the Canadian author Lucy Maud Montgomery, published in 1908, which is set on Prince Edward Island, was so popular that it turned the island into a famous tourist spot, much in vogue among Japanese tourists. In both cases school education plays a big part.

As emphasized already, *tabi* can be associated with travelling outside Japan. The chapters in this volume deal with the present and focus on travellers not only inside Japan but outside (Korea, Palau, Britain and Italy). They underline that somehow history, tradition, fantasy, playing, the making of Japanese identity, etc. are well mingled and are the main reasons for leaving one's own place.

Part I focuses on travelling history in the present. Nelson Graburn's chapter opens it, and he considers Japanese antiquity or even before, focusing on some of the foreign origins of Japanese identity. The chapter deals with a neighbouring country, Korea, whose influence on Japan has been tremendous in the forming of its most original characteristics. Korean potters compelled to settle in the Satsuma fief (present-day Kagoshima prefecture) at the end of the sixteenth century produced Satsuma ware, one of the most representative ceramics of the Japanese archipelago, largely exported to Western countries during the second part of the nineteenth century. Domesticated foreignness forms the core of this chapter, which implies two kinds of attraction for today's Japanese tourists. Visitors are looking not only for their own roots, but also for the familiar with a foreign origin.

Millie Creighton builds a bridge between the Edo period (1603–1868) and today, stressing that a nostalgic feeling is still strongly prevailing among Japanese visitors for that period, when Japan was not yet Westernized and not yet industrialized. Today the Edo period is considered as the one when Japanese identity completed its development. She insists on the deep meaning of the association between a Japanese Japan, if we dare term it so, and a Japan internationalized as in the present. There is a nostalgic feeling for this vanished and idealized Japan, rather than for the authenticity of the past as it actually was, compared to the Japan Japanese people are living in today, which corresponds to a rational present open to the outside and full of uncertainty. She points out that people are travelling not only in place but in time, looking for a place located centuries ago and still supposed to be closer to themselves than the environment in which they are living their everyday lives. We have to agree with her that Japan has experienced a huge evolution in all aspects, and that it might retain a feeling of uncertainty about a present so different from the past.

Sylvie Guichard-Anguis points to the same phenomenon, underlying the search for a Japanese identity in so-called Japanese inns (*ryokan*) which offer all the amenities of the present but in a culturally Japanese construction. References to tradition make the core of the attraction of these Japanese inns, but they are invented ones. Their combination helps to construct Japanese beauty as one of the main components of Japanese identity. No authenticity is sought there. References to local history, Japanese nature and the culture of hospitality so important in social relations in Japan are present everywhere.

Part II deals with tradition, time and fantasy, through the evocations of two kinds of destinations inside Japan. Markus Oedewald focuses on school excursions, a well-rooted institution in the Japanese schooling system. He shows how these trips are used to introduce some symbolic materials for the formation of Japanese identity to young Japanese. Historical Japan is still central among the destinations, and these travels help to reinforce handed-down traditions. He points out also that students of senior high schools write diaries during school excursions. The short accounts of the excursions are published as a book. So we find again the tendency to write while travelling in order to be read by others, and this phenomenon underlies how much travelogue is still alive, well and even fostered during the school years in present-day Japan.

Joy Hendry deals with another kind of destination, that associated with fantasy and which combines travel in time and space. Here again the search for authenticity is denied in the locations associated with theme parks. She introduces the contemporaneous notion of *reija* (leisure) to explain these trips, whose ultimate purpose is playing and learning. Theme parks versus museums have roots in internationalization, but at home. The foreign is well packaged, but in a Japanese parcel. Easy access is allowed to these unknown, made-familiar and indigenous worlds. Here again domesticated foreignness plays a part in forming the attraction of these tourist destinations.

In Part III we consider Japanese travellers looking for the familiar overseas, whether their destination is a natural, rural or urban environment. In other words this part centres on Japanese tourists travelling to foreign countries, including Asia, the Pacific region and Europe. Okpyo Moon analyses the evolution of Japanese tourism in Korea in the twentieth century against the background of the tumultuous relations between the two countries. She focuses in particular upon how different images of the ex-colony have been invented, appropriated and consumed by different segments of the Japanese population in various tourist contexts. Despite the considerable transform-ation of Japanese tourism to Korea from mostly male pleasure seekers of the colonial period to mostly female 'Korean wave' (*hallyu*) tourists in search of an alternative modernity at the beginning of the twenty-first century, what is sought after largely remains with the familiar and the ordinary rather than otherness and change, a mundane urban pleasure rather than a fantasy world or a created past in the rural.

Shinji Yamashita insists on the fact that the South, as in the case of

Bali island, too is often viewed as a place that makes travellers feel a degree of familiarity and even nostalgia. Contact with the Palau islands gives birth to feelings of exoticism and nostalgia. Japanese travellers are looking for something which has vanished from their archipelago, and nostalgia is stressed again as a strong factor among the travel motivations.

The next two chapters deal with Japanese tourists in Europe and show how much their behaviour in the two countries selected in this volume (Britain and Italy) is deeply rooted in the culture of travel (*tabi no bunka*). Bronwen Surman analyses the destination choice of Britain by Japanese tourists. The association with literature cannot be overlooked, for example William Shakespeare, the Brontës and Beatrix Potter. It goes without saying that Japanese tourists are not alone in terms of this association but it seems deeper as far as they are concerned. Facing this kind of rather unfamiliar demand from foreign tourists, the destinations tend to develop special products targeted to those visitors. In the same chapter the author also stresses the importance of education concerning those literary works and the creation of some expectation among the coming visitors, a very important factor which should not be overlooked considering the choice of destinations.

Unexpectedly Merry I. White speaks of nostalgia in considering Japanese travellers in Italy. In this case too Italy looks like a bygone imagined past for Japanese tourists, but this time they are in quest of a foreign cuisine. Escaping from the social and domestic demands on them at home, these travellers tend to professionalize their own travel experience. This tendency seems quite close to the one of writing about travelling. Again, travelling inside Italy allows the Japanese person to transform into a new person, a global one.

Notes

1 The *Tosa Nikki* is the first diary literature, written in 935, by Ki no Tsurayuki, governor of Tosa, on his return to the capital of Heian (today Kyoto). It is written in the name of a woman of his entourage and includes 57 *waka* (a 31-syllable form of poetry).
2 The *Ise Monogatari* is a mid-tenth-century collection of around 110 to 140 brief lyrical episodes of anonymous authorship; familiarity with it was necessary for courtiers in the late Heian period (794–1185).
3 The *Izayoi Nikki* [Diary of the Waning moon] was written around 1280 by Abutsu ni, a *waka* poet and secondary wife of Fujiwara no Tamei, on her way to Kamakura.
4 *Uta makura* (pillow words) are place names associated with certain standard images and feelings in classical Japanese poetry.

References

Anno, M. (1977). *Tabi no ehon* [My journey]. Tokyo: Fukuikan-shoten.
—— (1978). *Tabi no ehon* II [My journey II]. Tokyo: Fukuikan-shoten.
—— (1981). *Tabi no ehon* III [My journey III]. Tokyo: Fukuikan-shoten.
—— (1983). *Tabi no ehon* IV [My journey IV]. Tokyo: Fukuikan-shoten.

—— (2003). *Tabi no ehon* V [My journey V]. Tokyo: Fukuikan-shoten.

—— (2005). *Tabi no ehon* VI [My journey VI]. Tokyo: Fukuikan-shoten.

Anonymous Japanese ([1242] 1999). *Voyage dans les provinces de l'Est* [*Tōkan Kikō* (Travel in the Eastern Provinces)], trans. Jacqueline Pigeot. Paris: Gallimard.

Fukuda, H. and H. E. Plutschow (1975). *Nihon kikō bungaku henran* [A handbook for the study of classical Japanese travel diaries]. Tokyo: Mushashino-shoin.

Graburn, H.H.N. (1995) 'The past in the present in Japan'. In B. Richard and D. Pearce (eds), *Change in Tourism, People, Places, Processes*. London and New York: Routledge, pp. 47–70.

Guichard-Anguis, S. (2002). 'Communications as connections to different realms, through young Japanese children's illustrated books'. In Ray T. Donahue (ed.), *Exploring Japaneseness: On Japanese Enactments of Culture and Consciousness*. Westport, CT, and London: Ablex Publishing, pp. 89–101.

—— (2004). 'A propos des 90 ans de la revue japonaise "Tabi" (voyage)' [About the 90 years of the magazine 'Tabi' (travel)]. *Le Globe: Revue Genevoise de Géographie*, 144: *Voyage, tourisme, paysage* [Travel, tourism, landscape], pp. 85–102.

—— (2007a). 'Voyager sur la Nakasendō (Japon)' [Journey on the Nakasendō (Japan)]. Transport et tourisme, Actes du colloque de Chambéry, 13–15 September 2006. Collection EDYTEM, *Cahiers de Géographie*, 4, pp. 221–30.

—— (2007b). 'Pilgrimage, space and identity: Ise (Japan) and Santiago de Compostela (Spain)'. In P. Ackerman, D. Martinez and M. Rodrigez del Alisal, *Pilgrimages and Spiritual Quests in Japan*. Richmond: Curzon Press (JAWS series), pp. 16–26.

Ishimori, S. (1989a). 'Tabi kara ryokō he' [From journey to travel]. In Moriya Tsuyoshi (ed.), *Nihonjin to asobi* [Japanese people and playing]. Gendai Nihon bunka ni okeru dentō to henyō 6. Tokyo: Domesu shuppan, pp. 92–112.

—— (1989b). 'Popularization and commercialization of tourism in early modern Japan'. In *Japanese Civilization in the Modern World*, IV: *Economic Institutions*, Senri Ethnological Studies, 26. Osaka: National Museum of Ethnology, pp. 179–94.

—— (1995). 'Tourism and religion: from the perspective of comparative studies'. In *Japanese Civilization in the Modern World*, IX: *Tourism*, Senri Ethnological Studies, 38. Osaka: National Museum of Ethnology, pp. 179–94.

Iwai, H. (2002). *Tabi no minzoku shi* [Records on folk customs concerning the journey]. Tokyo: Kawadeshobo shinsha.

Jippenshā, I. ([1806] 1992). *A pied sur le Tōkaidō* [*Tōkaidōchu hizakurige* (Walking along the Tōkaidō)], trans. J. Campignon. Arles: Philippe Picquier.

Kanpo, O. and H. Itō (2006). *Enpitsu de Oku no hosomichi* [With a pencil the Narrow Road to the Deep North). Tokyo: Popurasha.

Kanzaki, N. (1990) *Kankō minzokugaku no tabi* [Journey to the folklorist studies of tourism]. Tokyo: Kawadeshobo shinsha.

—— (1995). 'A comparative analysis of the tourist industry'. In *Japanese Civilization in the Modern World*, IX: *Tourism*, Senri Ethnological Studies, 38. Osaka: National Museum of Ethnology, pp. 39–49.

—— (1997). *Omiyage* [Presents]. Tokyo: Seikyūsha.

Kitakawa, M. (2002). *Kankō: Tabi no bunka* [Tourism: the culture of the journey]. Kyoto: Minerva shobo.

Okada, K. (1975). *Tabi ni tsuite* [About the journey]. Tokyo: Daishindō.

—— (1977). *Kokoro no nokoru fukei (Tabi no hakken)* [Landscapes which remain in the heart (Discover on the journey)]. Tokyo: Kawade shobō shinsha Shohan edition.

—— (1991). *Tabibito Sora to Basho* [Travellers Sora and Basho]. Tokyo: Kawade shobō shinsha Shohan edition.

—— (1992). *Rekishi no naka no tabitotachi* [From inside history travellers]. Tokyo: Tamagawa daigaku shuppanbu.

Pigeot, J. (1982). *Michiyuki-bun (Poétique de l'itinéraire dans la littérature du Japon ancien)* [Poetic of the itinerary in the literature of ancient Japan]. Paris: Editions G.-P. Maisonneuve et Larose.

Plutschow, H. (2006). *A Reader in Edo Period Travel*. Folkestone: Global Oriental.

Sadler, A.L. (trans.) (1940). *Saka's Diary of a Pilgrim to Ise*. Tokyo: Meiji Japan Society.

Satō, Y. and C. Fujiwara (2000). *Ukiyoe ni miru Edo no tabi* [Travel during the Edo period through prints]. Tokyo: Kashutsu shobō shinsha.

Shiba, R. (1971–1996). *Kaidō o yuku* [Going along the highway]. *Asahi Weekly*, January 1971 to March 1996. Tokyo: Asahi Shimbunsha.

Shirahata, Y. (1996). *Ryokō no susume* [Recommendation of travel]. Tokyo: Chuōkōronsha.

Tabi [Journey] (1924–2004, monthly). Tokyo: JTB.

Tabi to iu na no jōseishi [Women's magazine called Tabi] (from May 2005). Tokyo: Shinchosha.

Toraya Bunko (2006). *'Wagashi de tanoshimu dōchū nikki' Ten* [Exhibition on 'Travel journal that can be savoured with sweets']. Tokyo: Toraya.

Vaporis, C.N. (1994). *Breaking Barriers: Travel and the State in Early Modern Japan*. Cambridge, MA, and London: Harvard University, Council on East Asian Studies.

Yamamoto, H. (1998). *Sankin kōtai* [Alternate attendance]. Tokyo: Kōdansha.

Part I

Travelling history in the present

1 The past and the other in the present

Kokunai kokusaika kanko –
domestic international tourism

Nelson Graburn

With a candor far removed from the usual poetic fog of the imperial court, Emperor Akihito, in remarks to the news media that took Japan by surprise in December, all but declared his own Korean ancestry. Speaking of the culture and technology brought to Japan . . . [he] said that 'it contributed greatly to Japan's subsequent development.' Then, he added, 'I, on my part, feel a certain kinship with Korea,' and went on to cite an ancient chronicle that says that the grandmother of his eighth-century imperial ancestor, Kammu, was from a Korean kingdom.

(Howard W. French, *New York Times*, 11 March 2002)

Introduction [1]

It is not often that, in my career as an ivory tower social scientist, I have been scooped by a member of the imperial family. This quote refers to a particular strand in the complex phenomenon of Japan's relations to outside peoples and nations, the cultural and now it appears 'filial' ties between Japan and Korea. This particular strand has been neglected, avoided and denied by most Japanese until recently (DeVos and Lee 1981; Ohnuki-Tierney 1990). The story that I relate here involves two places where the relations of Japan to Korea in the historical past – one where Koreans settled in Japan four centuries ago, and the other more than 1,300 years ago – have been recognized and promoted for a complex set of reasons, and whose present sites are the targets of domestic and international tourism.

The point in this experimental chapter on tourism and foreignness is to show how the usual construction of spatial identity by which places and regions get themselves 'on the map' (Graburn 1995) has been expanded by the inclusion of domesticated foreignness. In this case we may reverse Lowenthal's dictum (Lowenthal 1985) by stating that 'a foreign country is the past'. In this case the insertion of Koreanness into the structured panoply of *meibutsu* (things to be famous for) has reflected with both the ideological trend towards liberal multiculturalism in Japan (Graburn 2002, 2003; Graburn *et al.* 2007; Lie 2001) and pragmatic responses to Koreans' emergence as the leading sources of foreign tourists entering Japan since the early

1990s. A unique feature of one of the following cases is the asserted connection between core features of Japanese culture and antecedent features coming from Korea and the implied relationship between the Korean connection and the mythological, archaeological and historical origins of Japan's imperial family.

Those aspects of Chineseness and Koreanness coming from the dawn of Japanese civilization are not commonly recognized as 'foreign' except in the analytical sense. Foreignness consists of the frequent and remembered incursions and borrowing from the outside world within recorded history. Until the Tokugawa shoguns closed Japan at the beginning of the seventeenth century, the Japanese were often in trade (or at war) with overseas civilizations, and the Japanese countryside is marked with sites and memories of these contacts. Historically remembered events or sites are part of the fabric of today's Japan; most places have special events or products which contribute(d) to the organic whole. Thus each location has one or more allegedly unique characteristics, *meibutsu* (things it is famous for), which are key tourist attractions, *even if they are non-Japanese* (cf. Hendry 2000 for a slightly different version of foreignness as Japanese). It is the uniqueness of a place that is its particular part in 'making Japan' (Wigan 1997). Thus different areas are known by different events, characteristics and products.

It happens that the southern island of Kyushu 'is unique' for its multiple non-Japanese historical events and characteristics. According to a typical Japanese guidebook for domestic tourists (Ikuchi 1999: 18), 'Kyushu has always been a window on other cultures', i.e. its 'near foreignness' is its *meibutsu*, the thing for which it is famous within the Japanese system.

This is particularly true of the southernmost *daimyo*ship, known as Satsuma province (centred on but covering more than present-day Kagoshima), which is famous not only for spearheading the revolution which toppled the shogunate and put the emperor back on the throne in 1868, but also for its long history of foreign contacts. Some people of that area today are proud to say that they were far from Tokyo and Kyoto so their *daimyo* could get away with things that other Japanese could not.

Miyama: domesticated Koreanness

Prime among the historical evidence of foreignness and hence the sources of many 'foreign attractions' for domestic tourists are: Christianity, brought by the Portuguese Jesuits led by Saint Francis Xavier (Nagai 2001; Turnbull 1996; Whelan 1997) in the fifteenth century (leading eventually to their expulsion and the 'closing' of Japan); the long history of trade and eventually incorporation of the Ryukyuan kingdom of Okinawa in the eighteenth century, a direct source of trade and products from China and South-East Asia; and the Imjin War when Shogun Toyotomi Hideyoshi invaded Korea in the 1590s. The seventeenth *daimyo*, Shimazu Yoshihiro of Kagoshima, accompanied Hideyoshi to Korea and, when the invasion was eventually repelled, he had 80 Korean potters brought back with him. They were set up in three towns in Satsuma where there were suitable clays and minerals, in order to produce superior porcelain and pottery, known as *Satsumayaki*, as sumptuary goods for the *daimyo* and nobility. This 'stolen' Korean tradition is so important to Koreans that the invasion is sometimes called the 'pottery war', especially as Korea lost its best traditions and skills in later history (Geon-Soo Han, personal communication, 2000).

The town of Miyama (Beautiful Mountain), formerly known as Naeshiro-gawa, about an hour's drive west of Kagoshima City, is famous for two phenomena of 'national' importance. Firstly, it is the site of the manufacture of *Satsumayaki*, a distinctive kind of pottery characteristic of Satsuma (see above), in its 14 working kilns. Secondly, there is a memorial hall dedicated to the life and works of the infamous former minister of foreign affairs in the Pacific War, Togo Shigenori[2] (Ikuchi 1999: 336–7).

There are two major forms of pottery produced in Miyama today. The more famous and expensive form is called 'white' *Satsumayaki*, which includes pottery with painted decorative motifs over a 'crackled' golden-yellow base colour; it looks distinctively Japanese yet, when compared with now more popular and stereotypical, stark, *shibui* (simple yet refined) asymmetrical pottery, one might suspect some Chinese influence. For even less utilitarian purposes there is another more purely white unpainted form of pottery, usually in the form of sculptural figurines rather than dishes. In the less expensive register is 'black' *Satsumayaki*, which the promotional brochures say 'is widely cherished among the common people [consisting of] items such as tea pots, tea cups and such . . . deeply rooted to the people's daily lives'. Of course many readers will recognize such phrases as reminiscent of the language of Yanagi Muneyoshi, who 'created' the idea of the artless peasant craftsman and popularized his *mingei* (folk art) products (Moeran 1981). Like nearly all such contemporary pottery in Japan, it is consumed by middle-class urbanites for its slightly nostalgic '*furusato*-like' (like the rural village community where most ancestors of the Japanese originally came from) qualities.

Primus inter pares among these 14 potters – all of Korean descent – (and one guitar maker) in the village is the 'house' of Jukan Toen (Jukan Chin Satsuma ware factory).

When one enters the formal gate of the huge compound of old-fashioned wooden houses which constitutes the 'factory', one is greeted by masts with equal-sized flags, Japanese and Korean, flying side by side. Further inside, one of the side buildings is labelled 'Honorary Korean Consulate'. The major garden decoration is a large white-flowering bush, the *mugunghwa* (hibiscus syriacus), the national flower of Korea.[3]

The publicity tells that for 400 years the enterprise has been run by a Korean family, the Chin Ju Kan family (Shim Su Kwan in Korean), of which the present head goes by the 'professional' name Shim Su Kwan XIV. Since my first visit there in summer 2000, he has passed the baton on to his son Kazuteru Osako, now Shim Su Kwan XV.

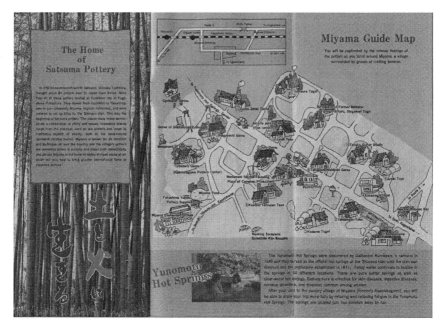

Figure 1.1 English-language tourist map of Miyama (note Jukan Toen on the main
street).

These 'professional immigrant' families used to wear Korean dress up until
the beginning of the Meiji period (1868–1912), and they used the Korean
language even longer (Brian Moeran, personal communication, 2002). The
Shim (also named Osako) family remained under the Shimazu patronage
for nearly 300 years. After the opening of Japan their wares were shown at
European expositions, where the *daimyo* often mounted his own Satsuma
pavilion (Graburn 1991: 241) and exported through to the 1870s. However, as
the *daimyos* were divested of their landed property, their sponsorship ceased
in 1875 and the family had to go it alone. Shim Su Kwan XII restored the
technique and reputation of *Satsumayaki*, and found or renewed patronage
by nobility and rich buyers abroad. He was suitably rewarded with a distinguished service medal from the export-minded Meiji government in 1885.
He even gained the patronage of the imperial household and was visited by
the prince and princess in 1893. One book emphasizes that Shim Su Kwan
XIV 'contributed significantly to cultural exchange and goodwill between
Japan and Korea' (Chinjukan 2001) and was the first Japanese to be
appointed as the honorary consul-general of Korea.

In 1998 he planned and promoted the four-hundredth anniversary of
Satsumayaki and was lionized after an exhibition in Seoul, where he received
Korea's highest cultural award, the Silver Crown medal of the Order of
Culture. Shim Su Kwan's pottery exhibition in Seoul drew 50,000, and was

accompanied by many articles, a book, and visits by many upper-class people and government officials to Miyama (Geon-Soo Han, personal communication, 2000). On the four-hundredth anniversary of the arrival of the original 80 potters by ship, the town was unusually bustling; a Korean reproduction of a sixteenth-century sailing ship came directly from the Korean coast, bringing 'fire' from the supposedly original pottery kilns there. When Korean potters carried the 'sacred fire' to Miyama, they were, according to Korean reports, reclaiming the pottery tradition by asserting that the kilns were now fired by Korean flames. The Japanese newspaper said this was the 'fire of friendship'.

Naturally, the Higashi Ichiki town office, within which Miyama falls, has latched on to these distinctive traditions, alongside its other attractions, including the Yunomoto onsen, the birthplace of Boku Heii, the grave of Shozaemeon Zusho and, of course, the commemorative hall celebrating the former minister of foreign affairs in the Second World War, Togo Shigenori.

To draw attention to the centrality of pottery in the village and regional identity, they built an imposing multi-purpose community centre beside a restored old *noborigama* (climbing kiln) on a small hill near the centre of Miyama (Naeshirogawa Pottery Center on the map in Figure 1.1). Between the centre and the old kiln is the memorial proclaiming 400 years of Korean–Japanese friendship, consisting of hundreds (perhaps 400) of clay tiles each with the hand impression of a child with its name (all Japanese as far as I could make out). Next to the hands-on clay memorial is a larger wooden plaque in Nihongo (the Japanese language) and *hangul* (the uniquely Korean form of syllabic writing) recalling the glorious relationship, erected by the Japan–Korea Friendship Society, of which our family leader, Nozoesan,[4] was an active member.

The large wooden building that serves as the community and tourist centre has in one large room pottery wheels and a kiln, for the use of amateurs such as schoolchildren, old people and tourists. It also has an impressive permanent exhibition of local pottery, as well as a gallery of local products and a shop selling ceramics as *omiyage* (souvenir gifts) and serving refreshments.

Preceding my second visit, in 2002, Shim Su Kwan XIV and his pottery were featured in the World Ceramic Exposition 2001, held in Ichon, Korea, which was the site of the Japanese–Korean revival of classical Korean pottery in the 1920s (Moon 1997). Already renowned in Korea, he was accompanied from Japan by a number of delegates from the Japanese–Korean Friendship Association from the Kagoshima area. And, expectedly, Korean-language travel literature on Japan features this 'local hero abroad' as one of the main attractions of the island of Kyushu.

The second paragraph in the Korean-language pamphlet is the statement that the Seoul-based Korean baseball team, the Lotte Giants, have been staying at the nearby Yunomoto onsen hot spring resort as their training camp since 1990! This inclusion of multiple attractions in the 'selling' of Japanese tourist locations is typical (Graburn 1983, 1995), as seen in the Miyama map

Figure 1.2 Four hundred years of friendship memorial next to *noborigama* (climbing kiln).

(Figure 1.1), which 'sells', alongside *Satsumayaki*, not only the old historical sites mentioned above but the local shrine, the guitar studio, the Togo Shigenori hall and the (road to) the Yunomoto hot springs. In the same way, the Korean-language pamphlet emphasizes the multiple 'Korean' attractions of the region, at the same time 'familiarizing' the atmosphere with the name of a 'home' team.

Koreanness emergent

Now let us step back nearly another thousand years to the tourist site of Nango Son (village) in Miyazaki prefecture, where allegedly the defeated seventh-century emperor of the Paekche (*Kudara*) kingdom sailing from the Korean peninsula found refuge in the village of Nango 40 kilometres inland from the ancient town of Hyuga on the south-east coast of Kyushu (Ikuchi 1999: 290–1). Hyuga itself recalls an almost pre-nostalgic past, for it is the present-day bearer of the surviving name of the ancient province of Hyuga, which was to the present prefecture of Miyazaki what Satsuma was to the prefecture of Kagoshima. As one follows the twisted road inland, up the valley from Hyuga, all the road signs are in Japanese and Korean *hangul* syllabic characters.

As one arrives in the small village of Nango and turns into the broad car park between the main road, running along the bottom of the hillside, and the small river which forms the other boundary, one can see the *annai*, the signboard showing the major tourist features of the place: the *Kudara* Restaurant, Kudara no Mori (the Mikado Shrine), the new 'Western Shosoin'[5] and the Paekche Palace. This small village once had a population of 7,000, but, as is typical in rural Japan (Graburn 1997), it suffered a continuous exodus and by 1990 this had dropped to 3,000; by 2002 it was about 2,500.

The Nango Restaurant is constructed in a modern 'retro-style' typical of country eating places – black beams and white registers with unpainted wooden pillars inside. Although it has 'Korean hot tables' in the middle for Korean foods, it has other attractions than Koreanness, for in Korean cuisine the menu actually only runs to something like '*Kimu Chi Setto* [set meal with the Korean pickled vegetables *kim chi*]', but it also advertises other local delicacies including a unique delicacy called *kodawari* made of *konyaku* (devil's tongue root). Next door to it is an alcohol and packaged goods store in a similar architectural style, and another larger establishment, which sold souvenirs but was not open in the winter season when I first visited.

Across the road from the restaurant, stores and large car park are the main 'attractions' of Nango. Next to the road, there are more wide car parks below the new 'Western Shosoin', and as one walks up the approach road one passes sets of the Korean folk totem-pole-like guardian spirit figures. Pairs of such figures – denoting male/heaven and female/earth – are frequently found in Korea protecting the boundaries of village communities, and their presence here signals the boundary of the Kudara no Sato 'Korean' ritual site within the Japanese village of Nango.

Figure 1.3 Brochure of Western Shosoin and Kudara Palace Pavilion.

At the top of the road is a ticket office at the edge of the broad plaza featuring this magnificent new wooden building, the 'Western Shosoin'. The building cost 16–17 *oku-en* (*oku* is 100 million; therefore it cost approximately US$14 million). It is identical in measurements and structure to the famed seventh-century Shosoin of Nara; the timber for its construction was brought all the way from the virgin forests in the mountains of Nagano, and the 38,000 tiles on its sweeping roof were specially made in Kyoto. It was built with grant monies from Tokyo in the first half of the 1990s both to serve as a tourist attraction in its own right and to display the material evidence of the Paekche–Kudara connection. This enormous building is divided into three main sections. One enters by climbing the wooden steps into the central room, as the whole building is raised on posts.

The purpose of the room to the right is to house and celebrate the 33 royal bronze mirrors found in Nango. These bronze discs have the well-known Chinese designs on the back, typical of those belonging to the ancient Korean and the Japanese royal family. These mirrors could have been made in either Korea or Japan (it appears that there has been no attempt to extract data from metallurgical analyses which might decide this question).[6] Seventeen of these mirrors were found in the Mikado Jinja (Shinto shrine) next door. Actually this part of the Shosoin contains replicas of 31 of the royal mirrors, out of a total of about 300 found in Japan, and two of the actual specimens. Publicity states emphatically that most of the other royal mirrors are found in Yamato, the original heartland of Japan centring on the Nara plain; this link with Nara and the imperial family is alluded to not only in Nango but in other tourist prehistoric sites in Miyazaki prefecture (see below). These mirrors are also connected with the imperial family through the *Kojiki* myths (a collection dating back to the beginning of the eighth century CE), which state that the heavenly goddess Amaterasu gave her wayward son Ninigi (grandfather of the first emperor, Jinmu, see below) a bronze mirror named *Yaata-no-kagami* and ordered him to worship her through worshipping it.

This huge room in the Shosoin also contains 'evidence' of the landing of the Paekche royal family by ship in the seventh century after their defeat in Korea by the combined forces of the Silla kingdom, the Tang dynasty and other Japanese; it is believed that Paekche was always the one of the three 'Korean' kingdoms most closely allied to Japan (Hong 1996). The Koreans were received on the coast of Hyuga as political refugees and given this inland spot to settle. Other evidence in this section includes archaeological Korean pottery and weapons from the appropriate period, found in the vicinity. There is also a large imaginative painting of what the scene of coming ashore may have looked like.

The centre section of the Shosoin is devoted entirely to a display of the traditional methods of construction and tools used to build it in the 1990s.

The third room, on the left, is devoted to explaining the relation with Korea and further evidence of the Paekche connection. Some of the evidence is historical, such as early Japanese travellers' accounts of the area. Presented as the definitive proof of the 'truth' behind the 'myth' of Korean origins is the research on a small piece of ancient cloth by noted historian Prof. Fukushuku, retired from Miyazaki University, as described in the *Miyazaki Daily Shimbun* (newspaper) (1996).

And dominating this section is an explanation of the local Shiwase festival which takes place every December in which the local farmers, dressed in ceremonial costumes, bring produce and compete. A special three-day section of the festival (it used to take nine to ten days in the past) is the meeting of the *goshintai* (physical abode of the *kami*, or god-spirit, within the shrine) from the Mikado Jinja in Nango and from the Hikki Jinja north of the village of Kiji some 90 kilometres to the south. On the first day they shout 'Light the fire for the *matsuri* [prayer festival].' The local officials take the wrapped *goshintai* from the Mikado Jinja and walk to the coast at Hyuga. They are met by a similar group coming from Kiji. On the middle day the two *goshintai* are introduced to each other; this is said to replicate and memorialize the annual meeting of the Korean emperor and his family, who had settled in Nango, with the party of his son, who had settled at Kiji. The third day is the goodbye ceremony, in which the two groups put on 'blackface' using charcoal. It might be suggested that this blackface, a unique and much played-up feature of this festival, may represent the 'mourning' of the 'family' groups about to part again for a year. But these days it is also a playful free-for-all in which the tourists or sightseers, especially Korean visitors, are blackened by the locals.

It is the modest but important Mikado Jinja which is central to this story. This is where some of the bronze mirrors were found under the floor and, it is rumoured, wrapped up as *goshintai*, as well as the 'proof' of the Paekche connection. This proof consists of a 20- by 25-centimetre twill cloth on which are written 16 lines in *kanbun* style, titled 'Record of the country', including descriptions of the royal castles and a notice of attack (presumably from Silla and Tang). It is suggested it is a souvenir or item of memorabilia brought to Hyuga by the Paekche emperor Nosho when he fled.[7]

Near the Shosoin but in a different compound down the hill from the Mikado Jinja is a building built as a replica of the guest house (part of an old national museum like the Shosoin?) of the seventh-century Paekche Palace, which was originally destroyed in a rout of 663 AD. After the 'proof' was established in the early 1990s, local Miyazaki delegations went to Puyo (the nearest modern town to the razed Paekche), where they held detailed discussions with Korean archaeologists and historians. They brought back the plans and reconstructed one of the pavilions of the palace.

The steps in front of the palace, leading down from the Jinja and up from the road, are pottery replicas of the decorated mirror backs. There is the entrance in the middle of the building, leading one into a central room which is the *omiyage* (gift) shop, full of Korean goods and postcards. The room to the left contains replicas of some old national treasures of Paekche. It also contains further archaeological, folkloric (the festival) and documentary evidence of the Kudara–Hyuga relationship, with geopolitical maps of Korea and sailing routes at that time.

The museum-like room on the right from the souvenir shop has a series of remarkable texts and displays showing the connections between Korean cultural features and those of early Japan. Rather than focusing on tangible, local stories and evidence, there seems to be an attempt to show that Japanese civilization *in general* is derived from nearby and slightly prior Korean civilization.

This evidence includes the overall distribution of the royal mirrors (a map of their distribution in Korea and Japan is provided) and other traits of material culture. The next three displays are separate segments, each showing similarities between key features of ancient Korean and original Japanese civilization. The first illustrates and maps the traditional construction of castles, foundations and moats. The second shows traditional Japanese agricultural implements against their counterparts in early Korea. The last section attempts to prove the similarities of Japanese Shinto shrines to their architectural and spiritual antecedents in Korea, by showing photographs and reconstructions, detailing the diagnostic identical features.

Although we might at first imagine that these mythical Korean features are played up as part of the entrepreneurial effort to attract Korean tourists, the prime source of overseas tourists to Japan, we should realize that the Koreans too, at both the popular and the scholarly level, are looking for 'stolen' or 'escaped' remnants of Korea's rich historical and cultural heritage in Japan. There is a very significant scholarship in Korean academia, which might be translated as non-anthropological 'folklore' but which might more fruitfully be compared to Japan's own nativist *minzokugaku* (nativist anthropology) followers of Yanagita (Timothy Tangherlini and Park Jeehwan, personal communications, 2004). Prime among these experts is the doyen Im, Tonggwon (Imu, Donguon in Japanese), who has published extensive research on the festival and material remains at Nango, as well as reputed Kudara material culture in Shiga prefecture, backing up the Japanese findings. He has not only published these findings in Korean (1994) but has himself translated these works into Japanese (2001). Thus the 'pressure to believe' these connections now exists on both sides of the divide.

Behind the material and historical 'Korean connection' between Miyazaki and Paekche is a complex of beliefs a lot older than this 'recently proven' discovery. Miyazaki is home to a number of important (pre)historical sites through which it claims originary priority with the Korean and/or Japanese imperial family/ies, whether as descendants of Korea or of the heavens. There are four major such sites which have been 'named, framed and elevated' (MacCannell 1989) as tourist sites, and the Nango (Kudara–Paekche) story is more recent than the other three in being put on the 'tourist map'. All of these sites are joined together on today's tourist maps of Miyazaki prefecture as *Shinwa: Dentsu no Michi roodo Chizu* (literally 'The road map of God's

Word: the Route of Legend', more colloquially 'The Road of Myth and Legend', perhaps modelled after the successful *Rekishi Kaido* (http://www.kiis.or.jp/rekishi/kaido-e.html, 2005) which was implemented by local governments to unite historical sites in the Kansai area into a 'tourist country'. This in turn was modelled on a Japanese examination of the Romantische Strasse (historic Romantic Road, a tourist route in southern Germany) in the German Rhine region (Shuzo Ishimori, personal communication, 1990)).

1   High on the Kirishima Plateau on the very border of Miyazaki and Kagoshima is Mount Takachiho, with the peak Takachiho-no-mine reaching 1,574 metres. It is upon this very visible peak that Ninigi, the

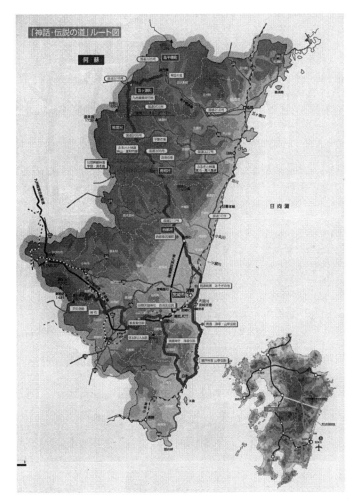

Figure 1.4 The past is a foreign country: the 'Road of Legend' map showing (south to north) Udo Jingu, Saitobaru, Nango Son and Takachiho.

grandson of the sky goddess Amaterasu, was supposed to have come down to earth and founded the imperial line. Indeed at the base of this mountain is the resplendent Takachiho Jingu (imperial shrine) commemorating the fact. Further material 'proof' is provided in the form of a slab of *sazare-ishi*, or conglomerate rock, the very kind featured in the national anthem, the *Kimigayo*, which wishes the emperor to reign 'as long is it takes small pebbles to become one rock'.[8]

2   Down the coast south of Miyazaki City is the spectacular Udo Jingu (cormorant shrine) in a cave by the sea. Here, according to the *Kojiki*, Ninigi's third son, Hoori-non-Mikoto, accompanied his wife Toyotama-hime, who gave birth to a son, Ugaya-Hukiaezu-no-Mikoto. However, Toyotama, daughter of the sea goddess, turned (back) into a dragon (*wani*, also crocodile or shark) and the poor child had to be nursed at the breast-like protuberances on the rock wall in the cave from which drip milky water even to this day. Udo Jingu is a popular and much photographed tourist attraction; it has long attracted honeymooners, and drinking the watery 'milk' which drips off the two stone 'breasts' is said to enhance fertility.

   The imperial connection is further amplified by the marriage of Ugaya to his mother's sister Tamayori-hime, who bore four sons, the last of whom, Iwarebiko, became known as Jinmu, the first emperor of Japan – to whom Miyazaki City's central shrine is dedicated. Emerging from 'mythology' is the story recounting how Jinmu assembled an army (or a navy) and fought his way north and east to the plain of Nara to found the Yamato state.

3   Moving from 'mythical protohistory' to 'protohistoric archaeology', the Miyazaki plain also contains 311 or more burial mounds at Saito-baru Kofun Koen (the Saitobaru Burial Mound Park). Archaeologists dug a few first in the late nineteenth century, and the whole site was recognized as a national property in 1952. The earlier ones are round and only a few metres across, whereas the later ones are keyhole-shaped and two of them are enormous, at 217 and 174 metres long. I was told by local scholars (in 1974) that these tombs show the earliest development of the imperial family, from early small chieftains with the round sites, growing larger over the centuries and culminating in 'imperial-sized' key-hole Kofun which resemble those found in the Nara plain which are directly attributed to named emperors. Indeed legend has it that the largest Saitobaru Kofun is the resting place of Ninigi. I was fascinated to find a brochure in *hangul* characters available for Korean tourists in Miyazaki in 2004 which set out in detail the whole genealogical history of the mythical ancestors of the Japanese imperium from Amaterasu on. So, just as the Japanese are expected to believe 'Korean' claims to the cultural history of the area, Korean tourists are expected to accept Japanese claims to the origin myths of this culturally numinous area.

Thus the entrepreneurs of Miyazaki are 'covering all bases' in connecting their semi-tropical territory both to the unchallengeable mythological origins of Japan as well as to the historically plausible connections to the Korean royal family in exile. The Road of Myth and Legend connects two mythological, and one archaeological, underpinnings of the imperial and hence national history, and the latest addition implies through its 'imperial mirrors' another historical, and foreign, connection to the same central theme. But no one so far has told the story of how the descendants of Emperor Nosho made their way from the villages of Nango or Kiji either to Takachiho or to the cave of Udo Jingu. Nor could one explain 'rationally' the connection between Jinmu's emergence, conventionally ascribed to 660 BC, and the fall of Paekche in AD 663.

Discussion

These data tell the visitor that the southern provinces of Kyushu were 'unique' in Japanese national history in being able to import foreignness and that in general some admired parts of Japanese civilization came from Korea to southern Kyushu. In this chapter and at the tourist sites, the Koreanness of these (pre)historic features is foregrounded. While the majority of the tourists are domestic Japanese, the Miyama family and tradition have been major news in Korea.[9] This mixed domestic–international attraction is visited both by international exchange students, being shown something 'uniquely Japanese', and by regular domestic tourists seeing something 'not quite Japanese'. Japanese guidebooks have increasingly played up the Korean connection and recognize this as an 'improved' kind of Korean pottery. This is relatively new compared with the chauvinistic expressions of the earlier part of the twentieth century. I contend here and elsewhere (Graburn 2002, 2003; Graburn *et al.* 2007) that these developments reflect a permanent change in attitude of the Japanese, with an acceptance of aspects of foreignness in spite of the politicians fighting a rearguard action. The soccer World Cup shared between Japan and Korea in 2002, which took place after my visit to Kyushu, showed that young people were more likely to sympathize with these new strands of internationalism. Japan has always been in the process of self-renewal (Vlastos 1999) and since the Meiji era, as Wigan has showed (1997), foreigners have been both passive and active players. This dialectic is now encouraged both by the successful efforts at *kokusaika* (internationalization) after more than two decades of official policy and by the equally powerful external incentive of Korea's new-found penchant for overseas tourism.

Notes

1 This is the kind of research where input from a network of friends is almost essential. In this case I am particularly grateful for assistance and communications from Jeff Hester (Kansai Gaidai), Geon-Soo Han (Kangwon University), Timothy

Tangherlini (UCLA), Shinji Yamashita (University of Tokyo), Hachiro Uchiyama (Kobe), Prof. Junko Habu, Mitzi Uehara Carter, Yuko Okubo, Maki Tanaka, Park Jeehwan and especially Kenji Tierney and Minkoo Kim (the latter five Berkeley graduate students at that time) and to my hosts in Japan in 2000 and 2002, the Obara, Ono and Yaguchi families. I also sincerely thank the editors for their guidance and patience.

2 Larger and more imposing than all the potteries is the newly built memorial hall for former foreign minister Togo Shigenori (1882–1950) erected near his birthplace (see Figure 1.1); he was born to a son of the Chin Ju Kan pottery family who had been adopted by a Japanese family. His brilliant scholarship in language and history led to his joining the Gaimusho (foreign ministry) after Tokyo University. As a Germanophile he became ambassador to Germany (married a German and trans-lated Fascist works into Japanese) and was twice minister of foreign affairs during the Second World War. He was tried and found guilty as a first-class war criminal and died in prison in 1950. Chin Ju Kan XIV spearheaded the fundraising to build the impressive hall.

3 The *mugunghwa* flower was adopted as the national flower in 1907, so we should not imagine that the Shim family planted them long ago to assuage their nostalgia for their lost homeland!

4 Nozoesan was a fan of Shim Su Kwan. As a relative of the Yaguchi family (my wife's parents) in Kamou-Cho, Kagoshima, he first introduced us to Miyama and the potters and accompanied us again on a second visit.

5 This wooden building (Figure 1.3) is an exact copy of the eighth-century royal treasure house of Todaiji temple, in Nara, which contains materials from the reign of the Emperor Shomu and materials from the construction of the Great Buddha. The Western Shosoin is constructed from timbers from the mountains of Nagano, where the original Shosoin timbers came from, and it has 57,000 ceramic roof tiles specially baked in a Kyoto kiln.

6 Berkeley archaeologist Prof. Junko Habu says that their 'country of origin' could probably be discerned by the style of the design on the back.

7 This kind of link to Korea through recently discovered material 'proofs' is not unique. For instance, I have another Korean-language pamphlet which claims a special relationship between Tottori-ken and the Korean region of Pyong Hae. A 'recently found document' with an explanation of *hangul* writing and an old picture of Japanese and Koreans in pre-modern dress tells the story of a Korean ship from Pyong Hae which was blown off course by a typhoon in 1819 and landed in Tottori, where the sailors were treated with great kindness and returned home.

8 The *Kimigayo* was 'invented' as a national anthem and put to music first by a British and then by a German adviser working with the imperial army in the 1880s, but the words were taken from a tenth- or eleventh-century poem.

9 During the Japanese occupation of Korea (1910–45) Japanese connoisseurs became very interested in developing Korean pottery that they had long admired (see the Miyama story). However, many of the kilns had closed down with the weakening of patronage from the Korean wealthy and nobility. One Japanese connoisseur devoted himself to a search for the courses of certain historically (and archaeo-logically) important glazes, e.g. green celadon, and working with local Korean potters found the old sources. In the 1920s a large ceramic industry grew up in towns such as Ichon, *ca.*50 kilometres south of Seoul, producing 'traditional' Korean pottery mainly for a Japanese clientele. The Japanese became assiduous admirers, collectors and exhibitors. After the Second World War, with Japanese patronage withdrawn, ceramic production nearly ceased, but was revived again in the late 1950s and early 1960s, at a time when some Koreans were getting wealthy enough to buy it and when the Japanese began to revisit Korea as tourists. Korean anthropologist Moon has analysed this process (1997) and concludes that this

Japanese colonial and touristic domination has distorted the pottery away from true Korean traditions and taste (though not all Koreans would agree). Having visited the area myself, I would add that for visiting Japanese (most of the buyers) it is like coming 'home' in that the ceramics are what they see exhibited and owned at home, and the prices are all displayed in yen (and US dollars) but at 25 per cent of the price demanded in Tokyo. Japanese tourists in Japan and later on Korea feel that the best of this ceramic tradition is a kind of Japanese cultural creation (or re-creation), which happens to be made in Korea.

References

Chinjukan (2001). *Ranko senri: Chinjukanke rekidai denseihin shuuzouku zuroku* [Orchid fragrance a thousand leagues: catalogue of the Chinjukan family archival records handed down through the generations]. Miyama, Kagoshima: Chinjukan-gama.

DeVos, G. A. and C. Lee (1981). *Koreans in Japan: Ethnic Conflict and Accommodation*. Berkeley: University of California Press.

Graburn, N.H.H. (1983). *To Pray, Pay and Play: The Cultural Structure of Japanese Domestic Tourism*. Les Cahiers du Tourisme, Série B, Numéro 26. Aix-en-Provence: Centre des Hautes Etudes Touristiques.

—— (1991). 'Tokubetsu supiichi' [Special speech at the symposium 'Why do flowers attract people?']. In Advanced Application Program Co. (T. Yoneyama) (ed.), *Report of the General Study of the International Garden and Greenery Exposition, Osaka, Japan, 1990*. Osaka: Advanced Application Program Co., pp. 240–51, 264, 273.

—— (1995). 'The past in the present in Japan: nostalgia and neo-traditionalism in contemporary Japanese domestic tourism'. Chapter 4 in R.W. Butler and D.G. Pearce (eds), *Changes in Tourism: People, Places, Processes*. London: Routledge, pp. 47–70.

—— (1997). 'Work and play in the Japanese countryside'. In S. Linhart and S. Freusteuck (eds), *The Culture of Japan as Seen through Its Leisure*. New York: SUNY Press, pp. 195–212.

—— (2002). 'When is domestic tourism "international"? Multiculturalism and tourism in Japan'. Paper for the International Academy for the Study of Tourism, Macao.

—— (2003). 'Communities of foreignness: models of cultural diversity in the new Japan'. Paper presented at the International Conference on Diversity: Peoples, Communities, Nations (organized by Paul James, RMIT, Melbourne), East–West Center, Honolulu.

Graburn, N.H.H., J. Ertl and R.K. Tierney (eds) (2007). *Multiculturalism in the New Japan*. New York and Oxford: Berghahn.

Hendry, J. (2000). *The Orient Strikes Back: A Global View of Cultural Display*. Oxford: Berg.

Hong, W. (1996). *Paekche of Korea and the Origin of Yamato Japan*. Seoul: Kudara International.

Ikuchi, N. (1999). *Hitori aruki no Kyushyu* [One person's walkabout in Kyushu]. Tokyo: Japan Travel Bureau.

Imu, D. (2001). *Nihon no naka no Kudara bunka: shiwasu matsuri to kishitsu jinja o chushin ni* [Paekche culture found inside Japan]. Tokyo: Daiichi Shobo. (Translated by the author from: Im, Tong-gwon (1994). *Ilbon an ui Paekche munhwa: Sajuje wa kwisil sinsa rul chungsim uro*. Seoul: Hanguk Kukche Kyoryu Chaedan.)

Lie, J. (2001). *Multiethnic Japan*. Cambridge, MA: Harvard University Press.

Lowenthal, D. (1985). *The Past is a Foreign Country*. Cambridge: Cambridge University Press.

MacCannell, D. (1989). *The Tourist: A New Theory of the Leisure Class*. New York: Schocken.

Moeran, B. (1981). 'Yanagi Muneyoshi and the Japanese folk craft movement'. *Asian Folklore Studies*, 40(1), pp. 87–99.

Moon, O. (1997). 'Tourism and cultural development: Japanese and Korean contexts'. In S. Yamashita, K. Din and J.S. Eades (eds), *Tourism and Cultural Development in East Asia and Oceania*. Bangi: University of Malaysia Press, pp. 178–93.

Nagai, A. (2001). 'Getting away: secret religious history reduced to a memory'. *Yomiuri Shimbun*, 16 June.

Ohnuki-Tierney, E. (1990). 'The ambivalent self of the contemporary Japanese'. *Cultural Anthropology*, 5(2), pp. 197–216.

Turnbull, S. (1996). *The Kakure Kirishtan of Japan: A Study of their Development, Beliefs and Rituals to the Present Day*. London: Curzon.

Vlastos, S (ed.) (1999). *Mirror of Modernity: Japan's Invented Traditions*. Berkeley: University of California Press.

Whelan, C. (1997). *Otaiya: Japan's Hidden Christians*. University of Hawaii, Department of Anthropology (34-minute video).

Wigan, K. (1997). 'Constructing Shinano: the invention of a neo-traditional region'. In S. Vlastos (ed.), *Mirror of Modernity: Japan's Invented Traditions*. Berkeley: University of California Press, pp. 229–42.

2 The heroic Edo-ic

Travelling the history highway in today's Tokugawa Japan

Millie Creighton

Introduction

In this chapter, I explore the present presence of Edo past in contemporary Japanese domestic travel and tourism campaigns, museum stagings and consumer-oriented re-creations of history for edutainment (education and entertainment, see Creighton 1992, 1994a, 1994b, 1998a, 1998c, 2001) purposes. In *Globalization and Social Change in Contemporary Japan*, Jerry Eades notes the growing rapprochement of anthropology, sociology and history. 'The stuff of history', he writes, 'has become the research material of anthropology' (Eades 2000: 4). This is particularly pertinent to anthropological research on contemporary Japanese tourism and other mass and popular culture offerings, in which historic eras have captured leading roles – staged for a nostalgic populace seemingly insecure about Japanese identity against a lifestyle now highly westernized and internationalized.[1] The Japanese historic epoch most prominently cast in the role of hero, offering reassurances of the continuity of a Japanese spirit and core, is Edo. The Edo era (1603–1868) is named for its focal city, Edo (present-day Tokyo), whose urban culture is strongly associated with its emerging commoner and middle-class culture. The period is also called Tokugawa after the ruling military shogunate government. To this period are attributed the unification of Japan and the corollary consolidation of a 'truly Japanese culture', the development of transportation and road networks, including five major 'highways', initially to service the system of alternate attendance, or *sankin kōtai*, but also resulting in the beginnings of travel and tourism for ordinary people, inns built throughout the country, commerce, the development of mass literacy, and along with it literature for the masses and advertising directed at them. The Edo era is famous for *sakoku*, the shogunate's policy of a 'closed country' through which interaction with the outside world was outside the range of ordinary Japanese and controlled for those among whom it was in a limited manner allowed.[2]

Edo as hero is not just an historic epoch, but a pre-eminent ingredient in modern Japanese identity constructions. Desiring further internationalization (*kokusaika*), Japan looks towards 'globalization' but seeks to centre itself first within its Edo-ic womb of domestic seclusion. Facing change and an uncertain future, Japan seeks continuity in Edo. In order to explore contemporary touristic forays into this historic Japanese epoch, I would like to first ask the following question. Is Edo a time or a place? For some, when the word 'Edo' is used, the first emerging association is a time frame, 1603–1868. For others, it is the idea of a place, the spatial location now thought of as Tokyo, Japan, which was called Edo during those years. There is a long-existing orientation towards establishing rank orders among things as seemingly diverse as siblings, educational institutions and types of retailing stores in Japan (see Nakane 1970; Creighton 1992). This extends to concepts of place and to tourism. Martinez (1990) found that an emphasis on ranking resulted in the designation of Kusaki as the number one traditional village for modern tourism in Japan. Through much of the Edo period, Edo was the number one location, the country's pivotal central core (a ranking that Edo's offspring, Tokyo, has retained and remains unwilling to relinquish). Edo, however, is also used to refer to the time period itself, an historic epoch delineated as lasting a bit more than two and a half centuries that was occurring everywhere in Japan *at the same time*.

In her essay 'The invention of Edo', historian Carol Gluck problematizes the collapse of Edo as era and Edo as urban forerunner to Tokyo. For Gluck (1998: 262), the Edo period signifies an historical imaginary of 'before-the-modern' that encapsulates a world 'identified as Japanese "tradition"' for contemporary ('modern') Japanese. She points out that this is 'Edo' the era, not the city later to be called Tokyo. Such reminders caution us about the tendency to associate Edo as time with Edo as place. When contemplating 'Edo' I often think first of Edo as the forerunner to Tokyo, not places known by such present designations as the Tōhoku region or Miyagi prefecture, nor areas outside Edo still vernacularly called by Edo era designations such as 'Awa' or 'Shinshū' or the Satsuma domain – places that in the mental imaginary all lived through the Tokugawa times. With prominent portrayals of urban-dwelling commoner and merchant classes, projections of the *Edo Edo Jidai* (Edo era of Edo the city) tend to be about the development of the city's merchant class, the city's emerging popular entertainments, the Yoshiwara or brothel quarters, and the newly evolving middle class of urban commoners. Areas outside of Edo during the Edo era are still pertinent to the mental imagining of an Edo-focused Edo era, because this was the period when a standardized form of money was established orchestrating national commerce, and also when the country was unified by road systems, so that the people of Edo who were not in Edo could get to Edo – hopefully in time, so they could be at the right place at the right time.

Part of the reason Edo is so prominent as historic hero is that the collapse of Edo as time and place makes the suggestion that one can travel back to Edo seem more plausible. Human beings have not yet invented the mechanism to physically travel through time, but they can travel to other places. Place locations that suggest a merging with alternative positions in time more easily allow for the suggested movement toward another temporal frame. Human beings have long contemplated the philosophical idea that time is but a place, suggesting that time is somehow analogous to place. Different times reflect different lifestyles, different cultures. Just as travel to different places allows people to experience such differences, there is the sense that we could do the same temporally if we but had a mechanism to travel through time. H.G. Wells suggested in his novel *The Time Machine* that 'Time is only a kind of Space' ([1895] 2001: 61). His fictitious time traveller proclaims: 'There are really four dimensions, three which we call the three planes of Space, and a fourth, Time. There is, however, a tendency to draw an unreal distinction between the former three dimensions and the latter' ([1895] 2001: 60). Wells' fictitious time traveller changes this by creating a time machine to allow travel along the fourth dimension.

Outside of fiction, human beings have not yet invented that particular machine, but they have created substitutes, referred to as the 're-invention of tradition' and the 're-creation of history'. My travelogue in this essay is precisely about the re-invention and re-creation of Edo as history and as repository of Japanese tradition. Along with assurances of cultural continuity and identity, the re-creation of Edo provides recreation for present-day Japanese through the offerings of contemporary domestic tourism and leisure industries.

I suggest three things about today's Tokugawa tourism to Edo. First, the terms Edo and Tokugawa, while referring to the same time period, are not completely synonymous, but evoke different connotations. Second, the appeal to Edo helps mediate the tension between the current quest for greater global participation on the part of Japanese and fears of a vanishing cultural identity thought to stem from strong local place connections, suggested in the contemporary nostalgic appeal of *furusato* (home village or home place) Japan. The juxtaposition of Edo/Tokyo as time/place helps offset concerns about the internationalized now of Tokyo and Japan, through the buffer zone of an internalized then of Edo Japan. Third, in Japan the merging of time and place travel is facilitated by parallel usage of temporal and spatial concepts. Japanese language usage suggests Japanese already have a cognitive understanding that, to paraphrase Wells, time is just a kind of space. The Japanese word *ma* means a space – a space in architecture such as a room, but also a space in time, such as a pause in music. The word *uchi* can refer to the inside of a space, the inside of a period of time, or the inside networks of human relationships.

When more than one term or label exists for the same item or phenomenon, often they are not simple synonyms, but have different connotative meanings. I suggest that the terms Edo and Tokugawa, although used to label the same era, evoke different associations in the historical imaginary of the time period. First, in scholarship on Japanese history, the term 'Edo' has been utilized more within Japan, while 'Tokugawa' has more frequently been used outside Japan, particularly in western scholarship. Within Japan there are suggestions, exemplified by literature for domestic travel campaigns focusing on the period, that 'Edo' and 'Tokugawa' differentially evoke period associations. 'Edo' is more strongly associated with the commoner culture as displayed in the large urban centre of Edo. The 'Edo' era is more often populated with themes and stories of the emerging urban middle classes, in their struggles to evade governmental authorities, and their escapes into pleasure and entertainment. In discussing the 'invention of Edo', Gluck (1998: 278) asks; 'but where have all the *bushi* [samurai or military class] gone?' I would answer that perhaps one should look for the *bushi* not in the Edo era but in Tokugawa times. The term 'Tokugawa' has stronger associations with the era's contrasting aspects, the shogunate, government authority, and the elite samurai or *bushi* class that served the shogunate.

In re-creations for touristic purposes, I noted that the term 'Edo' or phrase 'Edo era' occurred in discussions of merchant culture or lifestyle, whether in the city of Edo or elsewhere in Japan. Discussions about government outpost stations or castle towns often did not specifically use the phrase 'Edo era' and, although not using the phrase 'Tokugawa era', more often referred to particular Tokugawa shoguns. 'Tokugawa' suggests the hegemonic authority of the era, while 'Edo' suggests resistance to it by a newly rising literate middle class. That this differential association occurs in Japan is suggested by Japanese writer Haga Toru, who proposes that Japanese historians join their western counterparts in calling the period Tokugawa, because 'Edo' drums up associations of the urban *chōnin* (commoner) culture of Tokyo past, with images of Kabuki plays, and courtesans of the *yoshiwara* or pleasure quarters. Unlike many others, Haga does not value the commoner culture, but instead values the 'uniqueness' brought about through the long period of peace and tranquillity, secured by the Tokugawa shogunate. He writes:

> It is this bad habit [calling it Edo] of making the Tokugawa civilization's precious profoundness and unexpected universality, small and confining by constraining the Tokugawa period to the three-color drapery of the Kabuki theatre, and the kind of dandyism [of Edo].
>
> (Haga 1987: 68, my translation)[3]

Other examples show some Japanese scholars using the terms differentially. In discussing the diversity of the period, Shiba Ryotaro (1995: 14) uses the phrase 'Edo period' when discussing the flourishing merchant economy but refers to locations far from Edo in terms of the Tokugawa period, such as when he writes about 'feudal Saga of the late Tokugawa period' (1995: 15).

The modern Japanese travel and tourism industries seem just as guilty as Japan scholars of associating specific places with either the Edo era or Tokugawa times. If the Edo era took place everywhere in Japan (not just Edo), it can also be said that all of Japan went through Tokugawa times.

This means that if Japanese really wanted to reconnect with their past Edo/Tokugawa selves they would not have to go anywhere at all, but simply stay put wherever in Japan they are, because, as Lowenthal points out, 'the past is everywhere' (1985: xv). However, such awakenings do not propel promotional campaigns of travel and tourism industries, nor serve as an ideological force conjoining Japanese in a unified identity based on a sense of shared history that is also fused with the current geographical core of governmental power, authority and commerce, Tokyo.

In order to explore how Japanese tourism and other mass culture industries package and stage history travel to Edo, time and place, this chapter will discuss more fully the connections between nostalgic journeys and Japanese identity, looking at the symbolism of travel, roads and bridges in Japan. It will present the *Rekishi Kaidō*, or 'History Highway', travel campaign, emphasizing the occurrence of Edo, along with other historic epochs, in areas *other than* just Edo/Tokyo. The reader will be taken on a packaged magical history tour from the outside foreign now, through the Osaka *kuchi* (mouth or 'opening'), into Japan, to travel to some Edo/Tokugawa historic places, and then out again through another *kuchi*, the site of Edo/Tokyo, connector between Japan's internalized repository of its inner self of heritage and tradition symbolized by Edo past – espoused as still present – along with its internationalized gateway to the outer world and its modern self symbolized by Tokyo present and projected into the future.

Nostalgic journeys and Japanese identities

From the 1970s on, Japan became enmeshed in what one Japanese scholar called a 'retro boom' (Akatsuka 1988). Having emerged from the earlier years of post-war poverty to achieve the so-called economic miracle and a highly westernized lifestyle replete with consumer goods, Japanese began to wonder what had been sacrificed in the process and whether the basis of Japanese identity had faded with shifting lifestyles. Befu (1983: 259) claims that Japan's modern western lifestyle has 'brought about Japan's identity crisis on a massive scale'. Amidst this nostalgia for the lost past, a *furusato* (home village) boom ensued that sought out remote or rural areas thought to represent Japan's pre-industrial agrarian heritage.[4] Japan's pre-industrial history of urban centres was not entirely forgotten. Bestor's work shows that, even though it is a concentrated metropolitan area, Tokyo is conceptualized by local dwellers as 'neighborhood Tokyo' (Bestor 1989). '*Furusato* Tokyo' became a buzz phrase to represent the home 'village-like' life in neighbourhoods of Edo, the forerunner to Tokyo. Despite the nostalgic appeal of the lost village, Japanese also eagerly sought increased internationalization. From the mid-1980s, the Japanese government made *kokusaika* (internationalization) a national incentive, while ordinary Japanese were actively pursuing their own form of internationalization in the form of overseas travel, a trend that continued to increase throughout the 1990s.

Robertson points out that, despite their seemingly contradictory nature, *kokusaika* and the nostalgia for village Japan represent two complementary aspects of Japanese society. She writes:

> *Kokusaika* (internationalization) and *furusato* (native place) are perhaps the two most compelling and ubiquitous catchwords used in Japan today. On the surface they appear to represent opposite trajectories: a centrifugal movement in the case of internationalization, and a centripetal movement in the case of native place-making.
>
> (Robertson 1998: 110)

Internationalization is associated with opening up to the rest of the world, localism with a form of parochialism, nostalgically symbolized by Japan's semi-closure to the outside world during Edo. The appeal to Edo (more than Tokugawa) allows the mediation of the tension between these two seemingly contradictory desires for greater global participation and a return to the cultural identity signified by a Japanese past, and localized attachments to place. Edo's appeal lies in its ability to conjoin the era of Japan's pre-industrial, pre-opening to the west with the contemporary place of Tokyo, one of Japan's intense sites of interface with the international world. It does this through Edo/Tokyo's ability to represent both 'then' and 'now' in the same spatial location.

In contemporary Japan, the culture of travel involves both movements 'inside' and 'outside' Japan, echoing important Japanese spatial frameworks of *uchi* (inside) and *soto* (outside) (e.g. Bachnik and Quinn 1994). Major domestic travel campaigns promising a return to an encounter with a lost Japanese identity included the Japan National Railways promotion of 'Discover Japan' in the 1970s, and the self-exoticizing '*Exizochikku* Japan' (Exotic Japan) in the 1980s, analysed by Ivy (1988, 1995; see also Creighton 1997). Although the *furusato* or localism boom continues to be popular in domestic tourism (Creighton 1997, 1998a, 1998c, 2001; Robertson 1995), the focus shifted to Japanese history with the popular travel campaign of the 1990s, *Rekishi Kaidō* (History Highway or History Road). While domestic tourism has increased, Japanese travel abroad has also risen. In 1990 a seemingly phenomenal 10 million Japanese travelled abroad (Umesao 1995; Leheny 2003). This number had risen to over 17 million by 2000.

In Japanese concepts of space and relationships, *uchi* means inside. It is the inside space to which one belongs, and the inner group of people among whom one also experiences belongingness. It is also used to mean 'home'. This is contrasted with *soto*, the outside world. There are concentric frames of *uchi* and *soto*, reflecting degrees of intimacy. Scholars such as White (1988) suggest that ultimately all of Japan is an *uchi* space. While there is a fascination with *soto*, and particularly the outer foreign world, making travel abroad popular, the increasing popularity of nostalgia-laden domestic tourism in the closing decades of the twentieth century in Japan suggests a desire to return to *uchi*, or 'travel home' (Creighton 1997: 239).

However, as I have argued elsewhere, this is difficult because home is more than a geographical location. In a temporal sense, 'home' is the antithesis of the way most modern Japanese live, and something that seems to pre-date the struggle for economic parity with the west and the emulation of a western lifestyle (Creighton 1997). Returning 'home' in the collective Japanese nostalgic imagination suggests returning to a pre-western, pre-industrialized past Japan. Linguistic usage of *uchi* and *soto* again suggests that, cognitively, time represents a kind of space to Japanese. Common phrases using these terms delineate temporal spaces, such as *wasurenai uchi ni suru* – to do something within the inside space (or time) of not forgetting.

History tourism to Japan's Edo era appeals to both the desire to return inward to reconnect with Japan's 'inside' (*uchi*), by travelling to 'home towns' suggestive of a Japanese spirit and identity, and also to return to Japan's temporal *uchi*, or 'home times'. Gluck suggests Edo was created as a residual depository of pre-modern Japanese 'tradition' from early in the Meiji period (1998: 262). In this process, she contends, 'Edo became not only a historical time but a cultural space, a repository of traditions (*dentō*) associated with Japanese distinctiveness, both positive and negative' (1998: 263). Whereas most often, as Vlastos points out (1998: 2), the invention or re-creation of tradition involves a past temporal frame with no clear beginning or end, this is not the case with Edo. An added strength of Edo as historic symbol lies in its clearly framed temporal beginning and ending: boundaries which 'place it' between two times, the mythic ageless 'long ago' and the modern 'now'. This *placement*, both in time and in space, helps assuage contemporary concerns over identity *displacement*, offering reassurances of a persisting sense of Japaneseness that can be compatible with desires to further internationalize and fit among western nations. In order to show how the appeal to Edo serves this function it is important to consider the symbolism embedded in travel, roads and bridges generally and in Japan specifically.

Travel

Outlining an anthropology of tourism, Graburn points out that travel in the form of a journey is a cross-cultural metaphor for human life itself. He writes: 'An almost universal motif for the explanation and description of life is the journey' (1977: 23). This idea holds in Japan, where, Shirahata (1995: 54) says, *tabi* (travel) 'is often likened to life'. It fills the seventeenth-century poems of Basho. Graburn explains that travel goals may vary according to culturally specific values, but that travel in the form of the tourist journey 'must be morally justified by the home community' (1977: 24). Turner and Turner point out that, in many societies throughout history, travel was justified by pilgrimage (1978: 7) and – while pleasurable and restorative – was validated socially as a ritual activity equally essential to the group's welfare as arenas of 'work' (1978: 35). I think it valid to suggest it was considered equally essential to *other* forms of work, because ritual activity was valued as 'work'. The antecedent to Japan's modern travel industry is rooted in pilgrimage, which historically provided the edifying, or 'work', purpose justifying sightseeing trips. According to Graburn (1983) such travel in the guise of pilgrimage involves an attitude of 'pray, pay and play'. It is significant that, in Japan, travel as pilgrimage for common people emerged during the Edo era, now highlighted as a travel destination on a new form of pilgrimage, a journey into history to help Japan's contemporary middle class, analogous to travelling Edo commoners, meet their past selves. Vaporis (1994: 1) writes:

> The relative experience of travel in Tokugawa times may stand in contrast to the comfort that is the present norm, yet the experience of yesterday's and today's travellers is not totally dissimilar, for in Tokugawa times travel first emerged as a form of recreation that reached commoner masses.

Turner and Turner point out that, in post-industrial societies, pilgrimage often takes secular forms, with travel to places 'intimately associated with the deepest, most cherished, axiomatic values' of the collective (1978: 241), suggesting that for Americans this might mean travel to locations associated with the historical emergence of the US. I suggest travel to locations evoking the Edo era likewise constitutes a sort of secular pilgrimage for Japanese because the era is espoused to represent the fruition of a truly Japanese heritage and spirit. Whereas historically in Japan travel had to be cloaked as religious pilgrimage, the contemporary equivalent – the secular sacred – is the value placed on education and self-development. Travel that is edifying as educational, such as a journey into Japanese history, provides a similar cloaking of legitimacy to recreational travel, the legitimacy of which few would ridicule or question.

There are specific indications that travel is associated with human development in Japan. In a society where traditionally there were strong associations of inside and outside, and the idea that each person belonged to a particular inside place and inside group of people, maturity came about precisely by experiencing the world beyond one's expected place through travel. Tobin points to a Japanese belief that, to become a mature human being, a person needed to 'embark on a journey' (Tobin 1992: 26; see also Creighton 1998b: 212).

In the nostalgic cast of Japanese domestic tourism since the beginning of the 1970s retro boom, travel has also symbolized the means of offsetting the collective threat to Japanese identity that a modern, westernized lifestyle has wrought. If the west and westernization – forces to which Japan has been open since the end of the Edo era – have resulted in the estrangement of Japanese from their own Japanese cultural heritage and identity, travel is seen as the mechanism allowing them to reunite with their past Japanese selves, by *returning* to a Japanese *kokoro* (heart/mind). Ivy (1995: 42) explains the importance of travel as the mediator between modern Japanese and their sense of lost identity in earlier travel campaigns to rural areas. She writes:

> In this theory of travel and origins, the [traveller's] self equals an original Japanese self, which equals the authentic *kokoro*, which in turn equals the rural, remote, non-American, and non-rational. Travel is the operator which connects the terms by allowing the displacement of discovery, as it permits a temporary recovery of a lost self.

In the more recent, post-1990s, history tourism of the *Rekishi Kaidō* and other campaigns prominently featuring the Edo era, which are the focus of my research here, travel is again projected as the mechanism that allows Japanese to reconnect with their lost selves, but the focus is no longer only on the remote and rural. Edo era history tourism often takes travellers into the heart of their past urban heritage by emphasizing place locations in Edo/Tokyo or in other large cities already existing in the Edo era. Emphasized in Edo history travel is the possibility of travelling to places that allow travellers to reconnect with a time when they and Japan are conceptualized as having been more purely Japanese. The Edo era, in particular, symbolizes this as the era preceding Japan's opening to the western world. Thus time travelling to Edo, by visiting Edo-ic places, permits a temporary *temporal* recovery of a lost pre-westernized self.

Roads

Although travel can take many forms, particularly in an insular country like Japan where boat passages were important means of travel, the symbolism of human development associated with travel is most strongly suggested by the idea of roads in Japan. When Tobin claims that travel is necessary to become a mature human being in Japan, the emphasis is placed on taking to the road. In Japan, Tobin writes, 'the process of growing up and becoming a person was thought to take place metaphorically if not literally on the road' (1992: 26). The character for road, *michi*, in Japanese is used metaphorically for the concept of human development. Traditional forms of self-development by which individuals could enhance themselves through a form of discipline often include the character for road, *michi*, usually read in combination with other characters as *dō*. Thus the word for the martial arts, *budō*, and many of its specific forms, such as judo, kendo, and aikido, incorporate the idea of the path or road in the ending character *dō*, as do forms of the traditional arts, such as the tea ceremony, *chadō*, the way – path or road – of tea.

The *Rekishi Kaidō*, History Highway or History Road, campaign incorporates this idea of the road (*michi* or *dō*) in its name, and in its meanings, both in its literal sense of the road to travel and in the sense of road or pathway to one's development. The symbolic value of roads is again particularly pronounced in relationship to the history of the Edo period in Japan, during which the five major roadways connecting the country were established. Whereas metaphorically, and perhaps literally, maturity was thought to occur on the road in Japan, the development of this nationwide road system during Edo suggests to many the maturing of Japan during this period. Roadways in the Edo era were places where people of different ranks, backgrounds and statuses could meet and mingle, where information and knowledge were shared and transmitted. Thus, travelling the *Rekishi* Road, to reconnect with the historic Edo era, is rich with symbolic suggestions of finding, reuniting with and maturing in one's Japanese identity.

Associations with roads also reflect the emergence of Edo/Tokyo as pivotally central during this era. Just as the saying 'All roads lead to Rome' reflects the centrality of Rome during the Roman empire, in Japan there is a saying that 'All roads lead *up* to Tokyo' (my emphasis). The phrase reflects the concept of ranking in Japanese society, and that Tokyo's forerunner, Edo, emerged as the number one place location some time during the Edo era. The saying also reflects the Japanese culture of travel that began to emerge for the general populace during this era. With the system of *sankin kōtai*, alternate attendance, requiring regional *daimyo* (lords) to spend alternate periods of residence in the capital, Edo, and in their home regions, the five national roads built to accommodate this were thought of as all leading up to Edo.

Bridges

Bridges function in the movement of people to connect areas that would otherwise be inaccessible or the passage to which would be considered too dangerous. Bridges take on the symbolism of connection, not just between places but also between peoples. They also symbolize transition, not just between physical places but between states of being, stages in life, and from one time to another. Such symbolic associations are well developed in Japan. Nitobe Inazo was famous for his slogan 'I want to be a bridge across the Pacific' (Howes 1995: 10), indicating a commitment to facilitating intercultural understanding between Japan and North America.[5]

Bridges as motifs figure heavily in the ongoing portrayal of the Edo era. Bridges were a common feature of *ukiyo-e*, or woodblock prints, developed during the era. Certain bridges have a primary symbolic importance. One of these is Nihonbashi, which was located in the central commercial district of the city Edo, during the Edo era. Nihonbashi (which by itself literally means 'Japan bridge'), as an Edo-ic symbol, suggests connections between areas of the city at that time, along with connections between the city Edo and the rest of Japan. Hatano claims that 'the Nihonbashi Bridge graphically represented both the city of Edo and the whole of Japan' (1995: 31). Nihonbashi also symbolizes the temporal connection between the place of Edo and its successor, Tokyo, along with the connection between the time of the Edo era and the present.

Gluck points out that the Edo era itself has been conceptualized as a bridge or, as she calls it, the 'historical rainbow bridge' (Gluck 1998: 270). She references the work of Japanese scholar Fukumoto Kazuo, who characterized the Edo era as 'one great long bridge arched like a rainbow' connecting ancient Japan based on Chinese culture with modern Japan after the Meiji Restoration. Although Gluck appropriately scoffs at the dismissal of certain epochs of Japanese history in this poetic imagining of a historical rainbow bridge connecting epochs viewed positively in terms of cultural identity, I believe it is significant that the Edo era is positioned as a connecting bridge to deal with tensions between wishing to maintain an espoused cultural heritage seen as rooted in the past and wishing to embrace modern, westernesque attributes of identity.[6] Edo as bridge provides a connector of Japanese identity between a sense of cultural heritage anchored in a highly choreographed past and a contemporary westernized lifestyle. Edo as bridge connects Japanese to each other and to espoused values of community, while it serves to connect Japan and the Japanese to the outside world via the gateway of Tokyo (Edo's descendant), at one and the same time Japan's most central city and a prominent node in an international network of cities.

Thus, the particular evocative power of 'Edo' as symbolic travel trope for nostalgic journeys into the re-creation and recreation of tradition is that it conjoins the idea of time and place, allowing 'Edo' to operate as a pivotal travel stop. It connects local areas of Japan through its largest city, Tokyo, while connecting Japan to the outer world, and also serves as a bridge connecting a past, seen as imbued with icons of Japanese heritage and traditional identities, to a westernized present and sought-after internationalized future.

The '*Rekishi* Road' ('History Highway') travel campaign

From the 1990s on, nostalgia travels in Japan have emphasized history, exemplified by the *Rekishi Kaidō* campaign, officially launched in 1991. Ivy (1988) points out that, despite the rhetoric of getting in touch with a lost Japanese self, the 1970s 'Discover Japan' campaign title used English words and was a take-off of the US travel campaign 'Discover America', and that the 1980s '*Exizochikku* Japan' introjected Japan as the foreign by using the English word for Japan and the *katakana* syllabary used for things entering Japan from the outside. In contrast, *Rekishi Kaidō* shifts the emphasis back to an indigenous pre-western self by use of the Japanese phrase even in English descriptions. It suggests deeper connections to a prior Chinese influence on Japanese identity with *Kaidō*, a Japanese word based on combined Chinese character readings.

Many western observers in the 1970s and 1980s wrote about a vanishing Japan or lost Japanese identity. Significantly, the 1990s, as the first decade of the *Rekishi Kaidō* campaign, coincides with what the Japanese would label their 'lost decade', *ushinawareta jūnen*,[7] the decade of the post-bubble economic recession during which Japan could not get back on track. Nostalgic concerns with culture loss merged with a sense of economic loss, loss of purpose and loss of direction. *Rekishi Kaidō* offered a direction, a purpose and a route: a route one could travel through space and time to recapture something lost by directly experiencing Japanese history.

The official *Rekishi Kaidō* campaign is based in Kansai, the area which includes Kyoto and Osaka. While directed at recognizing the rich historical heritage of Japan in general, the campaign was designed to boost tourism to Kansai and help it regain something else Kansai people feel has been lost since 'Edo', the central prominence of Kansai, particularly Kyoto and Osaka, until well into the Edo era when this shifted to Edo/Tokyo. So while officially embracing, in the words of the *Rekishi Kaidō* campaign, 'the spirit of Japan', it was targeted at bolstering the spirit of Kansai, and reveals an aspect of Japanese diversity and persisting regional rivalries.

Brochures published by the Rekishi Kaidō Promotional Council describe *Rekishi Kaidō* as a 'new route that allows people to enjoyably experience Japanese culture while visiting [*tazunenagara*] the stage containing scenes of eternal historic significance' (Rekishi Kaidō Promotional Council, Brochure 2, my translation).[8] It consists of a 300-kilometre route that includes Osaka, Kyoto, Kobe, Ise, Asuka, Nara and eight theme routes associated with specific local histories. It is divided into five historical classifications, called 'zones' (*zo-n*). These are: 'Ancient Times Area', 'The Nara Period Area', 'The Heian Period to Muromachi Period Area', 'The Warring States to Edo Period Area' and 'The Modern Period Area'. Another brochure describes the purpose of those who created it: 'We are striving to create a new sightseeing route based on the places of the actual historical period as background, to make pleasurable travel where anyone visiting can experience intellectual excitement' (Rekishi Kaidō Promotional Council, Brochure 1, my translation).

Several things are apparent in these preliminary descriptions. One is that, despite the emphasis on history, 'newness' is important, indicated in the promotion of *Rekishi Kaidō* as a new route. In the naming of the time zones or areas, concepts of time and place (area or zone) merge and there is a suggestion that specific time eras occurred *more* in certain locations. All history is collapsed into four previous time areas, with a fifth area representing the modern to the present, and there is particular compression of all ancient and pre-history into one zone, seen as equal to the Nara period or Edo era. As Gluck contends, the Edo era is projected as the bridge connecting Japan's 'Modern Zone' directly to everything that – in a truncated manner – came before. As did earlier travel campaigns, *Rekishi Kaidō* emphasizes direct experience with Japanese history. The word for experience used, *taikan*, combines the characters for 'body' and 'feelings', meaning both emotions and physical sensations.

This idea of directly feeling, emotionally and physically, Japanese history and the spirit of Japanese identity reverberates in the campaign slogan, 'Touch the Spirit of Japan: Rekishi Kaidō'. This slogan appears on special logos designed for the campaign, consisting of a large round circle containing an outer and inner circle. The inner circle, in a lighter, aquamarine blue, is circumscribed by a bridge, with the central bridge post in the middle. The bridge outlines a smaller image of two hills surrounded by trees, with yet another circle – the sun – appearing between the two hills as if rising or setting. A circle in general, and a circle representing the sun, is a symbol used in Japanese identity constructions (Ohnuki-Tierney 1990; Creighton 2003). The outer circle is a darker, navy blue. Along the top half of this circle in the inner circle's colour is the English phrase 'Touch the Spirit of Japan', while along the bottom half are the capital Roman letters 'REKISHI KAIDO'. This circle links to the four Chinese characters that form the Japanese name *Rekishi Kaidō*, printed in the shape of a road leading out from the circle. To emphasize the campaign image of a road, the bottom line of the character for 'road', read *dō*, here changes to the romanized spelling of 'REKISHI KAIDO' such that the romanized form of the road becomes the road under-lying the Chinese character and Japanese word for road. In some versions another prominent navy blue wavy line, representing a road, lies under the characters for *Rekishi Kaidō* connecting everything emanating outward back to the circle of Japanese spirit.

Reflecting the importance of group involvement in Japan, popular culture and mass culture industries often provide opportunities to create a sense of

Figure 2.1 A *Rekishi Kaido* 'stamp point' in Kyoto shows the seal and logo of the *Rekishi Kaido* travel campaign. The stamp image, shown in the right corner, depicts a child or youth in front of Nijō Castle.

Photo by Millie Creighton.

belongingness to groups. For example, it is common for large retailing stores to offer shopping clubs based on participatory interactions of members (Creighton 1994a: 39, 1995). The same phenomenon is found in travel and tourism campaigns. In addition to establishing the *Rekishi Kaidō* travel route, the promotional council set up a History Road Club (*Rekishi Kaidō Kurabu*) that again offers direct physical contact with a Japanese spirit and history through experiential meeting with historic places and encounters with the nature of the Japanese islands, while also interacting with other club members (Rekishi Kaidō Promotional Council, Brochure 1). One pamphlet advertising for new club members asks: 'Won't you set out for travel on the history road to touch the various colourful aspects of [Japanese] history, physically experience the five eras, and the four seasons of nature?' (Rekishi Kaidō Promotional Council, Brochure 1). The Rekishi Kaidō Promotional Council also publishes a guidebook, a separate handbook and a magazine called *History Travellers* (*Rekishi Tabibito*). Rekishi Kaidō Club members receive these publications free, along with travel discounts at inns along the history road, often promoted as routes taken by Edo travellers. The Rekishi Kaidō Promotional Council supports small history museums and provides lectures on Japanese history and study sessions, reiterating the legitimating rationale of travel for educational purposes. The lectures and study sessions again highlight the idea of combining pleasure travel with socially valued education, and position learning about history as a connection to the future, and to meeting another self. One brochure states: 'Let's cultivate this rich historic culture with the purpose of nurturing it toward the future, and participate in these study sessions where people think together and experience meeting another more educated, enlightened self of yours' (Rekishi Kaidō Promotional Council, Brochure 1, my translation).[9]

Revealing the popularity of such travel incentives, the Council boasts over 6,000 members now supporting the organization (Rekishi Kaidō Promotional Council, Brochure 1).

Along with history, 'tradition' is emphasized in the travel campaign. Stops on the *Rekishi Kaidō* routes include 'traditional' calligraphy shops, and various small museums devoted to things considered icons of traditional Japanese identity, such as a futon museum, a sake museum, a tofu museum and a Japanese tea museum. Recommended eating locations include 'traditional-style' Japanese noodle restaurants. In contrast to earlier travel campaigns emphasizing remote areas, *Rekishi Kaidō* often highlights traditional aspects of a past urban life. Here again the implicit, and often explicit, emphasis is on the Edo era. Several brochures highlight the experience of living in *machiya*, urban or town dwellings, and one pamphlet is specifically entitled 'Discover Machiya – *Machiya Hakkenki*'.[10] These are described as Japanese traditional-style town dwellings of that (referring to the Edo era) past where merchants' and artisans' life and work were one ('sono mukashi, shōmin ya shokunin-tachi wa, kurashi to shigoto ga isshō ni natta Nihon no dentōteki na machiya') (Rekishi Kaidō Promotional Council, Brochure 2). *Rekishi Kaidō* brochures put the *machiya* in a positive light, saying they added to the ambience of the towns they were located in, and contributed 'great culture and history' (Rekishi Kaidō Promotional Council, Brochure 2). It is suggested that the dwellings themselves inherited and are inhabited by the spirit of Edo era artisans. It is also suggested that things of the past do not have to be left completely as they were to be appreciated, but rather that people understanding the true value of *machiya* are renovating them to retain their traditional value while enabling them to be utilized in a modern way (Rekishi Kaidō Promotional Council, Brochure 2).

Rekishi Kaidō travel promotion pamphlets emphasize the merging of travel through space and time. As for the idea of direct experiential meeting, this is particularly emphasized for Edo. One brochure says: 'koko o tazuneru to Edo jidai ni, taimu torippu dekiru' ('while travelling/visiting *here* one can take a time trip to the Edo era') (Rekishi Kaidō Promotional Council, Brochure 2, my translation and emphasis). For another location it is said that while walking about the town one can experience a direct meeting with Japan's Edo era ('machi o arukeba Edo jidai . . . no Nihon ni deaeru'). Although only one of five era areas of the *Rekishi Kaidō* campaign, Edo emerges as particularly significant given the focus on the period's urban life that is highlighted in the campaign.

The *Rekishi Kaidō* campaign was partly directed at regaining a sense of centrality for the Kansai region and cities of Osaka and Kyoto. It is suggested that in the 1990s Kansai, while not replacing the Kanto region which includes Tokyo as the country's core, did regain a stronger claim on national centrality. The dynamics of internationalism had a major influence on repositioning the regions as both being pivotally important in contrast to the previously overwhelming dominance of only Tokyo. What many observers believe had the greatest influence in this shift was the opening of the Kansai International Airport in Osaka. With both the Kanto region, represented by Tokyo, and the Kansai region, represented by Osaka/Kyoto, now having equally prominent international airports, both emerged as pivotally central nodes connecting domestic travel, communications and the flow of information within Japan. Thus, although the Kansai region did not replace the Kanto region as the pre-eminent core of Japan, it edged more closely in this direction than it had been since Edo emerged as central in the Edo era.

Although defined by its creators as oriented to the Kansai region and its outlying areas, the *Rekishi Kaidō* campaign became popular among travellers who either did not differentiate it from other travel promotions emphasizing Japanese history or, if they did know its specific boundaries, nonetheless connected it with other travel plans to visit period sites elsewhere. *Rekishi Kaidō* fitted a larger trend featuring history travel, particularly that focusing on the Edo era. For example, one Japanese television show featured a regular travel segment in which the announcers would travel to different locations of Japan showing buildings or other remains of the Edo era. In the *Rekishi Kaidō* campaign and in the television travel feature, time travelling to Tokugawa usually meant the era, as the locations were often outside present-day Tokyo. However, the re-creation of the Edo era was also intensely popular throughout the 1990s in Edo's location, Tokyo, as well. A popular television program, *Edo de gozaru* (This is Edo), featured Edo era life in Edo. A popular travel site capitalizing on the Japanese love of hot springs was built in the Tokyo area called Ōedo-Onsen Monogatari or 'The Great Edo Hot Springs Story', and the Edo-Tokyo Museum was completed and opened in this decade.

In the following section, I guide the novice history traveller along the *Rekishi* Road to connect with an Edo past. I choose some routes that follow the specified *Rekishi Kaidō* campaign, but also those that connect from these to areas outside of its target zones that travellers engaging in Edo history forays might be likely to follow, in order to route the traveller on to re-creations of Tokyo as Edo so travellers on this Edo 'time trip' can visit the era's namesake, Edo.

Time tripping on a magical history tour

Making a cultural analogy between time and place, the opening line of Hartley's nostalgic novel *The Go-Between* exclaims: 'The past is a foreign country: they do things differently there' (Hartley [1953] 2000: 5). Expounding on this, Lowenthal asserts: 'If the past is a foreign country, nostalgia has made it the foreign country with the healthiest tourist trade of all' (1985: 4). In Japan nostalgia has granted to the past a healthy tourist trade, but it might more appropriately be the present that seems like a foreign country where people do things differently. Time tripping offers Japanese a means to return to Japan – the country of the past – from their heavily westernized lifestyle in Japan, the country of the present. Thus time travel along the History Highway is projected as entering 'the real Japan' as if from a foreign country.

On this tour, readers will enter from outside through a now prominent *kuchi*, mouth or entrance, into Japan located in Osaka, the central base of the *Rekishi Kaidō* campaign and home of the Rekishi Kaidō Association and Rekishi Kaidō Promotional Council, via the *Kansai Kokusai Kūkō*, or Kansai International Airport, completed in 1994. This packaged magical history tour to the Edo era provides seven full stops. Seven is an auspicious or lucky number in Japan, and travel in the name of pilgrimage during the Edo era sometimes played on the auspicious suggestion of seven full stops. For example, it was common for people to try to visit the seven temples of the seven lucky gods during the first seven days of the New Year in Edo during Edo. From the Edo era merchant city of Osaka, the traveller/reader will travel directly to the central part of Japan, and the start of the Edo era, by visiting Hikone, where the Edo era is said to have both begun and ended, and then stop at another location in central Japan, Ōmihachiman, before travelling on to Hagi. From Hagi, the traveller/reader will come back on to the *Rekishi* Road for Kyoto, and afterwards make a brief downward pass to Ise. From Ise this modern travelgrim (travel pilgrim) will circle back up the *Rekishi* Road far enough to connect with the modern counterpart to the Edo era's Tokaidō (East Ocean Road), which linked Edo and Kyoto, for a final Edo era stop at Edo.

After passing through customs at Kansai's new international airport in Osaka, one sees sales stalls displaying Japanese souvenir T-shirts. The T-shirts reveal the dual assertions of a present and futuristic internationalized Japan, alongside iconic images of a past Edo era Japanese self. T-shirt choices on display show the new Kansai International Airport character mascot, emblem of the modern internationalized Japan, or images of an espoused Japanese past self symbolized by recognizable Edo era *ukiyo-e* (woodblock prints) images – the courtesan, the Kabuki actor, Hokusai's Mount Fuji. Although seemingly putting the spotlight on the city of Edo which, according to Vaporis, became associated with *ukiyo-e* from the end of the eighteenth century, the *ukiyo-e* motifs are another way of reclaiming the Edo era for Kansai, because *ukiyo-e* originated in the Kansai area. Forms of popular theatre such as Kabuki and Bunraku were also based in Osaka early in the Edo period, only later moving to Edo (Umehara 1987: 104). From this international gateway into Osaka, one can transfer to the now more 'inside' Osaka airport, Itami. After disembarking, the traveller is again greeted by reminiscences of the Edo era in Osaka, in the form of a large oil painting of Osaka-*jō*, Osaka Castle, overlooking a previous town-like Osaka of Tokugawa times with *machiya*-style dwellings, and remaining fields along the hillsides.

Within Osaka the traveller should visit the castle, a reconstruction built in the mid-twentieth century because the original castle used during Tokugawa was destroyed. Osaka Castle was renovated in the mid-1990s so that, despite its old-looking exterior, the interior now has the modern look of a sleek office building or department store, with shiny marble-like walls with recessed encased exhibits – replacing the previous ones which people could directly view while going through the castle – and lifts to the top lookout floor to replace the previous flights of worn narrow wooden stairs. Having experienced Osaka Castle before (when it was still an experience), I was totally disappointed with the renovations resulting in entry into an interior space more like a fancy hotel or other modern city building in Japan. I tried to get an explanation for this seemingly contradictory modernization of the castle interior which has resulted in people now being passively pulsed through the castle and eliminating the feeling of directly participating in some kind of antiquity. The decision to modernize the inside of the castle – a building used to suggest Japan's pre-industrial past – was justified by an information counter worker who said that, after all, the castle building itself was not the original but a reconstruction.

After alighting from the castle's new lift, from the top vantage point one can view the modern mega-city of Osaka, a scene very different from that in the painting at Itami airport.[11] Having 'done' the castle and castle grounds, in intense heat and humidity in summer, the modern traveller may wish to spend

Figure 2.2 In an Osaka shopping street, the Edo era castle theme is shown by the metalwork image of Osaka-*jō* (Osaka Castle) on Osaka's sewer hole covers.

Photo by Millie Creighton.

time protected from the sun shopping under the covered canopies of Osaka's shopping streets. This can be justified as a sort of pilgrimage, because Osaka was home to a strong merchant culture that flourished in the Edo era. The modern merchant culture of Osaka pays tribute to the icons of Osaka's past. Sewer hole covers in the shopping areas have artwork depicting Osaka Castle surrounded by the blossoms of spring.

From Osaka the time traveller heads towards Hikone, near Lake Biwa in Shiga prefecture, called Omi during the Edo era. This is a pragmatic stop early in the tour. On the shore of Lake Biwa is the temple Ukimi-do, where travellers come to pray for safe journeys. A Shiga guide boasts that Lake Biwa, Japan's largest lake, is said to be five million years old (Shiga-Ken n.d.: 1), in a way that seemingly links Japan's antiquity to the lake's. If Lake Biwa is Japan's largest lake, and Lake Biwa is five million years old, then 'Japan' is projected pastward five million years.

Again reminiscent of Gluck's suggestion that the Edo era bridges the present to everything before it, the descriptive statement of Shiga jumps from Japan's five-million-year-old Lake Biwa to the Edo era, with a statement about how the area, then called Omi, produced a thriving merchant culture. One of the Edo era's main five highways, the Nakasendō, traversed old Omi. Today, Edo period 'historical scenes' remain which, the guide claims, 'cannot help but appeal to the traveller's sentiments' (Shiga-Ken n.d.: 12). It states:

'where the old highways passed' you 'may perhaps experience a time-travel to Japan's olden' and will encounter 'sightseeing points promising you deep emotion' (Shiga-Ken n.d.: 6). Other references to the Edo era indicate that, by visiting the sites of the lords of feudal days and the many former Omi merchants, 'you may feel the roots of the Japanese spirit' (Shiga-Ken n.d.: 8).

Central Japan of the old Omi area near Hikone is associated with the beginning and the end of Edo, circumscribing the temporal boundaries of the period. In this area is Nagahama Castle (Nagahama-*jō*), where Tokugawa Hideyoshi is said to have taken control of the country to begin the era. Hikone City helps perpetuate the idea that this era represents true Japanese identity and is the true mother of modern Japan. The *Guide to Hikone* says that the prolonged peace of the period, combined with national isolation, 'led to a flowering of unique cultural and art forms that still exist today, making the Edo era the birth of modern Japanese culture' (Hikone Municipal Office n.d.: 4).

The Hikone Castle is a central tourist feature of national renown, and is always lit up at night. The sounds of the Hikone Castle grounds – such as the timekeeping bell that has rung out the time to the entire castle town since the Edo era, and the sounds of the castle ground's insects – were chosen to be among the 100 sounds of Japan, in the national 100 soundscapes project. The turret style of Nagahama Castle, where the Edo era is said to have begun, is replicated in Hikone Castle, now the only remaining castle in Japan with this feature. In addition to the castle, emblematic of Tokugawa authority and the samurai class in the period, the city of Hikone retains many areas of merchant town dwellings and businesses. Hikone has more remaining architecture from the Edo era than any other part of Japan, including Edo/Tokyo where most remaining era buildings were lost during the Kanto earthquake of 1923 or the bombings of WWII. The Hikone guide points out that a visit to Hikone allows one to travel back in time, stating: 'A walk through the city takes you back in time to Japan's Edo era, for Hikone has maintained the look and feeling of Edo more than any other city in Japan' (Hikone Municipal Office n.d.: 3).

Stretching out from Hikone, along the Kyobashi Castle Road, a city association has embarked on a plan to build 'the Heisei version of a castle town' (Hikone Municipal Office n.d.: 13). Heisei is the current Japanese era, which began in 1989 with the death of the former Showa emperor and the assumption of the reign of his son as the Heisei emperor. Thus, the suggestion is something of a temporal oxymoron, since 'castle town' involves a form of past municipal organization no longer contemporaneous in Japanese towns or cities (including Hikone) today. A 'Heisei version' of a castle town is by definition a simulacrum. In this case, it consists of an entire area where buildings are being created in the style of merchant houses and businesses from the Edo era. These are intended for use as private homes, tea shops, restaurants, craft shops and boutiques, with the intention that those travelling through will be entertained while reminded of past times. A large signboard displayed in the area announces it as the 'Old New Town'. The signboard explains the purpose of this project as 'making the city's life spirit anew utilizing the value of its oldness' (*furui yosa o ikashita atarashii seiki no aru machi zukuri*). Robertson (1987, 1988) has written about the oxymoronic naming of Japan's *shinfurusato zukuri* (making new *furusato*, or 'new old villages') campaigns. In this case the oxymoronic label of the town area is even more direct. There is also an inherent irony that Hikone, the city of Japan containing more intact architecture from the Edo era than any other, is the city that has erected a simulacrum to re-create an Edo-like townscape, despite the presence of its actual Edo era town streets.

Hikone and surrounding areas are also strongly associated with the ending of the era. Here again themes of domestic Japanese identity get combined with internationalization, while the strong cultural value on education is reiterated in the historic figure of Ii Naosuke, thirteenth lord of the Hikone clan. Ii attained the high rank of chief minister to the shogun at the age of 43. As a Hikone hero, Ii has a statue standing in Hikone's Children's Park. His academic accomplishments are applauded along with his warrior skills. He was successful, children and others are informed, because of his dedication to education and becoming a Japanese classical scholar as well as government minister. Reiterating the contemporary proverb on achieving academic

Figure 2.3 Although Hikone has more remaining Edo era buildings than any other part of Japan, such as the ones pictured here, it has also constructed a new city street area designated the 'Old New Town' of modern-made buildings intentionally designed to look like those from the Edo era.

Photo by Millie Creighton.

success told to Japanese children, 'with four [hours of sleep] you pass, and with five you fail', it is pointed out that Ii mastered both worlds by sleeping only four hours a night. The descriptions for children of Ii as a local historic hero emphasize how education contributed to his gaining career success, and tend not to mention how executing his enemies contributed to his maintaining it.

Ii was credited with an interest in the outside world as well as Japan. Ii supported the opening of the country and the path to internationalization, making strong seminal efforts against isolationists. Ii was credited with helping open Japan by supporting the Japan–American Amity and Trade Treaty after the visits of Commodore Perry (Japan Times 1986: 46). Many credit his decisive personality and ideology with a large role in bringing a swift end to the Tokugawa period. Others believe these had a large role in bringing a swift end to ill-fated Ii himself, who was assassinated on a state visit to the shogun's castle near the end of the era in 1860.

The next stop is Ōmihachiman, which flourished as a town of Ōmi merchants. Through merchant efforts, the city built a canal system, still seen today, linking to Edo's major highways, as a transportation route to the less easily traversed Ura Nihon ('back side of Japan') on the Japan Sea. Ōmihachiman has many remaining cobbled streets and merchant houses from the Edo era, and maintains a museum specializing in roof tiles. Again, linking Japan's Edo past with the present interest in internationalization, this museum along the History Highway shows Edo era roofs in one exhibit area and, in another, the rooftops past of peoples from other places in the world.

Travelling toward Ura Nihon, the traveller reaches Hagi. Hagi represents one of those remote, difficult-to-get-to locations where the *furusato* campaigns suggest the spirit of the 'real Japan' can still be found and experienced. In a country with a rank consciousness even in tourism, Hagi attempts to bill itself as number one in something. Signs along the scenic ocean landscape of the Hagi area declare that this is Japan's number one 'no rubbish town' (*Nihon ichi gomi no nai machi Hagi*). In addition to its beautiful location, Hagi has two other primary touristic appeals. Large parts of Hagi retain street walls and architecture remaining from Tokugawa times. Hagi is sometimes referred to in travel literature as 'the city of white walls' for the walls that line whole streets where samurai families dwelled during Tokugawa times. Hagi is also famous for the pottery named after it. Hagi pottery has a very high status in Japan and is immensely valued for use in *chanoyū* ('tea ritual') that developed during Tokugawa times. Consistent with *furusato*-like associations, this pottery is valued for its rustic nature. Around the year 1600, near the beginning of Tokugawa times, Koreans were brought to Japan to carry out the pottery-making traditions and instruct Japanese on these. They formed communities around Hagi, using the natural clay deposits of the area. Hagi represents one of the cases of likely interaction between Japan and Korea, despite Japan's supposed national isolation during the Edo era that commenced in 1600. In many cases, the Korean family lines were maintained separately from Japanese throughout the era and into the present. Hagi represents an interesting situation in ethnic relations in which the people making the pottery, Koreans or their descendants, faced a discriminatory attitude of social devaluation, while the product they made, Hagi pottery, was and is highly valued.

Hagi is also known and advertised as a 'castle town'. Hagi tourism posters often carry the phrase 'The Castle Town of Hagi'. Hagi is more often promoted as a castle town than Hikone, despite the fact that, unlike Hikone, Hagi does not have a castle – but it did during Tokugawa times. A Hagi tourist attraction is the place where the castle used to be in Tokugawa times.[12] A large signboard shows what the castle would look like if it were still there and one were able to view it. For modern travellers who would like a bit more castle in their castle town experience than seeing a depiction of what the castle might have looked like, lodging is available at the Hagi Castle Hotel. Hagi has not had a castle since the end of Tokugawa when the area lord of Hagi had the castle – a symbol of shogunate rule – destroyed because he thought the restoration forces were winning and wished to show he was on their side. This decision did not make him a hero, and did not result in the lord of Hagi being as gloriously remembered in local Hagi history as Ii Naosuke has been in local Hikone history. However, it might have been a factor in extending his own life and allowing him, unlike Ii Naosuke, to make the transition into the new era and his own continuing future.

Figure 2.4 Some of the famous white walls and remaining samurai areas of Hagi.
Photo by Millie Creighton.

Emphasis on tradition for tourists in Hagi goes beyond the walls of former samurai homes. Tourist offerings suggest that 'history has taste' and travellers are offered that direct experiential encounter with a past Japan through their senses of taste and touch. Souvenir shops offer over a hundred varieties of Hagi sake, often bottled in the famous, rustic Hagi pottery. Hagi reveals the attitude that a modern approach can sometimes be taken to tradition. Hagi hosts a ceramics competition. One winning entry in 1997, reminiscent of Cinderella's sisters attempting to squeeze their toes into the glass slipper, was an art piece made of Hagi clay, representing a high-fashion-design high-heeled shoe, bent back at the centre indicating the difficulties it would give its wearer, entitled *Ai no tame ni*, 'for the sake of love'. In an important social movement toward fuller internationalization, Hagi tourist signs, long written in Japanese and English, were replaced with those in three languages, Japanese, English and Korean. Whereas the first flush of the internationalization drive was really directed at western countries, Hagi, with a long history of intense interaction with Korea, began attempts to overcome discriminatory aspects of the past and ways countries like Korea have been ignored in the quest for an internationalized Japan.

From the castleless castle town of Hagi, the time traveller moves on to Kyoto. At the beginning of the era, the emperor and the *kuge*, the aristocratic class based on the emperor system, were banished to Kyoto. A pivotal centre before the beginning of the era, Kyoto, according to some scholars, still remained the cultural centre in the era during much of the seventeenth century, until this shifted to Osaka, which dominated in the eighteenth century, after which Edo emerged as the focal city for the last half of the period (Umehara 1987: 10). In a country that has long asserted a myth of homogeneity in terms of cultural identity, it is interesting that the modern quest to touch the spirit of a past Japanese identity draws so heavily on an interest in the Edo era, as an era that has been characterized by Shiba (1987, 1995) as an age of variety.

Although the concept of racial or ethnic diversity remains unaddressed and muted, there is much discussion of diversity during Edo in terms of social class and status. Unlike Edo during the Edo era where the emerging commoner culture of city dwellers is emphasized, unlike Hagi where the samurai class is emphasized, and unlike Osaka and Ōmihachiman where merchant culture is emphasized, Kyoto retained strong associations with aristocratic culture throughout the era. The touristic view of the era from Kyoto seems to flip the lens from the usual depictions of Edo culture. For example, frequent discussions of artistic developments in the era focus on emerging popular art expressions such as Kabuki and Bunraku theatre, and *ukiyo-e* prints. Discussions of *ukiyo-e* often suggest the art form was enriched by intense creativity at a time when the classical art schools, Kano and Tosa, were stagnating because of heavily conventionalized expectations. In contrast, the view of Edo from Kyoto upholds the value of these classic art schools during the period. Comparisons of Kyoto and Edo during the era suggest there were major differences due to Edo's newly emerging urban culture, in which people could live more freely because they did not have items and practices representing centuries-old traditions to protect. Kyoto, in contrast, did. In modern history tourism it is this lengthy, classical and aristocratic tradition of Kyoto pre-dating Edo that is emphasized as having still been present during the Edo past.

Kyoto is a favourite tourism venue for Japanese and for foreigners. It is also one of the commonest locations to be included in school *shūgaku ryokō* (school travel field trips) taken by nearly every schoolchild in Japan (see Oedewald, this volume). An inevitable destination for travellers visiting Kyoto is Nijō-*jō* or, rendered in its literal but less poetic English form, 'the Second Street Castle'. Nijō-*jō* is conveniently located on one of Kyoto's main roads. Nijō-*jō* was begun in 1603 at the beginning of the Tokugawa era by the first Tokugawa shogun, Tokugawa Ieyasu,[13] for the supposed purpose of 'protecting' the imperial residence and the *kuge*, and to serve as a second residence for the shogun in Kyoto. Nijō-*jō* incorporated another connection with the onset of the Tokugawa era, in that it was partly built with materials from Fushimi Castle, a castle bearing strong associations with Toyotomi Hideyoshi, who along with Tokugawa Ieyasu and Oda Nobunaga is considered to have unified Japan to commence Tokugawa times. As in present-day political justifications anywhere, the shogunate's espoused purpose of 'protection' probably had an underlying purpose of maintaining control of the Kyoto area and those associated with the emperor. Thus, Kyoto as a tour stop represents one of the tensions of the Tokugawa period, the lingering allegiance expected to the imperial family and aristocracy, along with the contrasting dominant political authority of the shogunate. Throughout Tokugawa times, area lords paid respects to the shogun at Nijō Castle, when it was in use as his secondary residence in Kyoto.

Nijō-*jō* has special architectural and art features highlighted for tourists. The 'nightingale floors' were designed so anyone walking or 'sneaking' across them would make a birdlike sound that would alert the guards. Stories of the nightingale floors evoke images of *ninja*, Japanese secret spies trained in stealth and the martial arts. Many walls of Nijō-*jō* are decorated with classic drawings of the Tosa and Kano schools, some rescued from the ruins of Fushimi Castle, dating back to an even earlier Momoyama era. So, whereas these schools are mocked in the literature about the emerging *chōnin* or commoner culture of Edo in Edo, here in Kyoto they are revered within the castle established to serve the shogun in Tokugawa times.

Kyoto, repository of Japan's ancient past, is projected as bearing the heart and spirit of Japanese traditional identity. This association with a core Japaneseness, which reverberates through cultural symbols occupying social space such as Nijō Castle, is nonetheless linked to the dynamic of internationalization. In tourism, a material example of this is found opposite Nijō-*jō*, in the form of a major hotel called Kyoto Kokusai Hotel (KKH).[14] KKH provides modern tourists, both Japanese and foreign, with a more convenient and updated castle accommodation experience. Like many period castles, including Nijō-*jō*, the hotel has a moat and waterway running through it, complete with swans. Once over the arched bridge that crosses the moat to the hotel's entrance, the taste of history merges with the taste of today for Kyoto's time travellers at the restaurant and refreshment area known as the 'Castle Beer Garden'.

From Kyoto the time traveller can prepare for the 487-kilometre journey up to Tokyo's Edo on the modern Shinkansen running near where Edo era travellers travelled the Tokaidō by foot. However, rather than embark for Tokyo directly, the *Rekishi* Road makes it easy to take a side trip to Ise. A trip to Ise, the home of the Ise Shrine, was one of the main legitimating reasons for travel during the Edo era, and often the only legal way to travel. Edo folklore includes a story of three headmen from Kyushu who got permits for a pilgrimage to Ise Shrine. They did travel the Tokaidō linking Kyoto to Edo (Tokyo), but did not bother to stop at the Ise Shrine (Vaporis 1994: 3–5).

Most Edo era travellers utilizing a pilgrimage to Ise as the culturally sanctioned rationale for getting away from the village and embarking on a journey to see what of the world they could did at least stop at Ise. However, as Vaporis (1994: 217) writes, 'Ise became less of a destination and more like just one attraction of the journey.' Recreational travel in the name of pilgrimage to Ise is thought to have sparked Japan's *tabi no bunka* (culture of movement). As many as half a million (Vaporis 1994: 242) travelgrims were visiting Ise each year, and as many as five million out of a total population of 30 million converged on Ise Shrine in 1830 (Vaporis 1994: 15).

For the modern traveller, tourism posters advertising Ise adorn Kyoto and Nara stations. Images of young women are common in Japanese advertising posters. Here, however, it is not the jeans-clad youth of other campaigns, but young women in kimonos, a focal symbol of Japanese heritage and traditional identity. Contemporary attractions at Ise reverberate with associations of history. A late-twentieth-century art exhibit at Ise was *e de miru Nihon no rekishi*, 'Japanese History, Viewed through Art'. Ise Shrine figures prominently in the symbolism used to construct a sense of Japanese state identity and of a lengthy history. Ise Shrine – like Japan – is said to be over 2,000 years old. It is the shrine of Amaterasu, the sun goddess, from whom the emperor is said to be descended. The linking of the emperor as a symbol of Japan, through Amaterasu, to the sun is another way in which Japanese identity partakes directly in symbolism of the sun. According to one version of the myth taught in the pre-WWII era, all Japanese were linked to Amaterasu and the sun, via the emperor, who stood in the role of father to the Japanese people. This version of the myth suggests the imperial family line is the highest family line, to which all others are linked. However, other interpretations point out that it is specifically the emperor and the imperial line that are descended from the sun goddess, not necessarily all Japanese. In this view it is the special connection to the sun goddess and divine status that differentiates the emperor from other Japanese and is used to legitimize his right to reign over them.

Given its asserted symbolic role, Ise – through its associations with the sun goddess Amaterasu and with the emperor – suggests the linkage spatially to all of Japan, as well as an historical continuity throughout the espoused 2,000 years of Japanese history and identity (Martinez 2004: 68). During the Edo era, Ise, like Kyoto, reflected the tensions between the shogunate-based political authority of the times and the marginalized but persisting imperial myth. Martinez points out that nearby villages like Kuzaki, which brought tribute to Ise, felt themselves caught throughout Tokugawa times by the twofold rule of Ise, symbolically representing the longer-standing imperial symbolism, and the feudal lord representing the Tokugawa system, a twofold rule that came to an end with the end of the Edo era. In constructing present-day identity, area dwellers 'celebrate their ancient connection with Ise and the feudal system' rather than recall its oppressive elements (Martinez 2004: 57). This selective viewing of a special role in Japanese history involves an impressive use of historical re-creation of the past to serve present needs or desires – in this case to create a positive local place self-identity and win a special 'place' in the larger construction of national Japanese identity. According to Martinez (2004: 57), 'Given the highly rigid structure of social organization during the Tokugawa era especially, this is a triumph of nostalgic mythologizing over grim historical reality.'

While the role of Ise in orthodox symbols of Japaneseness continues, modern travellers, like those during Tokugawa times, are often more interested in popular associations and attractions of the area. Near Ise is located the famous Mikimoto Pearl Island. The neighbouring fishing villages surrounding Ise are famous for *ama*, who are divers. They can be male or female, and usually are involved in diving for fish or other seafood such as abalone. However, in the invention of the present, *ama* are more romantically rendered and revered as pearl divers. Popular imagery often presents them as sexually alluring young women who dive for pearls – a more glamorous modern catch than abalone. Japan scholars such as D.P. Martinez (1990, 2004) and David Plath and Jackie Hill (1988) have debunked this myth of the *ama*, showing that men could also be *ama*, and that many female *ama* are heavily musculatured middle-aged women, not the willow-like sexy young women of popular depictions.[15] The myth-making machine of the Mikimoto Pearl Company, however, continues to contribute to the more tantalizing view of *ama* as pearl divers. It cleverly crafts the connection between pearls and the Ise Shrine in a large Mikimoto display at Ise. To the right of the display is a mannequin-like woman's upper torso draped in scarves, pearl necklaces and a pearl shoulder drop. The mannequin suggests the fashion and accessory desires of fashion- and consumer-conscious young Japanese women. To the left of the figure is a finely crafted miniature scale model of the Ise Shrine, made entirely of pearls. The model metonymically constructs the place association and identity of Ise more strongly with the nearby Pearl Island, as the pearls themselves construct in replica the space of Ise Shrine. This is Mikimoto's mythic linking of Japan's historical past to its modern consumption-oriented present.

As mentioned, an oft-reiterated Japanese phrase is 'All roads lead up to Tokyo.' Although the officially designated *Rekishi Kaidō* does not extend to the Kanto region including Tokyo, it, like other roads, is part of a national roadway system that does, for many Japanese, lead eventually to Tokyo. Hence Edo/Tokyo is to be the last travel stop on this modern history tour before exiting Japan for the outside world. Edo/Tokyo serves as model for the convergence of time and place. Instead of travelling to other, more remote places, which suggest an earlier time frame, one stays in place while attempting to travel in time. When Kodama (1995: 4) writes 'From Edo to Tokyo spans a history of over four hundred years', the distance between the two temporal spaces is being charted in terms usually used for geographical distances between physical spaces.

Edo/Tokyo provides an apt vessel for the Japanese contemporary pangs of nostalgia for a lost home – spatially and temporally. Tsuchida suggests that the nostalgia for a return to Edo is also a desire to return to the 'old Japan'. He sees nostalgia for Edo as not simply a modern phenomenon, but a recurring response to waves of modernization and westernization. He writes, 'whenever modernization and westernization appeared deadlocked for the moment, a resurgence of Edo nostalgia would occur' (Nishiyama *et al.* 1995: 11). Conveniently, Edo the place and Edo the time merge in this suggested recyclical nostalgia, such that Edo the place can serve as referent for Edo the time and thus symbolize the nostalgia for all of 'old Japan'. Sand concurs that 'Edo' is a convenient framing of nostalgia for a lost Japanese past. He writes, 'For critics of post-Meiji modernization, Edo provided the natural frame for the "world we have lost" ' (Sand 2001: 372).

The nostalgia for a lost Japan in late-twentieth-century Japan may have romanticized the rural, but it had its urban and specifically Tokyo manifestations. These took the form of a *'furusato* Tokyo' ('home town Tokyo' or 'home village Tokyo') campaign, and an 'Edo boom'. The 'Edo boom' involved revivals of crafts and culinary traditions from the Edo era in the Tokyo area. Large department stores rotated fairs of foreign countries, fairs of other regional areas of Japan, and fairs representing the old Edo of Tokyo (Creighton 1989, 1991, 1998a).

Along with tours of Tokyo that focused on revisiting remnants of its Edo past, special theme centres were constructed including the Edo Tokyo Tatemono-en (Edo-Tokyo Building Park) and the monumental Edo-Tokyo Museum. Both project the concept of edutainment, through an emphasis on combining education, in the form of transmitting historical knowledge about the Edo era, with an entertainment outing for both Tokyo dwellers and visiting tourists.

The Edo-Tokyo Tatemono-en set as its goal the preservation of Tokyo's historical buildings from past eras, particularly Edo. Despite being the offspring of the era's namesake, Tokyo, unlike Hikone, does not have many remaining structures from the Edo, or even the following Meiji, era, because most were destroyed by the great Kanto earthquake of 1923 or the bombings of Tokyo during WWII. The park thus emphasizes the importance of preserving the relatively fewer precious architectural examples from these past eras (Edo-Tokyo Tatemono-en n.d.: 1).[16]

Like travel campaigns in search of a Japanese self, the Edo-Tokyo Tatemono-en emphasizes direct experience and discovery. It also suggests this direct experience occurs while on a journey – walking along the museum created path. The guide tells its time-tripping visitors: 'This is the Edo-Tokyo Building Park. . . . While walking along one encounters the buildings of various eras – look at them, touch them, discover them, and also have a leisurely enjoyable experience' (Edo-Tokyo Tatemono-en n.d.: 2, my translation). Park exhibits show the making of Edo (*Edo no machi tsukuri*) and the making of Edo's heir, Tokyo (*Tokyo no machi tsukuri*).

The Edo-Tokyo Museum was a much more encompassing project that opened to the public in 1993. The Edo-Tokyo Museum was planned during the economic boom years of the 1980s as part of an attempt to highlight regional identities, while using these to serve in the bolstering of a Japanese national identity. It also represents the contemporary Japanese academic field of 'Tokyo studies'. With many historians and other academics as consultants, the Edo-Tokyo Museum again embraces the value of education, while suggesting that education can be made enjoyable. In the 'guide' to the museum – a lengthy book with several essays by prominent scholars – Kodama (1995: 4) points out that the Edo-Tokyo Museum counters the idea that museums are 'stuffy, stiff places' while aiming to be 'a place where the whole family can become familiar with and learn about history'. The reconstruction of the past, represented by 'Edo', is suggested to be important both to understanding the present, represented by 'Tokyo', and to building the future. Kodama (1995: 4) writes:

> This exercise transforms our understanding of history as a mere recollection of the lives of those who came before us into a dynamic process with the potential to shed light both on our lives today and on our future prospects.

The place of the Edo-Tokyo Museum, at Ryōgoku, itself suggests connections to travel in the Edo era. Ryōgoku, now accessible as a stop on the Tokyo transit system, was one of the 53 stages of the Tokaidō (the road connecting Tokyo and Kyoto), which were immortalized through Hiroshige's famous series of *ukiyo-e* prints. Thus modern time travellers to Edo via the museum make a stop in time at a stop in place that Edo era travellers used. The museum guide explicitly posits the museum as the vehicle for travel in the fourth dimension, defining it as 'a time machine to Edo' (Edo-Tokyo Museum 1995: 5). Like the Building Park, the Edo-Tokyo Museum creates a 'road' or 'path' for its time travellers, with the journey along this road more important than specific items on display. Sand (2001: 368) writes: 'By combining the open interior and the designated route, the museum creates an ordered walk instead of an ordered set of objects.'

Cultural meanings are communicated in the construction of space and spatial layouts. Mukerji points out that definitions of space create a physical reality heavily imbued with symbolic meanings (Mukerji 1983: 15; Creighton 1998b: 203; Seiter 1992: 233). The dualistic associations of the era with the Tokugawa authority and the culture of the emerging commoner class are both differentially communicated in the museum's physical structure and spatial layouts. In the end product, the building exterior expresses the Tokugawa times aspect of shogunal and government authority. The complex, while looking like a futuristic construction, represents in a modern sci-fi-like form a revised version of the shogun's castle from early in the period, with the height placed at the same point as the castle keep, the *tenshukaku* or main castle building (Sand 2001: 361). The interior spatial layout, in contrast, emphasizes the daily life of the commoner class of Edo and contemporary middle-class salary-based families of Tokyo. While the museum projects strong symbolic associations with travel and roads, the interior layout also strongly communicates meanings associated with bridges. The dominant visual structure of the museum interior is a simulacrum version of part of Nihonbashi, the bridge that was once the centre of old Edo. In his analysis of the museum, Sand describes the bridge as 'dividing the so-called "Edo Zone" from the "Tokyo Zone" ' (2001: 361). Although this is correct, I would like to suggest that the bridge is not just a boundary dividing Edo and Tokyo, but a transitional symbol *connecting* them. The sense of connection may not be as immediate, in that the bridge runs between the zones lengthwise, rather than the zones being at each end of the bridge. However, by crossing the bridge and then moving up or down along the designated path, it is possible to go between zones. Running lengthwise between them, the bridge connects them, not so much in the conventional sense, but by serving as the mediator between them, with the bridge as boundary shared by each side. Nihonbashi here emerges as a pivotal symbol, first of the world of Edo itself, and then of the suggestion that one can travel to otherwise inaccessible spaces by bridges, and metaphorically reconnect with other times through the symbolism of the bridge as mediator and connector.

Nihonbashi as symbol of the very Japanese city of Edo past also becomes the symbol of world city Tokyo. Nishiyama (Nishiyama *et al.* 1995: 5) cites Edo era intellectual Hayashi Shihei, who said that 'the water passing under the Nihonbashi Bridge flows to London'. The idea is that Edo was connected to the sea, from which Japan was linked to the world. Thus, despite the Edo period policy of *sakoku*, national seclusion, Nihonbashi bridge is symbolically used to reaffirm the international prominence of Tokyo as a world city, by granting a form of 'internationalness' to its predecessor, Edo. Shiba (1995: 14) performs a similar intellectual sleight of hand, to transform an Edo (both city and era) secluded under national isolation into an 'international Edo', by claiming that the regional diversity of the country and the fact that all regional lords served alternate attendance in Edo meant that 'Japan was an international society unto itself during the Edo period'.

Two significant – seemingly contradictory but actually complementary – messages are voiced in the design and layout of the museum, and they capitalize well on the convergence of Edo as both a spatial and a temporal referent. One of these is that Edo comes to represent the city itself, but with the suggestion of its connections to all other parts of Japan during the Edo era. Thus Edo, along with descendant Tokyo, is projected as a very Japanese city for all Japanese to identify with. Sand points out that the museum reveals the extent to which 'Edo-Tokyo studies made possible the slippage between the local and the national "us" shoring up the foundations of a cultural nationalist vision' (2001: 373). The Edo-to-Tokyo connection is thus used to reaffirm the identity of a localized *furusato* 'home village' Japanese identity.

Complementarily, the Nihonbashi bridge serves as a symbol of the international connections of Edo, despite national seclusion. Bridging Edo to Tokyo thus also highlights the connections of Tokyo to the global context. It reaffirms Tokyo as a world city, while positioning an international aspect of Japanese identity. Within the space and time of the Edo-Tokyo Museum, the conflict between the two desired identity statements is diminished as they merge into an identity suggesting both aspects can be *bridged* into the future. Edo as a place that is connected to other localized places of Japan connects in time to Tokyo as place, and Tokyo the place in current time connects with the international world. Edo as time past that is connected to other times in which Japaneseness is thought to have been forged connects to Tokyo of today, granting assurances that a Japanese home village identity persists despite westernization, and Tokyo today thus connects with a less threatening future of an increasingly internationalizing *furusato* Japan.

Since Edo-Tokyo is the last stop on this packaged magical history tour, before heading for the Tokyo international airport, actually located in the nearby city of Narita, to make that final connection between Tokyo and the outer world, our time travellers can 'wash' their 'worldly cares away' (Ōedo-Onsen Monogatari advertising poster) by a Japanese *sayonara* bathing experience. The Tokyo area now not only re-creates itself as Edo through the reinvention of history, but it re-creates bath experiences, which are popular tourist attractions elsewhere in Japan, through the reinvention of tradition. Edo meets Tokyo, and the rural meets the city, in the simulacrum of a Japanese *onsen* – since the area does not have an actual *onsen* – or hot springs, at the invented tourist bathing centre, Ōedo-Onsen Monogatari, or the 'Great Edo Onsen Story'. Advertisements for the Great Edo Onsen Story re-present an urban scene of Edo from an Edo era *ukiyo-e* print. Visitors are told they can journey to the past, exemplified in statements such as: 'Stroll, snack and shop in a scene from a bygone era.' At the same time, they are reassured that the old Edo connects to the new Tokyo. The advertising headline reads:

'Redefining relaxation where Edo tradition meets Tokyo's cutting edge' (Ōedo-Onsen Monogatari 2003).

Experiencing a bath here has special attractions. The compound area has the 'white walls' of samurai neighbourhoods, looking just like those seen along the streets of Hagi. The bathhouse is built in the Edo period architectural style of a grand building (rather than an ordinary neighbourhood *sentō*, or bathhouse). Inside, before heading to the bath, time travellers choose their favourite *yukata* (light kimono for wear after bathing), from a selection of options all decorated with scenes of Edo life, taken from period *ukiyo-e*, or woodblock prints: geisha and courtesans, Kabuki actors, sumo wrestlers, Edo/Tokyo's Asakusa Shrine, and other Edo city landscapes with Mount Fuji in the background. Another special attraction at Ōedo-Onsen Monogatari is called *Sankin Kōtai no Yu*. *Yu* refers to hot water, in this case for bathing, and *sankin kōtai* refers to the Edo/Tokugawa system of alternate attendance. In this case, it is not the area lords that come to stay in Edo/Tokyo, but hot spring waters from different locations in Japan. This is a popular attraction because the hot spring waters of different locations are famous and favoured for their distinct qualities. Japanese popular culture and folklore extol the virtues of various area waters. One example is the song '*ii yu da na!*' ('Such good hot water!'). With a repetition of '*ii yu da na!*' the song chants about various specific hot springs in different regions of Japan. The *sankin kōtai* association creates a guise around which to enjoy feeling as though one can experience the hot springs of different regions without leaving Tokyo. Each month a different regional hot water is featured.

In Japan, bathing often marks transitions, for example from periods of sickness to health. Bathing also marks temporal transitions, such as between day and night (Clark 1994). In the case of travel, bathing can mark the beginning and end, the journey into and out of the liminal travel period (Creighton 1996: 23). In this case, bathing in an artificially constructed invented *onsen* marks the boundary of the journey, and the end of the simulated tour and transition back to the usual routine. It also marks another temporal transition, between the history traveller's journey into Edo past and subsequent return to the present.

Conclusions

In this chapter, I have explored the contemporary nostalgia for Japan's so-called pre-modern era, 1603–1868, known alternatively as Edo or Tokugawa. I have attempted to show that the two terms are often used differentially. 'Edo' serves as a trope of the emerging commoner class, the vitality of everyday artisans, merchants and other urban dwellers beginning to resist authoritative structures, creating new forms of commoner culture, and finding ways to embark on travel in widespread numbers for the first time in Japanese history. 'Tokugawa', in contrast, serves as a trope for the ruling shogunate, aristocratic elite and government authority that attempted to define and keep people in their place, or at least control their comings and goings.

I have suggested that the appeal to Edo helps address fears about a vanishing cultural heritage amidst increasing urbanization, westernization and suggestions of a 'lost Japan', by highlighting the continuing presence of that past era during which Japanese identity was thought to come fully to fruition under a policy of national isolation that minimized outside western influence. I have suggested that the conflation of Edo as time and place helps mediate tensions between a desire to more fully internationalize and a reverse desire to re-embrace 'home town' Japan. '*Furusato* Tokyo' projects the idea of a Japanese 'home village', showing that an appeal to a past village-like community can be sought in Japan's long history of cities as well as in agrarian villages. Metaphoric travel to Edo, the time, is seemingly more real because one can travel to Edo, the place. Travel along the spatial axis is 'displaced' into the temporal dimension, allowing for the rediscovery and enactment of a past self. Newly created urban history-scapes such as the Edo-Tokyo Museum and the Edo-Tokyo Tatemono-en suggest that while staying in place one can travel temporally to Edo past or Tokyo present. The cognitive similarity of 'time' and 'place' suggested by Japanese language usage, in which both are indexing locations, facilitates the projection of travel in place as analogous to travel in time. This conjunction of time and place is particularly appealing to the nostalgic sentiments underlying the popularity of time travelling in today's Japan. In *The Future of Nostalgia*, Boym discusses how the nostalgic rebel against the usual conventions positing 'time' as inherently different from 'space'. She writes (2001: xiv–xv):

> The nostalgic feel stifled within the conventional confines of time and space. . . . At first glance, nostalgia is a longing for place, but actually it is a yearning for a different time – the time of our childhood, the slower rhythms of our dreams. In a broader sense, nostalgia is a rebellion against the modern idea of time, the time of history and progress. The nostalgic desires to obliterate history and turn it into private or collective mythology, to revisit time like space, refusing to surrender to the irreversibility of time that plagues the human condition.

Japan's *tabi no bunka* (culture of movement/travel) for ordinary Japanese was ushered in during this era as commoners began to travel in large numbers, seeking novelty, pleasure and excitement. This travel had to be cloaked in a legitimating guise of religious pilgrimage. Now middle-class Japanese travelgrims pursue history tourism as edutainment (education and entertainment) by wrapping themselves in the legitimating cloak of education. Pleasure travel is now legitimated as education about Japan, and as developing a new sense of Japanese self by time tripping to Edo and other 'locations' along the History Highway.

In the travelogue presented here, some routes were designated by the

Rekishi Kaidō campaign, while others continued on to Edo/Tokyo. The *Rekishi Kaidō* routes emphasize the Kansai area, and represent such current attempts to win back the central prominence of this area, as it held it during the first part of Tokugawa times, from the Kanto/Tokyo region. Conversely, new developments such as 'Edo-Tokyo studies' as an academic subject and the new Edo-Tokyo Museum and Edo-Tokyo Tatemono-en show that the Kanto/Tokyo region is not willing to give up its claim to the title. Time tripping to Edo-Tokugawa reverberates with the resiliency and strength of this regional rivalry, and reflects its persistence into the present era.

If, as the saying goes, all roads lead up to Tokyo, all Tokyo roads also lead from Tokyo to other places, connecting inward to other parts of Japan and outward to the world. On the History Highway, all roads lead at some point to Edo the time, if not Edo the place. However, metaphorically, Edo, as time past, connects to Edo as place past; Edo the past place connects to Tokyo of the present; and Tokyo the present connects to Japan's future in time, as Tokyo the place connects all of Japan to the rest of the world. Travelling the History Highway in today's Tokugawa Japan allows an inward movement of reunion with a lost Japanese self while conversely allowing an outward movement towards a more internationalized self. Edo mediates desires to recapture a sense of small, Edo-ic village Japan, and desires for greater global participation.

Bridges also mediate, acting as connectors between places and symbolizing transitions in time. In Tokyo, the Nihonbashi bridge, constructed during the Edo era, continues to serve symbolically as the suggested connector between Edo past and Tokyo present. As it did in Edo the time, it also suggests the connections between the Kantō area, now represented by Tokyo, and the rest of Japan, as well as between Japan and the rest of the outer world.

Kansai has its own bridge suggesting the linkage between Tokugawa times, the present and the desire to face toward the future rather than the past. It is Osaka's Kōraibashi bridge, established as Japan's first iron bridge, built over the Higashi Yoko-bori Canal in the summer of 1870 with the ending of the Tokugawa regime. According to descriptions of the bridge put out by the Osaka Castle Museum, it 'was thought of by the people as the symbol of the arrival of a new epoch', a bridge leading from Tokugawa times into a future that was unknown but anticipated with hope. The symbolic associations of the bridge as a connector in both place and time are clear enough. To further these, the Osaka Castle Museum collection utilized an image from a woodblock print showing people crossing the bridge on a souvenir item sold to visitors at the Osaka Castle Museum. Highlighting the bridge's symbolic associations with time, the woodblock print image of the Kōraibashi bridge was used to decorate the face of a playful contemporary fashion watch. As people from a past age make their passage across the Kōraibashi bridge they do so symbolically, and with this watch, literally, in association with the hands of time.

There is another kind of bridge symbolically prominent in the heroic

Edo-ic history *monogatari* (story). Edo, the era itself, is the bridge connecting Japanese of the present to the era in which an imagined more complete Japanese identity and spirit are today most strongly romanticized, and a bridge between today and the massive repository of the more ancient past where assurances of Japanese identity are sought – and thought to be guaranteed. There was a time when the Nihonbashi and Kōraibashi bridges signified a glorious opening to not-yet-experienced places and the anticipated progress of the future. In the early twenty-first century, after waves of westernization, a fear of lost community, and a decade of economic uncertainty, confidence to step boldly into the future was compromised. Japan's nostalgic mood was more not less important in the 1990s, with a prolonged economic recession and a decade labelled the 'Lost Ten Years' (*Ushinawareta Jūnen*) that caused people to further question concepts of perpetual progress and left confidence in the future shaken. Such conditions tend to promote a backward glance to the past for reassurance. According to Lowenthal (1996: ix), 'In recoiling from grievous loss or fending off a fearsome future, people the world over revert to ancestral legacies. As hopes of progress fade, heritage consoles us with tradition.'

These bridges, and particularly Edo as history's rainbow bridge, symbolizing connections between the past and the present, and likewise between the present and the future, thus remain important in the mental imaginary. Like roads, bridges are thought to be connectors that can be travelled in both directions. By travelling the History Highway, modern-day Japanese travelgrims in search of a more complete self attempt to cross over Edo's rainbow bridge to visit Edo and other past eras promising the repository of Japanese identity. At the other side of the rainbow, if successful, they may be transformed by an encounter with another self of theirs. They do not, of course, return to the actual past days of Tokugawa times, but to the simulated past of the Edo era as re-created in the present to serve present needs. Primary among these is providing reassurances that *something* thought of as Japaneseness still persists and will be present in the future. Lowenthal (1996: 139) writes that 'coalescing past with present creates a living heritage that is relevant because it highlights ancestral traits and values felt to accord with our own'. Once refreshed, and reassured, the heroic Edo-ic's rainbow bridge will allow them to cross back over to the contemporary conundrum it is used to address – the place of now.

Notes

1 In this essay, I abide by the practice of rendering words like 'west', 'western' and 'westernization' in the lower case. Titles of wars, such as WWII, are also kept in the lower case, in consideration of the possibility that capitalization of wars reifies them and grants them importance, thus serving as an underlying force reinforcing rather than diminishing these in the human experience.

2 Although the policy of *sakoku* is said to represent a 'closed country', scholars have long understood that Japan was open to various forms of international

intercourse during this period in highly controlled ways. Hatano (1995: 81) points out that links to the Dutch, Chinese and Koreans remained strong throughout the period. One of the issues explored by the contributors to *Bridging the Divide* (Blusse *et al.* 2000) is the nature of such international interactions and the true meaning of *sakoku*. Kasaya (2003) documents the periodic hosting of foreign missions by the shogunate in Edo.

3 There are further suggestions in this article that Haga appreciates established symbols of governmental or state authority in the present time and repudiates resistance against them. He goes on to sarcastically suggest that those who hate the *Hinomaru* flag (a flag with a red circle representing the sun against a white background that has long been a contested symbol in Japan) should consider replacing it with the three-coloured green, persimmon and black drapery of the Kabuki theatre (Haga 1987).

4 The nostalgic appeal of the village occurred in other post-industrial countries in the late twentieth to early twenty-first centuries. It is also the case that enterprises emphasizing a Japanese heritage outside of Japan began to embrace this appeal to the village. An example is the store long known as Ūwajimaya, in Seattle, Washington. Founded in 1928, at that time largely to service the significant market of Japanese immigrants dwelling in the area, the store remained a well-known entity in Seattle's international district. In the late 1990s, in preparation for its autumn 2000 reopening after an expansion, brochures put out by Ūwajimaya adopted the nomenclature of the village. The heading of one such brochure reads: 'Ūwajimaya Village: Building on Tradition'. In addition to the store itself, the expansion involved parking, additional smaller shops, an Asian food court, banking services, and apartments. Now, tourist maps of the central Seattle area no longer refer simply to Ūwajimaya, but instead to 'Ūwajimaya Village'.

5 Nitobe is strongly associated with this phrase, and it is used in several books, articles and essays about him. Rendered in Japanese as 'Negawaku wa ware Taiheiyō no hashi to naran', it is inscribed on a stone wall within Morioka-*joshi* (Morioka Castle site) compound in Morioka, Japan, Nitobe's birthplace, and also inscribed in a stone within the Nitobe Garden, named after him, located in Vancouver, BC, Canada.

6 Leheny (2003) explores how leisure manifests the tension between these contrasting desires.

7 It is not clear whether this phrase was really invented in Japan or whether it was a phrase adopted from use in English. The great depression in North America was also referred to as the Ten Lost Years. For example, Broadfoot edited a collection of personal accounts of Canadians who had lived through the depression under the title *Ten Lost Years 1929–1939: Memories of Canadians Who Survived the Depression*. Broadfoot indicates that the phrase is not his own, but came from one of the people who lived through the depression that he interviewed. Since Broadfoot's book was published in 1973, the title and concept have been around on catalogue and search networks long enough to have possibly been picked up or influenced the usage of such phrasing. It is also possible that those other than the interviewee Broadfoot mentions talked about the depression years in terms of the lost ten years, before the analogous phrase was adopted in Japan.

8 I include the specific reference to *tazunenagara* because it has connotations of 'while visiting', in the sense of 'while travelling to'. The full quotation in Japanese is: 'Rekishi Kaidō to wa, yūkyū no rekishi no butai o tazunenagara Nihon bunka o tanoshiku taiken dekiru atarashii ru-to no koto desu.'

9 The full original quotation for this in Japanese is: 'Yutaka na rekishi o mirai ni mukete hagukumu tame ni, kangaeru benkyō kai ni, sanka shi mo hitori no jibun ni deaimashō.'

10 The title of this brochure appeared as listed here in both English and Japanese (with the Japanese written in characters). Unlike many of the promotional pamphlets this one offered some English translations of the descriptions presented in Japanese.

11 In addition to being highly populated, Osaka was ranked as the third most expensive city in which to live in the 2004 international rankings of cities. Tokyo was named as the most expensive city in the world, with London ranked second between them.

12 To be fair to projected representations of history, it should be noted that the characterization of a 'castle town' meant more than just having a castle. It also involved forms of social organization and trade interactions that were associated with castle towns. Thus Hagi retains in the minds of many Japanese a stronger sense of being a 'castle town' than other cities, even some that still have castles. However, it is probably the case that the constant reiteration of Hagi as a castle town by the tourism industry also helps maintain these associations among Japanese.

13 Nijō-*jō* was completed in 1626 by the era's third shogun, Tokugawa Iemitsu.

14 The name of the hotel is written on the building face in all-capital roman letters, with the word for hotel in the correct English spelling rather than in the spelling of the word when transferred into *katakana*. Thus it integrates Japanese and English designations within the same title as if one type of speech form.

15 Although depicting the female *ama* as catching seafood rather than diving for pearls, the movie *Tanpopo*, directed by Itami Jūzō, exemplifies the depiction of *ama* as young, alluring, sexually attractive and in this case innocently virginal. The movie's main male character, a gangster, eats the catch from her hand, in a manner suggesting sexual gusto, during which time the seafood is cut and bleeds (suggestive of blood due to rupture of the hymen at first intercourse) and the young female *ama* apparently undergoes a sexual awakening.

16 The park describes itself as an outdoor museum where the precious remaining architectural structures of Tokyo have been gathered ('Tokyo ni nokatta kicho na tatemono o atsumeta yagai hakubutsukan desu', Edo-Tokyo Tatemono-en n.d.: 1).

References

Akatsuka, Y. (1988). 'Our retrospective age'. *Japan Quarterly*, 35(2), pp. 279–80.

Bachnik, J.M. and C.J. Quinn, Jr (eds) (1994). *Situated Meaning: Inside and Outside in Japanese Self, Society, and Language*. Princeton, NJ: Princeton University Press.

Befu, H. (1983). 'Internationalization of Japan and *Nihon Bunkaron*'. In H. Mannari and H. Befu (eds), *The Challenge of Japan's Internationalization: Organization and Culture*. Kobe and Tokyo: Kwansei Gakuin University and Kodansha International, pp. 232–66.

Bestor, T. (1989). *Neighborhood Tokyo*. Stanford, CA: Stanford University Press.

Blusse, L., W. Remmelink and I. Smits (2000). *Bridging the Divide: 400 Years The Netherlands–Japan*. Leiden: Hotei.

Boym, S. (2001). *The Future of Nostalgia*. New York: Basic Books.

Broadfoot, B. (1973). *Ten Lost Years 1929–1939: Memories of Canadians Who Survived the Depression*. Toronto and New York: Doubleday Canada and Doubleday.

Clark, S. (1994). *Japan: A View from the Bath*. Honolulu: University of Hawaii Press.

Creighton, M. (1989). 'Japan's department stores: selling "internationalization"'. *Japan Society Newsletter*, 37(4), pp. 2–7.

—— (1991). 'Maintaining cultural boundaries in retailing: how Japanese department stores domesticate "things foreign" '. *Modern Asian Studies*, 25(4), pp. 675–709.

—— (1992). 'The depaato: merchandising the west while selling Japaneseness'. In J.J. Tobin (ed.), *Re-made in Japan: Everyday Life and Consumer Taste in a Changing Society*. New Haven, CT: Yale University Press, pp. 42–57.

—— (1994a). 'Edutaining children: consumer and gender socialization in Japanese marketing'. *Ethnology*, 33(1), pp. 35–52.

—— (1994b). 'The shifting imagery of childhood amidst Japan's consumer affluence: the birth of the "5 pocket child" '. In H. Eiss (ed.), *Images of the Child*. Bowling Green, OH: Popular Press (division of Bowling Green State University Press), pp. 75–99.

—— (1995). 'Socialization for consumerism: from infant shopping clubs to young adult consumer roles'. In D. Dicks (ed.), *Communication with Japan: Images, Past, Present and Future*. Montreal: Concordia University, pp. 79–96.

—— (1996). 'Travelling by choice: visiting Japanese Canadian internment sites'. *Geppo Bulletin: A Journal for and about the Nikkei Community*, 38(8) (August), pp. 22–3.

—— (1997). 'Consuming rural Japan: the marketing of tradition and nostalgia in the Japanese travel industry'. *Ethnology*, 36(3), pp. 239–54.

—— (1998a). 'Pre-industrial dreaming in post-industrial Japan: department stores and the commoditization of community traditions'. *Japan Forum*, 10(2), pp. 127–49.

—— (1998b). 'The seed of consumer lifestyle shopping: wrapping consumerism in Japanese store lay-outs'. In J.F. Sherry, Jr (ed.), *ServiceScapes: The Concept of Place in Contemporary Markets*, Chicago: NTC, pp. 199–227.

—— (1998c). 'Weaving the future from the heart of tradition: learning in leisure activities'. In J. Singleton (ed.), *Learning in Likely Places: Varieties of Apprenticeship in Japan*. Cambridge: Cambridge University Press, pp. 190–207.

—— (2001). 'Spinning silk, weaving selves: gender, nostalgia and identity in Japanese craft vacations'. *Japanese Studies*, 21(1), pp. 5–29.

—— (2003). 'May the Saru River flow: the Nibutani dam and the resurging tide of the Ainu identity movement'. In D. Edgington (ed.), *Joining Past and Future: Japan at the Millennium*. Vancouver: University of British Columbia Press, pp. 120–43.

Eades, J.F. (2000). 'Introduction'. In J.S. Eades, T. Gill and H. Befu (eds), *Globalization and Social Change in Contemporary Japan*. Melbourne: Trans Pacific Press.

Edo-Tokyo Museum (1995). *Guide to Edo-Tokyo Museum*. Tokyo: Edo-Tokyo Museum.

Edo-Tokyo Tatemono-en (Edo-Tokyo Building Park) (n.d.).

Gluck, C. (1998). 'The invention of Edo'. In S. Vlastos (ed.), *Mirror of Modernity: Invented Traditions of Modern Japan*. Berkeley: University of California Press, pp. 262–84.

Graburn, N.H.H. (1977). 'Tourism: the sacred journey'. In V.L. Smith (ed.), *Hosts and Guests: The Anthropology of Tourism*. Philadelphia: University of Pennsylvania Press, pp. 17–31.

—— (1983). *To Pray, Pay and Play: The Cultural Structure of Japanese Domestic Tourism*. Les Cahiers du Tourisme, Série B, Numéro 26. Aix-en-Provence: Centre des Hautes Etudes Touristiques.

Haga, T. (1987). 'Sekaishi no naka no Tokugawa Nihon'. *Asahi Janaru*, 29(1) (2–9 January), pp. 68–72.

Hartley, L.P. ([1953] 2000). *The Go-Between*, London and New York: Penguin Books.

Hatano, J. (1995). 'The view from the Nihonbashi bridge and the merchant class'. In Edo-Tokyo Museum (ed.), *Guide to Edo-Tokyo Museum*. Tokyo: Foundation Edo-Tokyo Historical Society, p. 31.

Hikone Municipal Office, Department of Industrial Affairs (n.d.). *Guide to Hikone*. Hikone: Tourist Guide Division.

Howes, J. (ed.) (1995). *Nitobe Inazo: Japan's Bridge across the Pacific*. Boulder, CO: Westview Press.

Ivy, M. (1988). 'Tradition and difference in the Japanese mass media'. *Public Culture Bulletin*, 1(1), pp. 21–9.

—— (1995). *Discourses of the Vanishing: Modernity, Phantasm, Japan*. Chicago: University of Chicago Press.

Japan Times (1986). *Japan's History as News: You Are There*. Tokyo: Japan Times.

Kasaya, K. (2003). 'The shogun's domestic and foreign visitors'. *Japan Echo*, 30(2), pp. 68–72.

Kodama, K. (1995). 'Foreword'. In Edo-Tokyo Museum (ed.), *Guide to Edo-Tokyo Museum*. Tokyo: Foundation Edo-Tokyo Historical Society, p. 4.

Leheny, D. (2003). *The Rules of Play: National Identity and the Shaping of Japanese Leisure*. Ithaca, NY: Cornell University Press.

Lowenthal, D. (1985). *The Past Is a Foreign Country*. Cambridge: Cambridge University Press.

—— (1996). *Possessed by the Past: The Heritage Crusade and the Spoils of History*. New York: Free Press.

Martinez, D.P. (1990). 'Tourism and the ama: the search for a real Japan'. In E. Ben-Ari, B. Moeran and J. Valentine (eds), *Unwrapping Japan: Society and Culture in Anthropological Perspective*. Honolulu: University of Hawaii Press, pp. 97–116.

—— (2004). *Identity and Ritual in a Japanese Diving Village*. Honolulu: University of Hawaii Press.

Mukerji, C. (1983). *From Graven Images: Patterns of Modern Materialism*. New York: Columbia University Press.

Nakane, C. (1970). *Japanese Society*. Los Angeles: University of California Press.

Nishiyama, M., M. Takeuchi and M. Tsuchida (1995). 'Welcome to Edo-Tokyo Museum'. In Edo-Tokyo Museum (ed.), *Guide to Edo-Tokyo Museum*, Tokyo: Foundation Edo-Tokyo Historical Society, pp. 5–7.

Ōedo-Onsen Monogatari (2003). http.//www.ooedoonsen.jp.

Ohnuki-Tierney, E. (1990). 'The ambivalent self of the contemporary Japanese'. *Cultural Anthropology*, 5(2), pp. 197–216.

Plath, D.W. and J. Hill (1988). 'Athletes of the deep: the *ama* as artisans and as emblems'. *Japan Society Newsletter*, 36(3), pp. 2–5.

Rekishi Kaidō Promotional Council, Brochure 1: 'Rekishi Kaidō ku-ra-bu-Nyūkai no Goannai: Yūkyū no jidai e no taimu toraberu' [History Highway club entering invitation: time travel to the eternal ages]. Osaka.

Rekishi Kaidō Promotional Council, Brochure 2: 'Discover Machiya – *Machiya Hakkenki*'. Osaka: Osaka International Convention Centre.

Robertson, J. (1987). 'A dialectic of native and newcomer: the Kodaira citizens' festival in suburban Tokyo'. *Anthropological Quarterly*, 60(3), pp. 124–36.

—— (1988). 'The culture and politics of nostalgia: *furusato* Japan'. *International Journal of Politics, Culture and Society*, 1(4), pp. 494–518.

—— (1995). 'Hegemonic nostalgia, tourism, and nation-making in Japan'. In T. Umesao, H. Befu and S. Ishimori (eds), *Japanese Civilization in the Modern World*, IX: *Tourism*, Senri Ethnological Studies, 38. Osaka: National Museum of Ethnology, pp. 89–103.

—— (1998). 'It takes a village: internationalization and nostalgia in postwar Japan'. In S. Vlastos (ed.), *Mirror of Modernity: Invented Traditions of Modern Japan*. Berkeley: University of California Press, pp. 110–29.

Sand, J. (2001). 'Monumentalizing the everyday: the Edo-Tokyo Museum'. *Critical Asian Studies*, 33(3), 351–78.

Seiter, E. (1992). 'Toys are us: marketing to children and parents'. *Cultural Studies*, 6(2), pp. 232–47.

Shiba, R. (1987). 'Edo Jidai ni Tsuite: Baraetii to Tōitsu' [Concerning the Edo era: variety and unification]. *Asahi Janaru*, 24(41) (2 October), pp. 6–10.

—— (1995). 'The diversity of the Edo period'. In Edo-Tokyo Museum (ed.), *Guide to Edo-Tokyo Museum*. Tokyo: Foundation Edo-Tokyo Historical Society, pp. 14–17.

Shiga-Ken Syoko-Rodo-bu Kanko Bussan-ka [Shiga Prefectural Government Tourism and Local Products Promotion Division] (n.d.). *Shiga Tourist's Guide: Shiga, the Central Part of Japan*. Otsu City: Shiga-Ken Syoko-Rodo-bu Kanko Bussan-ka.

Shirahata, Y. (1995). 'Information studies of tourist resources'. In T. Umesao, H. Befu and S. Ishimori (eds), *Japanese Civilization in the Modern World*, IX: *Tourism*, Senri Ethnological Studies, 38. Osaka: National Museum of Ethnology, pp. 51–63.

Tobin, J. (1992). 'Japanese preschools and the pedagogy of selfhood'. In N. Rosenberger (ed.), *Japanese Sense of Self*. Cambridge: Cambridge University Press.

Turner, V. and E. Turner (1978). *Image and Pilgrimage in Christian Culture: Anthropological Perspectives*. New York: Columbia University Press.

Umehara, T. (1987). 'Edo-Jomon teki naru mono no fukkatsu' [The revival of Edo-like, Jomon-like things]. *Asahi Janaru*, 29(1) (2–9 January), pp. 104–8.

Umesao, T. (1995). 'Keynote address: tourism as a phenomenon of civilization'. In T. Umesao, H. Befu and S. Ishimori (eds), *Japanese Civilization in the Modern World*, IX: *Tourism*, Senri Ethnological Studies, 38. Osaka: National Museum of Ethnology, pp. 1–9.

Vaporis, C.N. (1994). *Breaking Barriers: Travel and the State in Early Modern Japan*. Cambridge, MA: Council on East Asian Studies, Harvard University Press.

Vlastos, S. (1998). 'Tradition: past/present culture and modern Japanese history'. In S. Vlastos (ed.), *Mirror of Modernity: Invented Traditions of Modern Japan*. Berkeley: University of California Press, pp. 1–16.

Wells, H.G. ([1895] 2001). *The Time Machine*, ed. N. Ruddick. New York: Random House.

White, M. (1988). *The Japanese Overseas: Can They Go Home Again?*. New York: Free Press.

3 Japanese inns (*ryokan*) as producers of Japanese identity

Sylvie Guichard-Anguis

In the world Japan has the rare privilege of possessing two types of lodging, existing side by side: Japanese inns (*Nihon no yado* or *ryokan*) and hotels. Japanese inns, whose historical origins are rooted in the Japanese archipelago, have resisted the introduction of Western forms of lodging represented by hotels (Maeda 2001; Okubo 2001). In any Japanese bookshop one can find an enormous amount of literature displayed on these two kinds of lodgings. Generally speaking, hotels show less variety, with the only categories being resort hotels, de luxe hotels, nostalgic hotels and so on, if we put aside budget ones. On the contrary, magazines and guides dedicated to *ryokan* show an amazing number of extremely specialized categories, and these volumes may cover spa *ryokan*, *ryokan* associated with Japanese famous writers (Yajima 1998), secret *ryokan*, very famous *ryokan*, *ryokan* where the emperor of Japan has stayed, wooden-built and three-storey *ryokan*, *ryokan* for Japanese cuisine associated with the seasons, *ryokan* with thatched roofs, etc.[1] This incomplete list gives an initial idea of the great variety of Japanese inns and of the individualism which characterizes them, as they all look different from one another.

Considering that *ryokan* are generally small (they have an average of 14.9 rooms compared to 76.2 for hotels – Kokudo kōtsūshō 2004), very individualistic and deriving from different historical periods, what makes them resist the competition of hotels, which may offer hundreds of rooms and whose construction and management may be sustained by huge capital investments? In other words, what kind of needs are the *ryokan* satisfying?

This chapter will focus mainly on *ryokan* which are the most successful in the upper categories, that is to say the most expensive, elegant and famous among the 61,000 found today in Japan (Sōrifu 2004), or roughly the tenth of *ryokan* which favour ties with a travel agent. Three tentative explanations are given. First, *ryokan* are places associated with modernity and the invention of 'Japanese beauty' through most of the Japanese arts; in other words they play the part of some kind of local cultural centres. Second, there visitors meet with history and travel to some nostalgic past. Third, they are places where one can encounter nature and which shelter the culture of hospitality (*motenashi no bunka*), a fundamental aspect of human relations in Japan. It goes without saying that those reasons are well mingled, but for a clearer presentation I will dissociate them.

Ryokan, modernity and the invention of 'Japanese beauty'

Before going any further, some general facts about *ryokan* should be given in order to understand the context of the *ryokan* mentioned in this chapter. The law on *ryokan* enacted in 1948 and its following decree in 1957 focus on the improvement of health conditions (Maeda 1998). It distinguishes hotels from *ryokan* by the following criteria. Hotels mainly have Western-style rooms in terms of construction or equipment, with at least ten rooms of a minimum surface area of 9 square metres. *Ryokan* mainly have Japanese-style rooms (*wafu*), with at least five rooms of a minimum surface area of 7 square metres. The law for the improvement of international tourist hotel facilities in 1949 (largely modified in 1993) aims at providing decent facilities to foreign visitors. Registered hotels and *ryokan* under this law are supposed to be the most representative of their category. In 2002 *ryokan* in Japan numbered 61,583, but only 2,011 are registered in this category.

Two points should be made about these very loose definitions of accommodation types in Japan. First, there is no clear boundary between hotel and *ryokan* categories. Second, the law underlines the difference of size between hotels and *ryokan* as one of the main criteria. These two points help with understanding why a clear definition of *ryokan* is a real challenge. *Ryokan* have to be accommodation of a Japanese style, but trying to define this style, which is characterized by an endless evolution, is difficult. The following text will help to draw a picture of them little by little by providing clarification about their most remarkable features.

The selection of *ryokan* in this chapter comes from two main sources: first, specialized magazines, guidebooks or volumes found in bookshops or in the travel (*tabi*) library founded by the Japan Tourist Bureau (JTB) in Tokyo and, second, the *ryokan* registered with the two main travel agencies, JTB and Kinki Tourist. According to Maeda Isamu, one of the main academic experts on *ryokan*, roughly 7,000 *ryokan* belong to this category, with around 3,000 for JTB and 2,500 for Kinki Tourist.[2]

The high social status of the owners of these *ryokan* gives some idea of the part they play in today's society and illustrates the historical evolution of these types of accommodation from mere shelters to de luxe inns, which allows some of them to belong to the most prestigious groups of small de luxe hotels in the world.

The word *yado*, still largely used in Japan today, illustrates one of the main transformations of such places. Famous works of Japanese travelogue give an insight into their historical origins, as they describe very rustic shelters, such as that in *Travel in the Eastern Provinces* (Anonymous Japanese [1242] 1999). The word is formed from a Chinese character with the meaning of 'shelter, lodging, inn', and seemed not worthy enough for the new types of inns which came slowly from the merger of different traditions of lodging and began to appear with the creation of railways during the Meiji period (1868–1912). *Ryokan*, written with the two Chinese characters of *ryo* (journey) and *kan* (mansion), emphasized the level of facilities one was able to find in the new types of inns. The word began to be largely used around the Taishō period (1912–26) to name this rather de luxe kind of accommodation in which a visitor would stay mainly for leisure purposes, which is completely distinct from the several kind of inns (*yado*) still in operation (Okubo unpublished paper[3]). *Ryokan*, instead of playing the part of mere shelters along the road, began to be the purpose of the travel itself, a shift in the general use of inns which is still prevailing today for many of them.

Deliberately in this chapter I will leave aside the types of *ryokan* which cannot survive the present economic situation and are disappearing. They include *ryokan* close to railway stations which cannot compete with modern business hotels (which date from the 1970s) or city hotels and the like, or the ones which did not update their facilities and offered too old-fashioned an environment. New types of accommodation made competition fierce, with the opening in 1956 of national popular lodgings (*kokumin shukusha*), followed by Japanese-style bed and breakfast including dinner (*minshuku*) in the 1960s and small private Western-style inns (*penshion*) in the 1970s. These *ryokan* are facing bankruptcy one after the other, as shown by the dwindling number of *ryokan* in Japan. With 61,583 in 2002, the number of *ryokan* is gradually falling from its peak of 83,226 in 1980. Even in a city like Atami (Shizuoka prefecture), which was from the end of the 1950s to the beginning of the 1970s the most popular recreation place in Japan, the number of *ryokan* fell from 361 in 1972, the peak year, to 68 in 2003 (Guichard-Anguis 2007b).

This harsh economic environment does not prevent some of them from being very successful and a few newcomers making the headlines in newspapers and magazines. One of the keys to their vitality lies in the constant flow of invention of modernity, associated with so-called Japanese beauty (*Nihon no bi*). In brief, they have to offer the same level of amenities that hotels do, but in a different way which justifies their originality as *ryokan*. The invention of a Japanese style (*wafu*) always on the move has been one of the patterns followed by the most innovative *ryokan* for more than a century. In other words they take part in the process of creating Japanese identity by a paradox: they assert their historical and indigenous origins by creating a modernity supposed to be unique.

One of the most well-known *ryokan* owners, from the Tama no yū in Yufuin hot spring (Oita prefecture), ranking among the very first *ryokan* in Japan today, declares in an interview[4] that she considers it her job to be a producer of space. She even dares to stress the importance of privacy inside *ryokan*, a notion hardly known until a very recent period. In most of the *ryokan* people looking after clients come and go inside the rooms with little warning. As food and sleep are functions shared by the same space, bringing the tray of food or laying a futon on the tatami or putting them back are tasks which require the presence of a member of staff (generally a woman), who may invite the visitors to go out of the room to take a bath and leave her free to conduct her duties. This young owner dares to depart from some of the stereotypes associated with *ryokan* in a very inventive way, trying to satisfy the new needs of visitors whose expectations have largely evolved and been modified from those of the most prosperous years of the *ryokan*.

In another inn in Yufuin, also well known to the general public, Kame no i besso offers a second alternative to this innovative process. It was originally a villa (*besso*) built around 1922, which includes six rooms in its main building and 15 in separate outbuildings (*hanare*). Composed of small wooden buildings scattered among trees as in the case of Tama no yū, it offers all the amenities people expect to find at the beginning of the twenty-first century, associated with an environment which stresses local history and nature. The main building, built with old material from the farmhouse, emphasizes a European atmosphere. A coffee shop stands on the first floor of a reformed sake trade house dating back to the end of the Edo period (1603–1868), with a menu which includes some European-style coffee according to the pamphlet.

Not only local history but the history of other countries, European or Asian (Guichard-Anguis 2006), is sought to emphasize the unique atmosphere of these places. They make much use of the past (Japanese or foreign), through its most exotic aspects, to create innovation and modernity. Westernization and stressing individuality are definitely part of these very recent tendencies among the most successful *ryokan* (Kashiwai 2003). Since the beginning of the Meiji period (1868–1912) the merger of different traditions of lodging (examples of which will be analysed below) combined with an endless introduction of contemporaneous amenities has given birth to the several types of *ryokan* which still exist today (Guichard-Anguis 2003, 2007a). Opened mainly for the many foreigners who began to settle in Japan, the very first hotel, Yokohama Hotel, made its appearance in the Japanese archipelago in 1860. But staying in hotels at the turn of the nineteenth century meant a lot of adaptation for Japanese visitors. Hotels were first conceived only as a Western environment; customers had to sleep in beds, sit on chairs and dine at tables, etc., which meant learning those habits. Second, these hotels included new amenities which were introduced one after the other and resulted in a comfort unknown in the inns operating in those days: new kinds of lighting with gas, electricity, running water (cold and hot), general heating, etc. Third, the privacy of customers was emphasized, as they could stay in their own rooms, separated from the others by real walls. Last but not least, customers could close and lock the doors of their rooms.

At the end of the nineteenth century the three main functions which gave *ryokan* their originality – sleeping, eating and bathing – after being scattered for centuries among different lodgings became slowly incorporated inside the inn itself. The new inns which made their appearance in this period adopted some of the novelties found in hotels. Rooms became individual, with solid walls between them, a door with a key to close them and a corridor leading to them. Electricity, running water, heating equipment, etc. made their appearance in these individual rooms. Diversity was emphasized as the new types of inns began to correspond to different needs: *ryokan* in tourist spots (*kankō ryokan*), famous cuisine *ryokan* (*ryōri ryokan*), without forgetting the *ryokan* which sprouted close to railway stations, etc.

In 1955 around 100 hotels and 55,000 *ryokan* could be found in Japan. The first innovations in Japanese inns were followed by the introduction of private toilets, TV, cooler and even private baths in the most de luxe ones. Not only the rooms themselves but the general environment inside the *ryokan* was greatly modified with the introduction of a lobby, a coffee shop, a gift shop, a karaoke room, a bar, a swimming pool, tennis courts, meeting rooms, banquet rooms, restaurant, theatre, Noh theatre, etc. According to their size and the period of construction, they adopted one or several of the new facilities, which added to the great variety of types and scale. Wooden built during the Meiji (1868–1912), Taishō (1912–26) and the beginning of the Shōwa periods (1926–89), *ryokan* began to be built in concrete around the mid-1950s. The improvement in building techniques allowed the size of the *ryokan* to grow to that of hotels in the 1960s and the 1970s. The new volumes allowed new recreation facilities to be included in the *ryokan*. The new types of *ryokan* began to be characterized by the contrast between their Western exterior look and a Japanese style inside or a hybrid style (*wayō setchū*) still favoured in a lot of well-known de luxe *ryokan*. The introduction of these facilities had two very important consequences for the pattern of stay: first, the very large *ryokan* could accommodate large groups of customers; and, second, visitors could remain inside these *ryokan* without going out, as they could find all the amenities they were looking for there.

The interior designs of the inns underwent drastic change in the Meiji and the following periods, emphasizing a so-called Japanese style (*wafu*), a permanent creation of a tradition going on to this day. The new types of inns adopted the decoration used exclusively until then in lodgings dedicated to the social elite. Rooms began to include the decorative alcove (*tokonoma*) found until then only in the most elegant rooms of the inns and still the norm in most of the rooms today. Their style was that of the drawing room (*zashiki*) or of the guest room (*kyakuma*), reserved in the Edo period (1603–1868) for elite visitors. An intermediate room was added to separate the room itself from the outside (*engawa*), which plays the part of a sun room. This new style, which emphasizes its unique character, is very often associated in women's magazines like *Katei-gahō* and in the tourist literature on *ryokan* to Japanese beauty (*Nihon no bi*), a powerful concept which stresses the ability of Japanese culture to invent what is supposed to be perfection and at the core of Japanese identity. A lot of the *ryokan* which have existed for more than a century are still fascinating examples of such architecture and designs (Miyamoto and Suzuki 1999) and still attract visitors for their quality. Some of them have even been turned into museums recently.

The concept of maintenance (*iji*) (Muramatsu 1999; Kasai 1999) might play a very important part in these places, but it is to ensure a better future by introducing modern comforts and amenities rather than to preserve bygone days. Authenticity is not really valued, and the past is always reinvented according to present needs. Architecture and design evolve over the years and diversity increases, which is why literature about so many kinds of *ryokan* is found in bookshops.

Last but not least this beauty is also made up of other components like the food served, the arts displayed inside, the environment, the bath, etc. In other words the main attraction of these places lies in the following paradox: in Japan today the so-called Japanese interior or style of life has simply vanished from the environment of everyday life. *Ryokan* are becoming the only places where one can taste Japanese culture as a whole. *Ryokan* offer a unique experience for contact with some of the most revered Japanese traditions by visitors who lead a more and more Westernized style of life. Flower arrangement is part of the decoration in all the rooms where the visitors stay. Calligraphy is hung in the decorative alcove (*tokonoma*) and the menu is handwritten with a brush and black ink. Dressed in the kimono, the woman patron (*Ōkami-san*) may prepare a bowl of tea according to the ritual of the tea ceremony (*chanoyu*). These allusions to artistic traditions also involve a dynamic perception, which fosters creation, innovation and renewal. Many crafts go into the creation of this so-called Japanese beauty, whether they date back to olden times and are testimonies of the ancient origin of the *ryokan* or are contemporaneous, like lacquer ware, ceramics, textiles, wood crafts, bamboo crafts, etc. It goes without saying that all those testimonies of successive modernity and artistic creation speak of *ryokan* history.

Ryokan as historic places to visit and the culture of travel

The oldest Japanese inn is recorded in *Guinness World Records* among the oldest enterprises in the world, as its present owner belongs to the forty-sixth generation. With an origin in 718, Hōshi *ryokan* (Awazu hot spring, Ishikawa prefecture) today is very representative of a *ryokan* of the 1960s and 1970s accommodating large groups of visitors. To the old Japanese-style wooden building was added the present main one built of concrete with eight floors, and altogether it has around 80 rooms and a capacity of 450 visitors. Walking inside those buildings, which are connected, facing an old Japanese-style garden, means going to one of the several large inside or outside baths or to the swimming pool with its Noh theatre at the back, or entering one of the banquet rooms which can seat 100, 200 or 300 visitors, or one of the meeting rooms of 230- or 240-visitor capacity, or even spending the evening in the bar or karaoke room, etc. In other words, in spite of asserting the longest history among the *ryokan* still operating, Hōshi has little to offer in terms of historical evidence today, some historical documents apart. The following text shows how much it differs from a lot of other Japanese inns.

Several sources offer an insight into the history of Japanese inns, among which the travelogue and Japanese woodblock printings (*ukiyo-e*) rank first. A travel book like the one written by Jippenshā ([1806] 1992) and illustrations given in many of the woodblock printings dedicated to hot springs (Kogure 2003) or moving (Satō and Fujiwara 2000) etc. help to build a vivid image of how visitors used to lodge in these inns. Even old photos of the very first years of the Meiji period (1868–1912) testified to urban or rural landscapes directly inherited from the Edo period, before modernization took its toll (Kodama 2001). And last but not least, remaining buildings from those periods stand as material evidence of the wealth of structures dating back to the Edo period (1603–1868).

During those centuries people from different walks of life, for many different purposes, travelled in such numbers that it gave birth to the expression 'the culture of travel' (*tabi no bunka*) among historians (Vaporis 1994). This notion remains fundamental to understanding the present position of Japanese cultural heritage on a national level, and the behaviour of Japanese tourists today. The number of exhibitions in local museums dedicated to this topic seems to grow every year. Even material culture associated with travel can be the topic of exhibitions in these places, in the form of famous delicacies, different kinds of lighting, etc. Selected books and series (one of the favourite topics focuses on highways) come out every year to satisfy a curiosity on this aspect of Japanese culture which seems endless (*Taiyō korekushon Chizu Edo Meiji Gendai* 1977). Travelling in Japan today very often means discovering how people used to travel centuries ago.

Very briefly, who travelled and how during those two and a half centuries of the Edo period? In 1872 the first railway line was opened between Yokohama and Shimbashi in Tokyo, and from that time the network of railways which took shape slowly modified the pattern of travel and of course lodging drastically. Until the last years of the nineteenth century people travelled by walking along the roads, except a small minority, which explains the density of facilities along them. Travel during that period was strictly limited to a minority having a permit to do so, but the reality varied quite a bit and several purposes can be put forward. People compelled to travel included merchants, pedlars and the like, the *Bakufu* government officials and last but not least the lords of the fiefs (*daimyō*) and their escort. Being compelled to stay every other year in Edo, *daimyō* had to travel from the castle town centre of their fief to Edo with a group of vassals, fief officials, soldiers, servants, etc., which could number several hundreds or even more (Vaporis 1994; Yamamoto 1998). Other travellers had to have official permission to leave their home place: pilgrimage and bathing in hot springs were the most popular. Between those involved in alternate attendance (*sankin kōtai*) and others looking for motives to tour some part of the country, many common habits can be found. The one of pleasure seeking (*monomi yūsan*) developed in the second part of this period (Fukai 2000: 112) and added a lot of variety to travel, including visiting famous places (*meisho*) such as shrines, temples and theatres, savouring local delicacies and so on, which became part of enjoying the walk.

And very briefly, too, to respond to the needs of those travellers, where were the inns located? Besides the largest cities of that period (Edo, Osaka and Kyoto), harbours, places of pilgrimage like Ise (Mie prefecture) or Nagano (Nagano prefecture) and hot springs, inns stood along a network of highways which extended from Edo. The main five, Tōkaidō, Nakasendō, Kōshu Kaidō, Nikkō Kaidō, Ōshū Kaidō, were complemented by a network of shorter ones like Saikoku kaidō, Hokkoku kaidō, etc. (Miwa 2003a, 2003b). Extensively illustrated in woodblock printings these highways, which begin at Nihonbashi in the centre of Edo, were equipped with post towns (*shukuba machi*) at regular distances (Imado 1984; Kodama 1986; Takeuchi 2003). Most of the ancient post towns can still be found in remote areas today offering landscapes dating back to previous periods (mountains or highways of secondary importance in rural parts of the country). Some roads still offer a succession of post towns to tourists, as on the Nakasendō, which links Kyoto to Edo through the Japanese Alps, along the Kiso portion (*Kisoji*), which includes 11 of the 69 post towns of this highway, with Narai (a village of Narakawa), Tsumago (a town of Nagiso) and Magome (a village of Yamaguchi). The name of Tsumago was made famous when this post town became a forerunner in preservation movements in Japan and when in 1976 the Agency for Cultural Affairs designated it as the first 'preservation district for groups of historic buildings' (*jūyō dentōteki kenzō-butsu-gun hozon chiku*).

With Wada, Ashida and Mochitsuki, a different group of post towns can still be found on this same highway before its connection with the Hokkoku kaidō, which linked Edo to the Japan Sea shore. Close to these post towns the one of Unno *juku* is located on the Hokkoku kaidō leading directly to the pilgrimage place of the Zenkoji in Nagano before reaching the Japan Sea shore. As a very important stop during the Edo period it became a silkworm culture town during the Meiji era. Because of its landscapes which reflect these two periods of its development, Unno *juku* is also designated as a preservation district for groups of historic buildings. Other rather isolated post towns can be found, like the Kumagawa *juku* (Fukui prefecture) on the Wakakusa kaidō linking Kyoto to Obama on the Japan Sea shore, a highway famous for Japan Sea products, especially mackerel, which is brought to the capital, and therefore the nickname *Saba* (mackerel) *kaidō*. In Fukushima prefecture, Ōuchi *juku* offers a north-eastern example of a traditional place, as highlighted in Japanese guidebooks. Located on the Aizu Saikaidō, which linked Aizu Wakamatsu to the Nikkō kaidō, most of the buildings still retain their miscanthus-thatched roofs, which give an impressive look to the street, with very large houses on both sides. These last two places are also designated as preservation districts.

Among the different categories – harbours, mountain villages, religious districts, warrior districts, etc. – included in the preservation district for groups of historic buildings, which altogether number 62, post towns number six (Sōrifu 2004: 137). This attraction for the culture of travel goes as far as reproducing inns, evoking local history, as in Ishibe (Shiga prefecture), one of the post towns of the Tōkaidō. A recent community centre constructed in the mountains a few kilometres from the old highway evokes the old Ishibe of the Edo period, with a resource centre of the Tōkaidō, a full-service inn (*hatagoya*), etc. Associated with it are various sports facilities. These buildings show that nostalgia for a past that is no longer part of the present definitely plays a part in leisure activities in Japan today.

It goes without saying that the number of inns varied according to the importance of the highway. The first was the Tōkaidō, with an average of 55 full-service inns (*hatagoya*) among its 53 stations (1843) (Vaporis 1994: 228). The popularity of the post towns did not depend only on their location but also on pleasure seeking. Prostitution of the serving girls (*meshi mori onna*) cannot be neglected in the attraction of these places, considering that the vast majority of travellers were men (Usami 2000). Several kinds of inns corresponding to the different categories of travellers and of economic means can be found in these post towns (Miyamoto 1987; Fukai 2000). Successively from the top to the bottom of society the different travellers could find *daimyō* inns (*honjin*), auxiliary *daimyō* inns (*waki honjin*), full-service inns (*hatagoya*) and firewood inns (*kichin yado*) (where only firewood is provided). As the following examples indicate, nowadays a good number of the remaining inns of the Edo period have been turned into museums and represent a

Figure 3.1 The post town of Unno *juku* (Nagano prefecture).

Photo by Sylvie Guichard-Anguis.

fair share of the tourist spots in Japan, with their historic surroundings, in particular in the case of inns for *daimyō*.

The stay of the *daimyō* and his escort in the post town was planned well in advance among the several kinds of inns (*yado-wari*). A period of several days was chosen at least two or three months ahead, as the natural conditions could not allow a more precise date at a time when nearly everybody walked. The *daimyō*, some of his retainers and the people caring directly for his person had to stay in two kinds of inns: *daimyō* inns (*honjin*) and auxiliary *daimyō* inns (*waki honjin*), in which the rest of the retainers could be accommodated if the first one was not big enough. By their appearance and conception *honjin* were an exception, as they referred to two classes of Edo society: their guests were of the warrior class, but their owners were of a much lower class, that of craftsmen or merchants. They had a gate (*mon*), exclusively dedicated to the *daimyō*, an entrance, rooms opening one from the other leading to the *jōdan no ma*, a room elevated in a Shoin style characterized by a *tokonoma*, decorative shelves, and tatami on the floor, where the *daimyō* stayed. In Kusatsu (Shiga prefecture) the Kusatsu *jūku honjin* was designated as an historical landmark (*shiseki*) in 1949; complete restoration works were undertaken from 1989 to 1997 which give a fair idea of this type of inn. These inns offered very few facilities, as everything had to be brought by the *daimyō*'s escort. Sleeping, eating and bathing were functions dependent on the escort, while the owner of the inn took care of the building itself. His only duties included booking in advance, welcoming the escort, greeting the *daimyō* and bidding him goodbye. As *honjin* accommodated *daimyō* only, it goes without saying that making a living from this type of inn meant having a second source of income.

Some *honjin* still offer a wealth of historical documents about their use, for example Koriyama *honjin* (Osaka prefecture) or Yakage *honjin* (Okayama prefecture). Designated as the first *honjin* among historical landmarks (*shiseki*) in 1948, Koriyama *honjin* was restored to its present state (the main building dates back to 1721) in two stages, 1985–87 and 1993–2000, and opened to the public in 2001. Located on the Saikokku kaidō which connects Kyoto to Nishinomiya (Hyogo prefecture), although on a highway of secondary importance (Nihon no kaidō no. 74 2003) it received the visits of the *daimyō* from the Chūgoku and Shikoku island. It retains the gate for the *daimyō* (*onarimon*) leading to the private entrance and rooms where the *daimyō* himself was carried by palanquin (*kago*) and even preserves the rooms for the *daimyō*'s retainers and the lodging of the owner close to the large kitchen where food was cooked for the *daimyō*. Besides offering a fairly complete material environment as a *honjin*, it displays historical documents inside that help visitors to get a vivid image of the *daimyō*'s stays within these walls. From 1696 to 1869, except for 1803–18, which are missing years, the volumes of the inn give a lot of details of the visits, and record 1,360 rests and 2,040 nights altogether. March and May were the busiest months, as April corresponded to the change of residence of the *daimyō*. During the Edo period the

Figure 3.2 The *honjin* in Koriyama (Osaka prefecture).

Photo by Sylvie Guichard-Anguis.

Kaji family owner of the *honjin* was involved in wholesaling as a side business and had the status of the village headman. According to the present owner, the seventeenth generation still living there, around 50 persons could be accommodated inside, while the rest of the escort was distributed among the 30 *hatagoya* of the post station, as Koriyama lacked any *waki honjin*. Other historical documents give a wealth of details about the money paid by the *daimyō*, distribution of the escort among the post town inns, menus, etc.

In the town of Yakage (Okayama prefecture), a post town on the Sanyōdō, both the *honjin* house of the Ishii family (*Ishii-ke*) and the *waki honjin* house of the Takakusa family (*Takakusa-ke*) still exist, designated as very important cultural assets (*jūyō bunka-zai*) by the Agency of Cultural Affairs. Yakage *honjin* has been turned into a museum and offers a fairly complete insight into the stays of *daimyō*, as both the historical environment and its documents are well preserved (Take *et al.* 2002). Around 14 *daimyō* escorts with around 500 to 600 men stayed in the *honjin* every year. As a second source of income the owners brewed sake from 1687, which gave them the status of fairly well-off merchants. Most of the equipment is still preserved, which gives the rare opportunity to observe the activities of the *honjin* as a whole.

With the emergence of new means of transport the evolution of these *honjin* took different directions. Very few became inns during the Meiji period, as they lacked the basic facilities and their owners would have had to hire employees, as they did not have any. *Go-honjin* Fujiya in Nagano

(Nagano prefecture), a few metres from the Zenkoji, was in operation from 1661 until very recently, managed by the seventeenth generation, but retains very little of the Edo period. Its façade was rebuilt in Western style in 1923 and it was registered in 1997 by the Agency of Cultural Affairs. The inside dates from the 1920s and the back from the Meiji period. The pamphlet given out by this inn emphasizes the romantic atmosphere of those two bygone ages but makes very little allusion to the *honjin* period. Koriyama *honjin* turned into an inn at the beginning of the Meiji period before becoming just the home of its traditional owners. A fair number of *honjin* turned into elementary schools or town offices, as they offered ample space, corresponding to the new requirements of the Meiji Restoration. The present *honjin* in Wata *juku* (Nagano prefecture) dates back to 1861, when it was rebuilt after a fire. It was turned first into the town office and then into the agricultural co-operative office until 1985. Designated as an historical landmark (*shiseki*) it has been restored to its original state (*fukugen*) and shows the dwelling of the owner and the rooms of the *daimyō* sharing the same building, as was customary. The *honjin* in Mochitsuki met a completely different fate, as it is today hardly recognizable as the local paediatric clinic and lodging.

Honjin began to be turned into museums in the second part of the twentieth century, and in some cases local town planning, under a policy called 'the making of the city' (*machi zukuri*), focuses on them. In Shiga prefecture the city of Kusatsu enhances the culture of travel with a city policy aiming to foster a new cultural identity. In the Edo period Kusatsu developed as one of the most important post towns around the intersection between the Tōkaidō and the Nakasendō. Opened in 1999, the 'House of cultural exchange on the highways of the post town of Kusatsu' (*Kusatsu-juku-gaidō-kōryūkan*) dedicated its first exhibition, which took place in June to July, to one of the most famous products (*meibutsu*) of the Edo period: a local sweet, *ubaga mochi*, made of glutinous rice that one can still eat while travelling. A letter of information called 'The culture of the highway' is produced by the municipal centre of information and a *shukuba* festival takes place for two days every April in Kusatsu. In 2000 the House had an exhibition on full-service inns (*hatagoya*), which are the most numerous inns in every post town.

Ryokan as historic places to visit and stay: *hatagoya* and Japanese inns

The two Chinese characters forming *hatago* mean 'travel' and 'basket' respectively and refer to the origin of this type of inn: fodder carried in a basket and then food for the journey. *Hatago* or *hatagoya* corresponds to an inn largely depicted by woodblock prints and a type of accommodation used by most of the travellers of the travelogue. According to the document produced during the exhibition which took place in 2000 in Kusatsu, 72 *hatagoya* could be found in this post town in 1843, with 7 large ones, 16 medium-sized ones and

49 small ones, among which remains the Sendaiya today. Before entering the house visitors first had to wash their feet, a scene much depicted by woodblock prints or literary works. Contrary to the practice in *honjin*, visitors shared rooms and sleeping arrangements, but meals and baths were provided by these inns. The presence of these facilities allowed *hatagoya* to be among the traditions of lodging from which the *ryokan* came. The strong competition characterizing the *hatagoya* fostered the appearance of women beaters (*tome onna*) to draw in customers. Two kinds of *hatagoya* can be identified: plain *hatago* (*hira-hatago*) and *hatago* providing serving girls (*meshimori-hatago*) (Takeuchi 2003: 35), in other words prostitutes. Their auxiliary function was serving drinks and food, but their presence helped to bring in additional funds, as making a living by providing shelter and two meals was not generally enough.

Floors were covered with mats rather than tatami, and accommodation did not differ that much from other types available to travellers with very limited means, such as firewood inns (*kichin yado*). As their name suggests, only wood to cook the meal had to be paid for, and this kind of very rustic inn remained very popular with pilgrims. In Japan today, some hot springs, especially in remote mountain areas, keep their inns rather close to this ancient type, and these attract visitors because of their very rustic appearance, which suggests an exotic past, as in Togyo (Akita prefecture). Pilgrims could also stay in temple lodgings (*shukubo*), which can still be found in the twenty-first century in several places. In Tokage (Nagano prefecture) *Shukubo* Kyokui dates back 450 or 500 years, but its main building was rebuilt after a fire around the middle of the Edo period (Miyamoto and Suzuki 1999: 80–4). With its huge thatched roof protecting again heavy snow, this lodging is operating today as a *ryokan*.

The fate of these *hatagoya* differs from that of *honjin*, as many of them became inns during the Meiji Restoration, and some of them are still operating under the name of *ryokan*. A guidebook called 'Staying in *hatagoya*' published in 1995 selects 24 of them from all over the country. Shiroganeya in Yamashiro hot spring (city of Kaga, Ishikawa prefecture) has its main building registered by the Agency of Cultural Affairs, as it is more than 350 years old.

Preservation of the culture of travel involves not only cultural properties (*bunkazai*) associated with ancient types of inns dating back to the Edo period, whether they are designated by the country, the prefecture or the municipality, but some *ryokan* which symbolized modernity less than a hundred years ago. The carpenters and craftsmen who worked for the warrior class, the nobility, etc. during the Edo period had to find new clients after the Meiji Restoration. This phenomenon explains the remarkable quality of some of the most prestigious *ryokan* built during the Meiji period, the Taishō and the beginning of the Shōwa period. Some of them became museums, like Tokaikan in Itō and Kiunkyaku in Atami, both located in famous hot springs of Shizuoka prefecture. Tokaikan, built along the river in Ito, was opened in

1928 by Inaba Yasutaro, a lumber dealer. Turned into a *ryokan* for groups with the opening of the Ito line in 1938, it was enlarged several times. With its three floors entirely the work of famous master carpenters, Tokaikan is still a beautiful example of the *ryokan* of the end of the Taishō (1912–26) and beginning of the Shōwa (1926–89) periods. Closed in 1997, Tokaikan was presented by its owner to the city, which designated this *ryokan* a municipal cultural asset. After two years of dismantling and repairing, it was opened to the public in 2001. A visit to the present Tokaikan allows one not only to admire unique works from carpenters but also to enjoy sweets with tea on the first floor or the bath that is still in operation, savouring the atmosphere of this *ryokan*, which is still partly alive.

Kiunkyaku, one of the three most famous resort villas in Atami (Guichard-Anguis 2007b), built in 1918 by Uchida Nobuya (1898–1970), then national minister of railways, sold in 1925 to Nezu Ichiro (1860–1940), the founder of the Tōbu railways, who purchased land several times to enlarge the villa plot and added several buildings, was sold again in 1947 and opened as a *ryokan* in the same year. In 1999 Kiunkyaku closed for business, was bought by the municipality the following year, and reopened to the general public at the end of 2000 as a new local tourist spot. Only 16 rooms remain of the original *ryokan*, because the municipality chose to emphasize the most gorgeous rooms characterized by the unique blending of Western influence and Japanese style of the 1930s. Many historic documents displayed give a vivid impression of its golden period, as they come from its most famous visitors, who included writers such as Shiga Naoya (1883–1971) and Tanizaki Jūnichirō (1886–1965).

Remaining in operation means that inns have to adapt to the new amenities which have been introduced since the Meiji period, and therefore they could not keep their original character. But, as the female patron (*Ōkami*) of the Arai *ryokan* in Shuzenji (Shizuoka prefecture), which has several assets registered by the Agency of Cultural Affairs, stresses in an interview, there is a limit to modernization.[5] She was talking about her clients complaining that they could not use their laptops and get the internet in their room. How does one cope with modern comforts and amenities in registered buildings, without implying continuous investment by the owners of the inns? According to her, adding air conditioning in the old parts of the Arai *ryokan* was already a great source of difficulty, because the equipment had to be hidden. For various reasons (economic, age of the owner, etc.) a lot of *ryokan* cannot cope with visitors' changing habits; they refuse to add new amenities and comforts and are going bankrupt. Those built to accommodate large groups are the ones which encounter the most difficult times.

Owing to the great quality of their architecture and design some of the most representative of those *ryokan* are turned into museums, like the two mentioned above. Others find new economic functions and are turned into shops, restaurants or coffee-shops, like Hashimoto-tei, built in 1910 in Minō,

Figure 3.3 Tokaikan in Ito (Shizuoka prefecture): details of the inside.

Photo by Sylvie Guichard-Anguis.

Osaka prefecture. Others (even *hatagoya*) are turned into private homes, because of the quality of the wooden materials used, which stand for centuries, and the unique atmosphere they offer.

Others try to keep a balance between the new requirements and the preservation of an atmosphere full of memories. In Iizaka hot spring (Fukushima prefecture), Nakamura *ryokan*, which benefits from national registration, offers the choice between two kinds of baths, depending on the two buildings which make up the inn: the Edo period one and the Meiji one. Founded in 1872, Arai *ryokan* has 15 cultural assets dating from 1881 to 1943, registered by the Agency of Cultural Affairs in 1999. Besides offering a wealth of buildings of exceptional quality connected one to the other by covered corridors or bridges, looking over ponds or small portions of garden or the river, it displays documents about its famous visitors: painters, authors, film actors and

Japanese theatre actors who went there. A film of Ozu Yasujirō (1903–63), *The Taste of Ochazuke* (*Ochazuke no aji*), was shot there in 1952. To make this rather expensive *ryokan* affordable and allow visitors of more limited means to stay there, visits to the cultural assets are organized in the day. This *ryokan* adopts a formula which tends to be popular among de luxe *ryokan*, allowing visitors to use baths and get a full lunch there without staying the night, a new source of income for inns that are nearly empty in the daytime.

Generally speaking, cultural assets associated with inns are divided into several categories according to the Agency of Cultural Affairs. *Honjin* and *waki honjin* belong to the category of historic urban landscapes. Because of a law of 1996, registered *ryokan* are included as material cultural assets among buildings with economic functions. In 2003, 59 *ryokan* had cultural assets registered. In 2004, 155 cultural assets were registered altogether, among which only 14 belonged to hotels. For instance, Shiroganeya, founded in 1624 in Yamashiro hot spring (city of Kaga, prefecture of Ishikawa), has three cultural assets in this list: the main building, the tea house and a corridor. Being registered offers new criteria of selection for visitors, as is emphasized in the title of a magazine:[6] 'To stay in *ryokan* of hot springs registered as cultural assets'.

Basically today two types of *ryokan* still in operation offer this contact with the past: hot springs *ryokan* and urban *ryokan*, which often belong to the *shinise* type. This word *shinise* indicates shops, restaurants, *ryokan*, etc. which have been in business for several generations and specialize in selling products

Figure 3.4 Higashiya *ryokan* (Yamagata prefecture).

Photo by Sylvie Guichard-Anguis.

or services associated with a so-called Japanese tradition. A lot of hot springs are located in rather remote mountainous areas, and it may be that there lies one of the keys for the preservation of very old buildings. In Shirabu hot spring (city of Yonezawa, prefecture of Yamagata) the so-called West and East, Nishiya and Higashiya, *ryokan* offered the splendid sight of a huge thatched roof protecting wood constructions built side by side, until Higashiya was burnt down a few years ago. The remaining Nishiya was founded before the Edo period, and its present main building dates back to the eighteenth century. Visitors' rooms were an addition at the beginning of the Shōwa (1926–89), and they can accommodate around 65 visitors. In Bessho hot spring (Nagano prefecture), Hanaya is a beautiful example of a *ryokan* opened at the beginning of the Taishō period, in 1917. All the wood build-ings, including the different types of bath, are scattered about a Japanese-style garden and connected by covered corridors and bridges, and they can accommodate 150 to 160 visitors altogether. To give a further example, close to Tokyo and benefiting from many well-off visitors, Hakone hot spring (Kanagawa prefecture) offers a wealth of beautiful old *ryokan*, like the Hansuirōfukusumi, opened in 1625 and made famous for its building from the beginning of the Meiji period or Fukusumirō dating back to 1890.

In the heart of Kyoto, Tawaraya *ryokan* (Fiévé *et al.* 2003: 239–42, Korean trans. 2007) is one of the most famous of the urban *shinise* type. Located on a narrow street and surrounded by buildings on different scales, at first sight one may wonder why it has such a reputation. Entering into this *ryokan* allows the visitor to discover a labyrinth of corridors and staircases leading to varied rooms facing Kyoto-style pocket gardens. While sitting on the tatami in one of these rooms, visitors may forget about the urban surroundings and find themselves immersed in the kind of place imagined by the owners of the *ryokan*, based on the invention of a Japanese, more precisely Kyoto, tradition. Looking for excellence in all its details whether they belong to the design or the comfort of the room or the services, Tawaraya wants to be the symbol of Japanese hospitality. It emphasizes the work of the craftsmen who daily work in it and the fact that it could not exist without them (Muramatsu 1999).

But contact with the past is not restricted to ancient genuine inns. Some authentic pieces of architecture, whether vernacular (as we saw with Kame no i besso in Yufuin, Oita prefecture), high society residences (Kiunkyaku in Atami) or even shops, can be turned into *ryokan*, a process which helps to preserve a lot of old buildings, especially in small or medium-sized towns and in the countryside. In Kurashiki (Okayama prefecture) *Ryokan* Kurashiki opened only 40 years ago as an inn, having converted its buildings dating back over 250 years: the main mansion house and the three-storey houses associated with the wholesale trade of sugar and rice.

Not only the architectural environment, but all the decoration, especially in the decorative alcove (*tokonoma*), the works of art inside the inn, the dishes served and so on might make some allusion to the past, or even to local culture through festivals, local habits, etc. Last but not least the past also may be personified by the generation number of the woman patron (*Ōkami-san*) of the *ryokan*, who might embody a tradition of hospitality going back several centuries, as has already been noted.

Ryokan as places to encounter nature and as shelters of the culture of reception and hospitality (*motenashi no bunka*)

If the Japanese past seems to be enhanced through a great variety of means in *ryokan*, it is always merged with two other components. The result tends to give its original character to Japanese inns. Travel magazines and most of the programmes on Japanese TV channels dedicated to tourism, mainly hot springs and *ryokan*, tend to illustrate a similar perception, as nature and hospitality used to play the main parts. In previous works (Guichard-Anguis 2003, 2004a, 2004b), we have analysed how this perception works through two monthly magazines, *Katei-gahō* (The illustrated magazine of the home) and *Tabi* (Travel). First, it is obvious that the topic of *ryokan* is clearly associated with seasons, as far as the months of issue are concerned. For instance, *Katei-gahō* has dedicated a large number of autumn issues to *ryokan*, followed by winter and summer, while spring issues usually lack any allusion to them. To put it differently, *ryokan* look like the best places to savour the autumn colours, the feeling of coolness in summer and several festivals and traditions in winter. Culture and all its expressions are the main ingredients in the construction of those moments. Second, selected *ryokan* are always depicted by the same discourse, which emphasizes the hospitality of their owners or managers, always very personalized and very often illustrated by photos of them.

In the perception of the past the overwhelming presence of nature, whether wild or manmade, cannot be overlooked, as it plays a very important part in the attraction of *ryokan*. Through the sliding doors some of the *ryokan* offer spectacular views of their natural environment: mountain slopes, forests, rivers, mountain streams, seashores, etc., enhancing an ever-existing nature. *Ryokan* also may be nested inside this natural environment and offer outer baths among rocks, shrubs and trees, as is the case in many hot springs *ryokan*. Even in inns located in the middle of the city, like Tawaraya in Kyoto, all the rooms face pocket gardens. In fact gardens designed by famous artists are also parts of the image of some *ryokan* and associated with their history. If greenery is not available outside the *ryokan*, it is always present close to the bath, in which visitors can indulge themselves while watching some greenery planted nearby, through the glass of the sliding doors.

Besides being part of the surroundings, nature is always present through the allusion to the passing of seasons. Based on a clear distinction between cold and hot seasons, pieces of furniture are changed, fires lit in the hearth (*ro*) and a kettle put on to boil in the entrance during the cold season, while all sorts of means enhance freshness during the hot season. In the *tokonoma* a hanging scroll and a flower arrangement and on the dining table the several dishes and their recipients inform visitors about the local products and specialities associated with the seasons. Flowers for tea gatherings (*chabana*) and flower arrangement (*ikebana*) give the *ryokan* manager plenty of opportunities to make nature part of the decoration of the rooms. In the first case coming from the immediate surroundings and part of the natural environment in which the *ryokan* is located and in the second ordered in the local flower shop, flowers and branches are used to add a powerful sense of the seasons in each room. Conversely, the Western style of flower arrangement has taken root in most Japanese contemporaneous homes. Flowers and leaves do not remain in the *tokonoma* only, but enhance Japanese cuisine. *Ryokan* are definitely places where one can watch the flow of seasons while enjoying their tastes. There is a dynamic perception of those seasons, which draws out a lot of creative work in every aspect of the services offered by the *ryokan*. For instance, cuisine is Japanese style, but involves continuous innovations. Of the three main functions characterizing *ryokan*, bathing and eating are the ones most prone to developing this contact with nature enjoyed through all the senses.

Staying in *ryokan* usually follows the same pattern, and a brief description seems necessary before going any further. Visitors check in between three and four o' clock in the afternoon. Shoes are deposited in the entrance, to be found again when leaving the inn. A woman clad in a kimono leads the visitors to their room, where she serves tea and sweets, while explaining the schedule of their one-night stay, which is usual. Visitors are invited to change from their everyday clothes and dress in the cotton kimono (*yukata*) prepared for them, slip into clogs and have a bath in one of the inside or outside baths (men's and women's turns being clearly stated at this first meeting). While the visitors are away, the room is prepared for dinner, which is usually served between six and eight in the evening, but preferably around six, according to most of the *ryokan* managers. The number of small dishes and the sake or beer soon have an influence on the visitors, who tend not to stay awake late. A second bath might be encouraged while the room is cleaned after dinner and the futon spread on the tatami. Visitors can enjoy an early bath before or after breakfast, which is usually served around eight o' clock in the morning in their room or in a dining room, and check-out is completed before ten. Unlike baths, meals have to be taken at a given time, which leaves little freedom to the visitors. The number of dishes and the particularity of Japanese cuisine may help in understanding this unbreakable rule. On the contrary, visitors get more freedom with the choice of baths, their number and duration.

Today, baths play a major part in the selection of *ryokan*, as emphasized by the pamphlets related to them. Their surroundings, natural or manmade, their setting, their design (Arai *ryokan* in Shuzenji is famous for its Tempyō-style bath built in 1934 imitating an antique temple), the materials used (plain wood, tiles, marble, etc.), their number and the period when they were created (some of them may be cultural assets like this Tempyō-style one) are definitely criteria which decide the success of a *ryokan*. Baths (*furo*) were already found in the *hatagoya* of the Edo period (Maeda 2002: 44–63), a period when people already enjoyed the natural outside baths in hot springs. New techniques of drilling for water allowed each inn to get its own private inside bath during the Taishō and the beginning of the Shōwa periods. Three laws established in 1948 – the one on hot springs, the one on *ryokan* and the one on public baths – controlled baths in inns. With the boom of domestic tourism in the second part of the 1950s, baths tended to show diversity, between very large ones accommodating hundreds of people (influenced by the large groups staying in *ryokan* for one night), baths with a foreign design (Roman, tropical, etc.), or using expensive materials like marble. Later on, with the visiting pattern becoming more individual, baths tended to become smaller and even family sized, in order to be booked by one single family or a couple. In the 1980s, outside baths became the main amenity people were looking for in *ryokan*, as shown by advertising that focused mainly on them. A lot of visitors were dreaming of enjoying an outside bath in the evening under a bright sky full of stars, with a shining moon. The closeness of baths with nature enhances their attractive character, as some may be close to a mountain stream, a river, the sea or the ocean or set among rocks and trees. Moving from one bath to another depending on the wealth of baths in the *ryokan* is a way of spending the evening that is quite popular among Japanese visitors. Baths are the main places where visitors meet and talk while lingering in the hot waters or having a break outside on the rocks. As most of the *ryokan* still serve dinner and breakfast in private rooms, baths remain the main place of socializing among guests from different parts of Japan. The people in charge of the service used to come and go freely inside the rooms, a habit which is beginning to be seen as a lack of respect of privacy. But inside the baths or the adjoining rooms visitors are never bothered by these visits.

This contrast between the rooms, where visits from those providing the different services are numerous, and the baths, where the visitors find some kind of rest and peace, is based on a conception of hospitality nurtured in *ryokan* by a history more than a hundred years old. Today *ryokan* are places where the culture of hospitality (*motenashi no bunka*) finds its full development, at the core of Japanese culture and expressed through a lot of traditional practices, such as the tea ceremony (*chanoyu*), cuisine, entertainment, etc. *Ryokan* play the part of local environments which shelter excellence.

The *Ōkami-san* (woman patron of the *ryokan*) embodied these traditions and this spirit of innovation, as she always appeared dressed in the kimono before visitors. *Ryokan* were places where greetings (*aisatsu*) found their full development, as in the rooms for tea meetings (*chashitsu*). Walking, sitting, opening the sliding doors, etc. were gestures which belonged to the traditional practices. Working on the staff of a *ryokan* helped one to become familiar with all those body movements and cultural traditions and was considered a good training for young women. Politeness, a keen sense of hospitality and artistic gifts should characterize the *Ōkami-san*, whose presence influenced the well-being of the visitors in every aspect. She played the part of an intermediary between the local and the outside, the past and the present, nature and the outside, for visitors coming for the most part from the largest cities in Japan. *Ōkami-san* slowly became some of the main producers of Japanese cultural identity, as they invented a so-called Japanese beauty (*Nihon no bi*). Nowadays the artistic innovations made in these *ryokan* have become cultural references. Owners of *ryokan* may be personalities in the cultural life of their cities. The present manager of the *ryokan* Sumiya in Kyoto, an author of several books (Horibe 2001), is a well-known tea practitioner and organizes formal tea gatherings (*chaji*) in his *ryokan*. A great number of *Ōkami-san* are personalities, well known all over Japan; in their old age more and more are writing books of memories, and some of these works may include chapters on Japanese history.

The word *Ōkami-san* has the following meanings: wife, housewife, and woman patron dedicated to hospitality and reception (*motenashi*). How *Ōkami-san* came into being is a process that has not yet been well researched. It is generally admitted that different traditions merged and modelled for the present *Ōkami-san*. During the Edo period, the presence in inns of women looking after the well-being of guests, who used to be mainly men, entertaining them and even acting as prostitutes for them, is well documented in Japanese travelogue. But generally speaking managers were men. The *Ōkami-san* as the manager of a *ryokan* finds its closest historical origin in several women's roles dating from the Meiji and the Taishō periods, at the same time that *ryokan* began their appearance (Okubo 2002, 2003a). In the Meiji period women were employed in de luxe restaurants, and this association with women clad in the kimono and Japanese cuisine might have influenced the conception of hospitality in *ryokan*. These women needed experience, education and elegance to fit in with the de luxe environments, and a gift for conversation with the guests. Being the wife of the manager or the manager herself, they began slowly to personify the *ryokan* itself by having direct contact with the visitors. According to Okubo (2003b), a very popular serial drama on television in 1970, *Hosoude hanjōki* (The dwindling period of prosperity), fostered the role of *Ōkami-san* in *ryokan*. Through the enormous popularity of this programme they became the 'face' (*kao*) of the *ryokan*, symbolizing its characteristics. In the 1980s *Ōkami-san* became part of the image of the Japanese style (*wafu*) of hospitality offered by the *ryokan*. Several publications (*Nihon no yado* 1 1985; *Nihon no yado* 2 1985; *Nihon no meiryokan* 1986) began to place the *Ōkami-san* at the core of the *ryokan*, as the person in charge of protecting Japanese traditions in local inns. As a wife and a mother she was introduced as a woman completely dedicated to her work and her family. Programmes on TV followed this same trend, and the *Ōkami-san* was always shown dressed in the kimono, greeting visitors in the entrance or explaining the menu to the guests, while introducing her *ryokan*.

From 1990 *Ōkami-san* could attend a yearly national meeting, 'The national summit of the *Ōkami*', managed by them, which broke with this very individualistic world. It gave them an opportunity to exchange a lot of information about their personal experience. According to Okubo those participating in the meeting seemed very well aware of the importance of being the producer of the originality of their *ryokan* and creating their own style following modern trends and demands. Being an *Ōkami-san* is passed down through the generations in the same family (the number belongs to the image of the *ryokan*), and training is part of the life of the next *Ōkami* from a very young age. Managing a *ryokan* means an enormous amount of daily work, with very little holiday, a deep knowledge in very different fields such as finance, ikebana, cuisine, etc., and a good sense of human relations with the staff and all the people supplying the various goods to the *ryokan*. Published in several books (Shūkan hoteru resutoran 1995, 1997, 1999), personal stories always give the same image of a self-dedicated woman able to sacrifice herself to the well-being of the visitors, creating smooth relations with the staff and caring for her family. Recently the number of *ryokan* going bankrupt or without a successor has created a demand for these women managers. A private school of *Ōkami* has even appeared and trained candidates, generally among urban young women willing to have a complete change in their working life. In the hot spring of Kinosaki (Hyogo prefecture) the *Ōkami-san* of the *ryokan* Ginka opened a training school, the *Ōkami juku* (the private school of *Ōkami*), where after a very tough selection process she trained women in the different jobs in the *ryokan*. According to her, cuisine, private rooms and the baths are the three main fields in which the *Ōkami-san* has to develop her taste. After several years of hard training the candidates are sent to *ryokan* looking for dynamic managers able to solve all the economic problems they are facing. A TV drama was based on the story of this *Ōkami-san*, and a book, *I Will Work as an Ōkami in a Japanese Inn* (Kurasawa 2002), was published. It tells of the creation of the private school of *Ōkami-san* and personal stories from several successful candidates who speak about their new working life and their hard training. This new phenomenon tends to break the hundred-year-old rule of passing the job from mother or mother-in-law to daughter or daughter-in-law. It is obvious that, owing to today's economic conditions, managing a *ryokan* means breaking with traditional rules, an initiative which may often not be accepted inside the family circle. This recent phenomenon is one more testimony to the capacity of *ryokan* to adapt to new economic conditions.

The culture of travel (*tabi no bunka*) on which a large part of Japanese cultural heritage is based and the culture of hospitality and reception (*motenashi no bunka*) in which a large portion of Japanese cultural identity finds its meaning help *ryokan* to stay dynamic in a very severe economic environment. In spite of very strong competition from hotels and their continuous innovations, Japanese inns still retain some original and unique features which are sought after. The very long historical evolution they experienced explains some of their characteristics, but the never-ending 'invention of traditions' which is fostered in the *ryokan* justifies their attraction. Japanese inns introduce visitors to an experience of collapsing time and place, inside their own culture. Being more and more familiar with the world outside Japan, the Japanese visitor is looking for a new kind of exoticism, but this time at home, where the other is supposed to be himself.

Notes

1 See 'Selected magazines on *ryokan*' in the References.
2 These figures were given during an interview in November 2001.
3 'Kindai ni okeru Nihon ryokan no naritachi to henyō' [Origin and changed appearance of Japanese *ryokan* in modern times'), Rikkyo University (date unknown).
4 *Asahi Shimbun*, 17 April 2004.
5 This interview took place on 25 November 2003.
6 *Recruit*, vol. 69, March 2004.

References

Selected magazines on ryokan

Aera Mook (2002). *Kankōgaku ga wakaru* [Understanding the science of tourism]. Tokyo: Asahi Shimbun Extra Report, Analysis, Special 81.
Gokujō no hoteru [First-class hotels] (2000). Tokyo: Neko.
Gokujō no yuyado [First-class inns in spas] (2000). Tokyo: Neko.
Hatago ni tomaru [Staying the night in *hatago*] (1995). Shotor Travel. Tokyo: Shogakukan.
Hi yu no yado 70 [70 inns from secret spas] (1998). Tokyo: Seibido.
Kayabuki no yado [Miscanthus-thatched inns] (1997). Shotor Travel. Tokyo: Shogakukan.
Kisetsu o taberu yado [Inns with seasonal menus] (1995). Shotor Travel. Tokyo: Shogakukan.
Mokuzō sankai tate no yado [Wooden inns on three storeys] (1995). Shotor Travel. Tokyo: Shogakukan.
Nihon no meiryokan [The most famous *ryokan* in Japan] (1986). Kotsu kosha no Mook 1. Tokyo: Nihon Kōtsû kōsha.
Nihon no yado [Inns of Japan] 1. (1985). Būru gaido mukku 7. Tokyo: Jitsugyo no Nihon-sha.
Nihon no yado [Inns of Japan] 2. (1985). Būru gaido mukku 8. Tokyo: Jitsugyo no Nihon-sha.
Tenno-ke no yado [Inns of the imperial family] (2001). Tokyo: Kawade-shobō.
Tōji Jisui no yado [Inns where one can have therapeutic baths and cook] (1998). Tokyo: Kinki Nihon tsûrisuto.

General reference

Anonymous Japanese ([1242] 1999). *Voyage dans les provinces de l'Est* [*Tōkan Kikō* (Travel in the Eastern Provinces)], trans. Jacqueline Pigeot. Paris: Gallimard.
Fiévé, N., F. Ged, V. Gelézeau, S. Guichard-Anguis and T. Sanjuan (2003). *Les grands hôtels en Asie: Modernité, dynamiques urbaines et sociabilité* [Grand hotels in Asia: modernity, urban dynamism and sociability]. Paris: Publications de la

Sorbonne. Also published as: V. Gelézeau *et al.* (2007). *Toshi eui Chang, Gogeup Hotel* [The grand hotel: a window above the city], trans. Yang Jiyeu. Seoul: Humanitas.

Fukai, J. (2000). *Edo no yado* [Inns of the Edo period]. Tokyo: Heibonsha.

Guichard-Anguis, S. (2003). 'Feuilles d'érables, terres cuites et poissons grillés: une alternative de la sociabilité offerte par les ryokan au Japon' [Maple leaves, potteries and grilled fish: an alternative to sociability found in the *ryokan* of Japan]. In N. Fiévé, F. Ged, V. Gelézeau, S. Guichard-Anguis and T. Sanjuan, *Les grands hôtels en Asie: Modernité, dynamiques urbaines et sociabilité* [Grand hotels in Asia: modernity, urban dynamism and sociability]. Paris: Publications de la Sorbonne, pp. 217–51.

—— (2004a). 'The tourist as a reader of a Japanese women magazine: Katei-gahô'. In R. Aparna (ed.), *Tourist Behaviour: A Psychological Perspective.* New Delhi: Kanishka Publishers, pp. 248–63.

—— (2004b). 'A propos des 90 ans de la revue japonaise "Tabi" (voyage)' [About the 90 years of the magazine 'Tabi' (travel)]. *Le Globe: Revue Genevoise de Géographie,* 144: *Voyage, tourisme, paysage* [Travel, tourism, landscape], pp. 85–102.

—— (2006). 'Japanese inns (*ryokan*) and an Asian atmosphere: always east of somewhere'. In W. Dixon and J. Hendry, *Dismantling the East–West Dichotomy: Essays in Honour of Jan van Bremen.* Anthropology Japanese Studies. London and New York: Routledge, pp. 69–74.

—— (2007a). 'New traditions and successful Japanese inns (*ryokan*)'. In A. Raj (ed.), *Sustainability, Profitability, and Successful Tourism.* New Delhi: Kanisha Publishers, 2 vols, pp. 180–97.

—— (2007b). 'Japanese inns (*ryokan*) in Atami (Japan) and the shaping of coming "traditions" '. *Tourism Review International,* Special issue: *Japanese Tourism, Part 2,* vol. 11, pp. 19–31.

Horibe, K. (2001) *Kyo. Sumiya Motenashi no chanoyu* [The way of tea and hospitality from Sumiya of Kyoto]. Kyoto: Tankosha.

Imado, E. (1984). *Me de miru Nihon no fūzoku* [Japanese customs watched with the eyes], 6: *Shukuba to kaidō* [Post stations and highways]. Tokyo: Nihon hōsō shuppan kyōkai.

Jippenshā, I. ([1806] 1992). *A pied sur le Tōkaidō* [*Tōkaidōchu hizakurige* (Walking along the Tōkaidō)], trans. J. Campignon. Arles: Philippe Picquier.

Kasai, K. (1999) *Kyo no daiku tōryō to shichi nin no shōkunin shū* [Carpenter in Kyoto and the group of the seven craftsmen]. Tokyo: Sōshisha.

Kashiwai, I. (2003) *Kiwami no Nihon ryokan Ima doko ni tomaru bekika* [The Japanese inns of the highest rank – now where should we stay?]. Tokyo: Kōbunsha.

Katei-gahō [The illustrated magazine of the home], monthly. Tokyo: Sekai bunka-sha.

Kodama, K. (1986). *Shukuba to kaidō* [Post stations and highways]. Tokyo: Tokyo Bijutsu sensho.

—— (2001). *Gaidō to shukuba machi: Furu shashin de miru* [Highways and post stations: seen on old photographs]. Tokyo: Sekai bunkasha.

Kogure, K. (2003) *Nishikie ni miru Nihon no onsen* [Japanese spas shown in woodblock colour print]. Tokyo: Kokusho.

Kokudo kōtsūshō [Ministry of Land and Transport] (2004). *Kankō Hakusho* [White book on tourism]. Tokyo: Okurashō.

Kurasawa, K. (2002). *Ryokan no okami ni shūshoku shimasu* [I will work as an Ōkami in a Japanese inn]. Tokyo: Bajiriko.

Maeda, I. (ed.) (1998). *Gendai kankô-gaku kîwādô jiten* [Encyclopedia lexicon of modern tourism]. Tokyo: Gakubunsha.

—— (2001). 'Ryokan no miryoku nikansuru kenkyu' [Some research about the charm of *ryokan*]. Rikkyo daigaku kankōgaku kenkyūka Maeda sensei kenkyûshitsu (unpublished).

—— (2002). 'Ryokan no tokuchô toshite no "aimaisei" nikansuru bunseki' [An analysis of vagueness as the charm of *ryokan*]. *Rikkyo University Bulletin of Studies in Tourism*, 4, pp. 1–18.

Miwa, A. (2003a). *Zen koku gaido jiten: Higashi Nihon hen* [Dictionary of the highways in all Japan: East Japan]. Tokyo: Tokyodō shuppan.

Miwa, A. (2003b) *Zen koku gaido jiten: Nishi Nihon hen* [Dictionary of the highways in all Japan: West Japan]. Tokyo: Tokyodō shuppan.

Miyamoto, K. and S. Suzuki (1999). *Ryohaku no kukan* [Space in the travel inns]. Tokyo: Shōten kenchiku-sha.

Miyamoto, T. (1987). *Tabi no minzoku to rekishi* [Travelling people and history], 1: *Nihon no yado* [Japanese inns]. Tokyo: Yasaka shobō.

Muramatsu, T. (1999). *Tawaraya no fushigui* [Strangeness of Tawaraya]. Tokyo: Sekai bunkasha.

Nihon no kaidō no. 74 (2003). *Kyoto. Saikoku kaidō* [Kyoto: the Western Provinces highway]. Tokyo: Kodansha.

Okubo, A. (2001). 'Nihon ryokan no myrioku bunseki (II) Kindai Nihon bungaku ni okeru ryokan no hyogen' [An analysis of the attractions of *ryokan* (II) From the scene on the works of the modern Japanese literature]. *Nihon kankō kenkyūgaku gakkai zenkoku taikai*. Tokyo: Rikkyo University, Japan Institute for Tourism Research, pp. 16, 17–20.

—— (2002). 'Nihon ryokan hyogen ni taisuru rekishi shakaigakuteki kōsatsu' [Representations of *ryokan* in Japanese serial stories in newspapers from 1880 to 1974]. *St Paul's Annals of Tourism Research*, 4, pp. 19–26.

—— (2003a). 'Ryokan imēji keisei katei ni okeru medeia no eikyō' [The image of *ryokan* influenced by the media]. *Journal of Japan Institute of Tourism Research: Tourism Studies Quarterly*, 14 (2), pp. 19–26.

—— (2003b). 'Ryokan to Ōkami' [Japanese inns and *Ōkami*]. In I. Maeda (ed.), *21 no kankōgaku* [Tourist science for the 21st century]. Tokyo: Gakubunsha, pp. 213–31.

Satō, Y. and C. Fujiwara (2000). *Ukiyoe ni miru Edo no tabi* [Travel during the Edo period through prints]. Tokyo: Kashutsu shobōshinsha.

Shūkan hoteru resutoran (1995). *Ōkamisan kara no atsui messēji 1* [Warm messages from women managers of hotels and inns 1]. Tokyo: Oota paburikeshon.

—— (1997). *Ōkamisan kara no atsui messēji 2* [Warm messages from women managers of hotels and inns 2]. Tokyo: Oota paburikeshon.

—— (1999). *Ōkamisan kara no atsui messēji 3* [Warm messages from women managers of hotels and inns 3]. Tokyo: Oota paburikeshon.

Sōrifu (2004). *Kankō Hakushō* (White book on tourism). Tokyo: Okurashō.

Taiyō Korekushon Chizu Edo Meiji Gendai (1977). *Edo. Tokaidō*, vol. 1. *Kyoto. Osaka. Sanyōdō*, vol. 2. *Saikaidō. Nankaidō*, vol. 3. *Nakasendō. Oshudō*, vol. 4. Tokyo: Heibonsha.

Take, Y., K. Nakayama, K. Ikeda, T. Okada and N. Shitaguchi (2002). *Yakage no honjin to wakihonjin* [The *honjin* and *wakihonjin* of Yakage]. Okyama: Nihon bunkyō shuppan.

Takeuchi, M. (ed.) (2003). *Edo no tabi to kōtsu* [Travel and transport during the Edo period]. Tokyo: Gakken.

Usami, M. (2000). *Shukuba to meishi mori onna* [Post towns and the *meishi mori* women). Tokyo: Doseisha.

Vaporis, C.N. (1994). *Breaking Barriers: Travel and the State in Early Modern Japan.* Cambridge, MA, and London: Harvard University, Council on East Asian Studies.

Yajima, Y. (1998). *Meisaku o unda yado* [The inns which gave birth to famous literary works]. Tokyo: Shogakukan.

Yamamoto, H. (1998). *Sankin kōtai* (Alternate attendance). Tokyo: Kōdansha.

Part II

Travel in tradition, time and fantasy

4   Meanings of tradition in contemporary Japanese domestic tourism

Markus Oedewald

General discourse of tradition in contemporary Japan

Modern Japan is widely regarded as a society saturated with traditions. This is a notion which has often been emphasized both in Japan and in Western countries – in discourses and in narratives. The notion of culturally especially powerful traditions in Japan is intensified by the modern media, which often shows us the stereotypes of a culture (e.g. Moeran 1996).

Many discourses and narratives are connected to the dialogue between 'tradition' regarded as Own and the Other. The appearance of numerous 'traditions' has been connected to the creation process of national identity but also to the legitimating of power. In many cases it can, however, be noted that many of these 'traditions' are modern constructions, although they are presented as much older (e.g. Vlastos 1998). The past has been interpreted and constructed from the present time point of view. Recent examples of this can be found in *nihonjinron* literature[1] and the *furusato* movement[2] as well as in many other different areas of culture.

As traditions are so popularly discussed it is important to find out how traditions are understood. What are these traditions of the discourses? How are the notion and content of tradition understood? In this chapter I shall introduce different general notions of tradition. As I will show, the concept of tradition is used rather differently depending on what kind of topic is under discussion. Also the notion of tradition depends on the perspective from which tradition is observed. I will examine the ideas of tradition in the context of Japanese domestic tourism. What is the position of tradition in Japanese domestic tourism? And, more particularly, what are the position and meaning of tradition in the school excursion, *shūgaku ryokō*?

Perspectives on understanding tradition

The concepts of tradition and culture are central in this study. The prerequisites of culture are certain common codes or systems of meaning, but there is also space for making differences so that culture can be understood as a dynamic system. Although we talk about cultural patterns it is important to keep in mind that human behaviour is inherently extremely plastic (see for example Geertz 1973). Cultural patterns give meaning to social and psychological reality both by shaping themselves to it and by shaping it to themselves (Geertz 1973: 93). In other words, identity is strongly influenced by the social structure, but conversely identities react upon the social structure, maintaining it, modifying it and reshaping it (see for example Berger and Luckmann 1967). In the context of modern society it could be stated that, by knowing and using the codes of consumption of my own culture, I reproduce and demonstrate my membership of a particular social order.

Notion of tradition

With interpretations of understanding culture and social reality in this sense we should also consider traditions as something including both stasis and change. However, this is only one point of view in the analysis of tradition. I will present here some of the major perspectives of tradition.

Tradition as opposition to the modern

Perhaps the most common notion of tradition focuses on the view that tradition is opposition to the modern. Modern or often also Western societies are viewed as being innovative, rational, empirical, etc., and traditions or traditional societies supposedly are not those things, thereby implying that they're normative, conservative, belief oriented, etc. Anthony Giddens (1994: 68) describes it by saying that during modern times tradition or old customs were understood as something opposite to something based on the mind. This kind of idea of tradition was developed to serve the descriptive purposes of proponents of the Enlightenment (Shils 1981: 18). From the late eighteenth to the early twentieth century, as the achievements of the Enlightenment were assessed, a new romanticized notion of tradition also appeared. This romanticized notion of tradition was alleged to be the guarantor of order and of the quality of civilization (Shils 1981: 19[3]).

This kind of perspective of tradition usually supports the idea that tradition refers to something which has existed from time immemorial, something age-old, or that it marks a historical period preceding modernity. Also rather common is the notion that *before* is traditional society and the *after* is that which is 'other', that which is not tradition (Adam 1996: 143). Adam argues with good cause that the prefixes 'de' and 'post' (as in detraditionalization and post-modernity) delimit the substantive scope of the subject matter and transform ongoing and embedded processes into disembedded, static states. In this sense the characteristic of tradition is invariance (see Hobsbawm 1983: 2).

In Japan the recent attempts to conquer the modern by returning to an age of culture, *bunka no jidai*, have ahistorical implicit references (see for example Vlastos 1998). Marilyn Ivy (1995: 33) stresses that the cultural policy of the Meiji state and after must be seen in relation to cultural encounters with the Euro-American nations. In this sense the emergence and resurgence of traditions are results that derive from the cultural encounters in modern society.

Tradition as part of culture including change

However, traditions as cultures in general are always changing in one way or another. This becomes a major touchstone of analysing tradition. Raymond Williams (1981: 187) has stated that traditions are renewal of action. Williams also points to the selective nature of what is known as tradition. What we have to see is not just a tradition but a selective tradition: an intentionally selective version of a shaping past and a pre-shaped present, which is then powerfully operative in the process of social and cultural definition and identification (Williams 1977: 115). From this point of view, cultural traditions are 'chosen' not inherited.

Alice E. Horner (1990: 31–5) has emphasized that tradition can be, or is, an inventive process including imagining and creation. Culture is continually re-created by the people who live it, and it is this very quality of inventiveness that gives culture its power (Horner 1990: 33; see also Wagner 1981: 89). In this sense tradition can be understood as an ongoing symbolic creation and re-creation. According to these examples a concern with stasis should be replaced by a concern with process. In the Japanese context throughout history the religious and political authorities have very often been so closely tied that religious institutions were at the same time political and political institutions religious. The rites in political and religious institutions were also closely tied, and this explains why rituals changed when the social order changed (Grapard 1992: 47). In travelling or the history of tourism this meant that some famous sights, *meisho*, might lose their importance and correspondingly some sights' popularity might increase. This occurred with Ise when Kumano became popular before the Edo period (1600–1868) (see for example Ishimori 1989; Gorai 1989: 155–242).

Content and meaning of tradition

Edward Shils (1981) has created some general conditions for tradition. He describes tradition very similarly to the common notion of culture. To simplify, Shils (1981: 12) states that tradition is all that a society of a given time possesses, which already existed when its present possessors came upon it. On the whole, according to Edward Shils (1981: 12), tradition:

> means simply a *traditium*; it is anything which is transmitted or handed down from the past to the present. It makes no statement about what is handed down or in what particular combination or whether it is a physical object or cultural construction; it says nothing about how long it has

been handed down or in what manner, whether orally or in written form. . . . The conception of tradition . . . is silent about whether there is acceptable evidence for the truth of the tradition or whether the tradition is accepted without its validity having been established.

This kind of idea of tradition would follow the common idea of Japanese tradition, *dentō*, which is often connected to certain concepts such as *dentō geijutsu* (traditional art), *dentō geinō* (traditional entertainment) or *dentō bunka* (traditional culture).[4] *Dentō* tradition implies those things and customs that have been transmitted through a line, or passed down through the generations, which will be passed on in the future (e.g. traditions of painting, *kaiga no dentō*). Traditions may be passed, for example, through family tradition, *kaden*. When referring to literary material (e.g. legends) *densetsu* is very commonly used. The English word 'traditional' is commonly understood to be very similar to the Japanese *dentōteki*.

Pascal Boyer (1990) has made a noteworthy attempt to find out the content of tradition. Boyer (1990: 1–2) stresses three important elements or prerequisites of tradition: 1) they are instances of social interaction (actual events); 2) they are repeated (reference to previous occurrences of the same type of social event); and 3) they are psychologically salient (attention-demanding, focalizing people's attention more than ordinary discourse or actions).

Anthony Giddens (1994: 63–4) says that tradition is bound up with memory, and especially the 'collective' variant of it. It is connected with a phenomenon which he calls the formulaic notion of truth. This formulaic notion of truth is available only to a few, and tradition leans on guardians. The content of tradition has both moral and emotional validity, and this is one of the differences between tradition and custom. Giddens draws a conclusion (1994: 65) that traditions are effective because their moral character offers ontological security for people. Altogether, the attempts to classify the general content of tradition include the following examples (e.g. Giddens 1994; Shils 1981; Hobsbawm 1983; Boyer 1990[5]): it is attached to places; it includes the notion of formulaic truth; it involves rituals (and ritual gestures); it is esoteric; it is repeated; it has guardians (custodians or licensed speakers) as mediators; it has a normative and moral content; it is active and interpretative; it is a tool for organizing collective memory; it is connected strongly to emotions and senses, and symbolic material; it is described as invariant; it is formal; it is characterized by literalism on repetition; it is understood as knowledge which has passed for knowledge in a society, regardless of the ultimate validity or invalidity of such knowledge.

In order to get a clearer picture of what is involved in the existence of tradition, John B. Thompson (1996) has distinguished four aspects of tradition: hermeneutic, normative, legitimating and identity. The hermeneutic aspect refers to the idea that 'tradition is an interpretative scheme, a framework for understanding the world. . . . All understanding is based on presuppositions, on some set of assumptions which we take for granted and which form part of a tradition to which we belong' (Thompson 1996: 91). For example, the Enlightenment is not the antithesis of tradition but is one tradition among others – that is, a set of taken-for-granted assumptions which provide a framework for understanding the world (Thompson 1996: 92).

The second, normative aspect contains:

> sets of assumptions, forms of belief and patterns of action handed down from the past that can serve as a normative guide for actions and beliefs in the present. . . . Material handed down from the past can serve as a normative guide in the sense that certain practices are *routinized*.
>
> (Thompson 1996: 92)

The third, legitimating aspect emphasizes that 'tradition can, in certain circumstances, serve as a source of support for the exercise of power and authority' (Thompson 1996: 92). In tourism the meaning of the legitimating aspect can be noted excellently in the *furusato* campaign. In 1984 finance minister Takeshita Noburu introduced *Nippon rettō furusatoron* (the proposal for *furusato* Japan: *furusato tsukuri*). This still continuing project has been criticized for presenting *furusato* villages as places providing access to another, presumably more 'authentic' world. For natives and tourists, what is experienced in the *furusato* village is not village life, but constructed imaginary village life (see for example Ota 1993; Robertson 1995; Ishimori and Sakaue 2000; Moon 1997). As Jennifer Robertson (1995) and Ota (1993) have noted, the important task of the still continuing, also politically oriented, campaign is to activate a nostalgia informing the imagination of a traditional, authentic, more Japanese future.

Fourthly and finally is the identity aspect, referred to 'as sets of assumptions, beliefs and patterns of behaviour handed down from the past, traditions provide some of the symbolic materials for the formation of identity both at the individual and at the collective level' (Thompson 1996: 93). Giddens (1994: 80) also emphasizes that tradition as a medium of identity is a prime requisite of ontological security. For this reason, Giddens argues, the threats to the integrity of traditions are often experienced as threats to the integrity of the self.

According to Thompson (1996: 93) 'tradition retains its significance in the modern world, particularly as a means of making sense of the world (the hermeneutic aspect) and as a way of creating a sense of belonging (identity aspect)'. Thompson (1996: 94) continues that the decline of traditional authority (legitimating aspect) and the traditional grounding of action (normative aspect) does not spell the demise of tradition but rather signals a shift in its nature and role.

Invented tradition

One way of describing the position and role of tradition is to explain differences in the concepts of tradition and invention of tradition. Separation of these two concepts is not an unambiguous task, paying attention to the argument that traditions and the meanings of traditions also change.

'Traditions', which are attempts to establish continuity with a suitable historical past, are often called 'invented traditions' (Hobsbawm 1983). Hobsbawm (1983: 2) states that 'the peculiarity of invented traditions is that the continuity with it is largely factitious'. In Japan as in many other countries you can see the selected symbols of 'history' or 'tradition', selected as appropriate to the particular group at particular phases of its history. In Japan some aspects have been analysed, such as the 'invented' meaning of village life (e.g. Scheiner 1998; Robertson 1998; Yoshino 1992). For invented traditions invariance seems to be an emphasized characteristic (see Hobsbawm 1983; Vlastos 1998).

An important issue is that invented tradition is presented (or tourists are given to understand that it is) as an 'old tradition'. These kinds of examples can be noted, for example, in *furusato* villages (e.g. Robertson 1995; Moon 1997; Kajiwara 1997), in the construction of a tourist village of *ama* divers (Martinez 1996), in the creation of Tōno city in the image of folklore (Ota 1993: 392–4) and partly in the creation of the touristic History Road, *Rekishi Kaidō*, in the late 1990s in Kii peninsula (see Creighton, this volume). In these examples invented tradition must be seen particularly as a political or commercial tool.

Conclusion

As we have noted, the entity of tradition is a very complex phenomenon. From all the points I have presented I would like to draw some conclusions. The aspects or meanings of traditions show that dynamics are part of tradition, although constancy is often emphasized as a characteristic of tradition.

Instead of underlining the stasis of traditions we should emphasize the processual aspect of tradition. This notion makes it possible to examine tradition as a natural manifestation of culture, including for example the idea of renewal, handing down or protecting. In this chapter tradition itself is considered as a visible structure or process of culture. Tradition may include underlying ideas, but they as such are not tradition; they lie as the cultural core under the tradition. Tradition is conceived here as a type of interaction which modifies people's representation in a relatively organized way. The models of interpretation used in society mixed with the personal identities constitute – that is produce and reproduce – culture or social reality and, as a part of this, tradition as well. The dynamic processual and contextual nature of tradition will be explored through examination of examples which focus on cultural behaviour, particularly in Japanese domestic tourism.

Tradition in Japanese domestic tourism

Japanese domestic tourism has increased significantly since the Second World War. According to research of the Japanese Ministry of Land, Infrastructure and Transport (Kokudo kōtsūshō 2001: 23–4), the Japanese made 325 million overnight trips in 2000. On average this means approximately 2.6 trips per person, with 51.6 per cent of the trips for pleasure, 19.5 per cent for family reasons, 15.6 per cent for business, 7.5 per cent for pleasure combined with other motives and 5.7 per cent for another reason.

The Japanese travel association Nihon kankō kyōkai has made a study (Nihon shūgaku ryokō kyōkai 1998, 2001) where they examined activities during overnight pleasure trips. The respondents (2,781) were asked what they do during overnight pleasure trips. The most popular choices (Nihon shūgaku ryokō kyōkai 1998: 102–3) were:

1　Hot spring *onsen* bathing: 45.8 per cent
2　Scenery viewing: 44.3 per cent
3　Viewing famous places and historic spots: 29.3 per cent
4　Buying special products, eating and drinking: 23.6 per cent
5　Zoological gardens (and information centres): 18.0 per cent
6　Leisure and theme parks: 12.7 per cent
7　Car ride: 11.1 per cent
8　Visiting shrines and temples: 8.3 per cent
9　Cherry blossom viewing, flower viewing: 7.6 per cent
10　Skiing: 5.7 per cent
11　Sea bathing: 4.9 per cent; painting nature, collecting plants as a hobby or study: 4.9 per cent
12　City sightseeing: 4.7 per cent; mountain climbing, hiking: 4.7 per cent
13　Watching, appreciation of drama or sports: 4.2 per cent
14　Golf: 3.6 per cent
15　Fishing: 3.5 per cent

Onsen bathing was in the top four in all age groups. It was especially popular in the age group over 50 years old. The most popular activities for young males 20–24 years old were skiing (25 per cent), scenery viewing (21.4 per cent), *onsen* bathing (20.2 per cent), viewing famous places and historic spots (17.9 per cent) and car ride (15.5 per cent). Females in the same age group appreciated scenery viewing (43.5 per cent), *onsen* bathing (29 per cent), viewing famous places and historic spots (28.3 per cent), car ride (23.9 per cent) and buying special products, eating and drinking (23.2 per cent). Visiting shrines and temples was above average in age groups over 60 years (males) and over 50 years (females). Cherry blossom viewing or flower viewing was especially popular with the female age group over 40 years old. In the young male age groups, sport activities such as skiing were especially popular. Buying special products or eating and drinking was above average in age groups 60–69 years (males), 18–19 years and over 35 years (females). Comparing the results of the 1992 and the 2000 survey some major changes can be noticed in the popularity of the options (Nihon shūgaku ryokō kyōkai 2001: 11). Activities which increased were *onsen* bathing (from 44.2 per cent to 51.3 per cent), scenery viewing (from 45.7 per cent to 49.4 per cent), leisure and theme parks (from 8.3 per cent to 12.9 per cent), and cherry blossom viewing, flower viewing (from 4.5 per cent to 10.2 per cent). Activities which decreased during the same time span were car ride (from 25.0 per cent to 13.3 per cent) and skiing (from 9.0 per cent to 3.6 per cent).

Both traditions and invented traditions are important parts of Japanese domestic tourism. They are attractions which have an enormous meaning for the whole of tourism. As the statistics show, history in general is very important. Tradition as presented in tourism more often has the character-istics of the invention of tradition, with emphasis on external circumstances. Tradition in tourism is often presented as the opposite of modern.[6] *Ofuro* baths are rebuilt, but they are considered as old and traditional, referring mainly to the habit of bathing which dates back approximately 2,000 years (see for example Shimomura 1993). In Japan there are dozens of examples of using the image of tradition as a tourist attraction. This can be noticed in large tourism campaigns. In 1970 Japan National Railway launched a cam-paign, *Jisukabā Japan* (Discover Japan), which inundated Japanese with images of 'authentic' Japan. This campaign was followed later by *Jisukabā Japan II* and in 1984 *Ekizochikku Japan* (Exotic Japan). In the *Jisukabā Japan* campaign the tourist attractions were intentionally promoted as the opposite of modern and Western (Ivy 1995; Shirahata 1996). The *Ekizochikku Japan* campaign described tourist attractions as exotic and strange.

Such examples of the use of 'traditions' in tourism are common in Japan as well as in dozens of other tourist attractions in the world. After visiting these kinds of tourist attractions, there is a strong inclination to say that the use of 'tradition' in tourism is just a phenomenon of fashion where the connections to the content of tradition are largely fictitious, artificial or non-existent. Many 'traditions' presented in tourism are constructed pictures of the imaginary past or the past proved real by historical methods but detached from their original contexts.[7] These latter ones could also be called relics or living museums (see Giddens 1994: 101–2). Connotations are basic instruments in the marketing of tradition in tourism, and as a result they might turn cultural categories into seemingly natural elements of the material world.

Furthermore in Japanese tourism it is worth noting that the meaning and purpose of rituals have changed. In many cases the ritual occasions have become mediated celebrations (of national or religious identity) which all citizens, wherever they may be, are able to witness and in which they are invited vicariously to take part. These are well represented in many *matsuri*, festivals. Umesao Tadao (Kanzaki 1991:35) has mentioned that certain *matsuri* are not festivals where people go to respect *kami*, gods (on the construction of *matsuri* see also Hendry 1993: 129).

Sets of values and beliefs that form part of traditions may alter in character, as they become increasingly remote from their contexts of origin. These symbolic contents of tradition become interwoven with local ones and this may produce new traditions or traditions embedded in new circumstances. Tradition does not get its authenticity because it is old or it encapsulates past events accurately. The authenticity of tradition depends upon the connection of ritual practice and formulaic truth (Giddens 1994: 94).

Tradition of Japanese domestic tourism

By the tradition of Japanese domestic tourism I refer to certain cultural patterns in contemporary domestic tourism which are reminiscent of tradition, with similar content and characteristics. I call these traditional aspects of tourism. They are essential in domestic tourism and have their origin mostly in the Edo (1600–1868) and Meiji (1868–1912) periods (see for example Graburn 1983; Ishimori 1989; Gorai 1989; Kanzaki 1997). The idea is also to examine how the culturally specific social structures define the character of the journey. I emphasize that the aspects presented here are the ones I consider as most important, and there are other aspects which are also very important (for more detail see Oedewald 2001).

An important historical aspect of travelling in general is the pilgrimage, which has many different concepts in Japanese, such as *mōde* (e.g. Mitake *mōde*), *junrei* (e.g. Saikoku *sanjūsansho kannon junrei*), *okagemairi* (Ise *okagemairi*), *henro* (e.g. Shikoku *henro*), *sankei* and *kodō*. As early as the Nara period (710–94) ascetics travelled to mountain areas for religious reasons (Swanson 1981; Kitagawa 1987; Blacker 1986). From the Heian (794–1185) to the Azuchi-Momoyama (1568–1600) period, pilgrimages got more popular, including an increasing number of pilgrims to 33 destinations in the Saikoku pilgrimage, *Saikoku sanjūsansho kannon junrei*, in western Japan (Foard 1982; Gorai 1989), to 88 holy places in the Shikoku pilgrimage, *Shikoku henro*, and to Ise (Ooms 1985; Ishimori 1989) as the most popular ones. During the Edo period (1600–1868) pilgrimages became mass pilgrimages as the number of Ise *okagemairi* pilgrims increased to 3.6 million in 1705 (Ooms 1985: 187) and 4 million to 5 million in 1830 (Davis 1992: 49). At least partly because of these pilgrimages, the idea of travelling is considered very natural in contemporary Japan.

The idea of worship at a series of temples, *junrei*, had been present in Japan at least since Ennin's (793–864) return from the famous journey to China in the middle of the ninth century and had been applied to a series of seven temples associated with Kannon in the capital (Foard 1982: 233). In the Kamakura period (1185–1333) the common view was that, as *mappō* (defined as the latter age or the latter day of the holy law) approached, a need to visit certain temples increased (Kitagawa 1987: 333). Visiting many places in one trip, or touring, has continued since then, although the meaning and motive of the trip may have changed.

Souvenirs, *omiyage*, have also been an important aspect of travelling for many hundreds of years. It was very important in the Edo period, when French leave pilgrims, *nukemairi*, for their part brought back presents or even money (as 'interest') for masters and relatives who had stayed at home (Kanzaki 1997). As a *kō* association sent its representative on a pilgrimage and paid his travel expenses it was expected that the pilgrim would bring souvenirs for the people in the home village. This has been continued in the *senbetsu–omiyage* relationship. When a person or a small group that is part of a larger group goes on a trip, they are given amounts of money or other travel accoutrements as a farewell gift, *senbetsu*, by those who are not travelling (Graburn 1983: 44). Reciprocally, the traveller must buy gifts, *omiyage*, to take back for those who gave *senbetsu*. Although this *senbetsu* custom is diminished, the *omiyage* custom is extremely important.

The social organization of tourism is an important factor which can be noticed in the number of travelling groups and also in the reciprocal nature of tourism, with the importance of the *omiyage* custom. Group travel is often associated with *kō* associations (e.g. Graburn 1983), but as the meaning of group culture in Japan is so widely discussed I would like only to emphasize that the meaning of group travel has been and still is extremely important in Japan, although small changes in favour of individual or small-group tourism have occurred in the past few years, as Table 4.1 shows (Nihon shūgaku ryokō kyōkai 2001: 11).

The number of small groups of two to three or four to five persons has increased significantly. This is explained by the fact that at the same time (1992–2000) travelling with the family has increased from 27 per cent to 41.8 per cent. Travelling with friends or acquaintances has decreased from 30.9 per cent to 27.3 per cent, and travelling with family and friends or acquaintances has decreased from 13.4 to 11.5 per cent (Nihon shūgaku ryokō kyōkai 2001: 11).

The idea of famous places, *meisho*, as tourist attractions is also one of the important aspects in Japanese domestic tourism. The word *meisho* was

Table 4.1 Size of groups during domestic trips

	1992 %	1994 %	1996 %	1998 %	2000 %
Alone	2.4	2.7	2.7	2.2	1.8
2–3 persons	21.5	25.0	24.9	25.5	27.9
4–5 persons	20.5	21.6	24.2	22.5	24.3
6–10 persons	14.2	15.8	14.0	16.1	13.6
11–14 persons	4.2	3.7	3.5	3.7	3.1
15–30 persons	14.9	11.2	11.8	11.3	10.1
31–50 persons	8.6	6.1	7.6	5.7	7.9
Over 50 persons	7.1	3.7	4.3	4.2	4.1
Unknown	6.6	10.1	7.0	8.8	7.1

originally *nadokoro*, literally a place of fame, and it existed solely as a poetic image or device until the middle of the medieval period. Even if one was not familiar with the place, one could use a specific place name one had heard as *utamakura* (set poetic phrase) or learned from poetry manuals.[8] In the Edo period the *meisho* became a visual, actual tourist destination (Ishimori 1995: 13), and the *meisho* places were emphasized in the *meisho zue* literature, which was much used as travel books.[9] This promoted and legitimated the idea of important places and others not mentioned which had no cultural importance.

A final special important aspect of Japanese tourism is the meaning of tour guides. The *oshi* priests of Ise became very active in the Kamakura period. Kanzaki (1991: 39, 1995) and Ishimori (1989: 186) have argued specifically that these priests had an important influence on the structure and development of travel and the institutionalization of group travel in Edo period Japan. This priest–parishioner institution, *shidan seido*, came into existence especially in the Kumano and Ise shrines. Shinjō Tsunezō (in Davis 1992: 284) has stated that by the end of the sixteenth century there were 145 *oshi* priests attached to the outer shrine alone and by the early eighteenth century their number had risen to 504. Kanzaki (1995: 48) has categorized the business activities of *oshi* in the Edo period as follows: 1) management of their own territory; 2) organizing *kō* associations (organized package tours); 3) management of the *kō* fund; 4) dispatching helpers for the journey; 5) welcoming (a meeting service); 6) prayer; 7) guiding the shrine visits (arranging guides); 8) entertainment at banquets; 9) looking after accommodation; 10) arranging souvenirs (recommending souvenir items and presenting memorial gifts); and 11) escorted introductions to the market (introductions to the local night life). The popularization of tour guides in the Edo period has supported the development of the social attitude that tour guides are important as mediators during tourist trips.

It has often been emphasized that Japanese domestic tourism is changing in character from seeing tourism, *miru kankō*, to doing tourism, *suru kankō* (see for example Shimomura 1993: 31; Knight 1996: 176; Moeran 1983: 95). There is a certain change going on, but the change is taking place very slowly, and what should be emphasized is that the role of *miru kankō* is still very strong in Japanese tourism. Another important point is that this active tourism is mostly a phenomenon of certain categories, such as young males, and it does not apply to all categories.

Case: school excursion (shūgaku ryokō)

This chapter introduces a particular case of tourism, as I examine what the role of tradition is in Japanese school excursions. The aim is to find out how tradition in Japanese domestic tourism and the tradition of Japanese domestic tourism can be noted in school excursions. What are the characteristics which reflect culturally important factors?

The school excursion dates back to 1886, when it was introduced as a means of physical and spiritual training for Japan's youths. Today the school excursion refers to organized school travel, funded by parents, by elementary, junior high and senior high school students to various destinations. Tokyo Normal School (now Tsukuba University) initiated the school excursion in 1886. The principal of the school, Takemine Hideo, planned to offer practical, on-site education in geography and science. He was influenced by the educational philosophy of Johann Heinrich Pestalozzi (1746–1827), whose ideas he studied at Oswego Teachers College in New York State. In 1888 the Ministry of Education decided to allocate funds for excursions as an official part of the normal-school curriculum. Middle-school students quickly adopted the custom. Group tours for the students of girls' schools began in the 1920s. In the 1930s, when educational policy came to be dominated by Japanese militaristic thinking, students headed mainly for *shintō* shrines. The original purpose of practical, on-site educational opportunity received a political nuance. Before that excursions had been carried out with relative freedom (Kasama 1987).

Nowadays almost every Japanese has visited Tokyo, Kyoto and Nara, often as a student on a school excursion. Japan School Tours Association publishes statistics on school excursions (Nihon shūgaku ryokō kyōkai 2002), and statistics show that, in 2001, 94.5 per cent of elementary schools, 97.5 per cent of junior high schools and 94.4 per cent of senior high schools made a school excursion. The length of the excursion was, for elementary school students, typically (74.5 per cent) one night and two days, for junior high schools two nights and three days (68.9 per cent), and for senior high schools three nights and four days (45.9 per cent) or four nights and five days (33.8 per cent) (Nihon shūgaku ryokō kyōkai 2002: 94–6, 103–5). School excursions were mostly done during the second year in senior high schools (95.3 per cent) (first year 2.3 per cent, third year 2.0 per cent), during the third year in junior high schools (80.3 per cent) (second year 17.8 per cent) and during the sixth year in elementary schools (93.1 per cent) (fifth year 4 per cent, other 3 per cent). In senior high schools the expenditure during school excursions on average was as follows (Nihon shūgaku ryokō kyōkai 2002: 108): transportation ¥45,600 (€387), accommodation ¥32,700 (€277) and other ¥20,100 (€170), or ¥98,400 (€834) in total. There were some differences between different kinds of schools. Students of national schools spent ¥106,600 (€903), public (full-day) ¥89,200 (€756), public (part-time) ¥78,000 (€661) and private ¥124,400 (€1,054). The spending money per student was in public (full-day) schools ¥25,900 (€219), public (part-time) ¥33,200 (€281) and private ¥26,000 (€220) (national schools' information was not available), or an average of ¥26,100 (€221) per student.

The school excursion is a very important part of Japanese schooling. The meanings of school excursions are various. Usually school excursions are something special that Japanese people certainly remember of their schooldays. As one teacher expressed it in research data (Saitama ken 1986a: 3):

Some time ago in the class reunion I met my school friends who graduated with me from senior high school 15 years ago. After talking a while about what we are doing nowadays, the conversation turned to the senior high school excursion.

This is also one of the most important aims of the school excursion. The aims, *nerai*, of senior high school excursions were various according to the study of Japan School Tours Association (Nihon shūgaku ryokō kyōkai 2002: 111).

As Table 4.2 shows, 'To form enjoyable memories of school life' is one of the most important aims of school excursions. (For aims, respondents could choose more than one answer.) The main purposes, *mokuteki*, for the senior high school excursion (where a single choice was made) were (Nihon shūgaku ryokō kyōkai 2002: 111): to study by observation and study directly (23.1 per cent) (in 1991 30 per cent), to raise awareness of nature and to train the body (19.2 per cent), to get experience of group life and public morals (18.5 per cent), to deepen human relations (17.5 per cent), to form memories (13.7 per cent), and to understand internationalization and other purposes (7.6 per cent).

The aims of the junior high school excursions were also various according to the study of Japan School Tours Association (Nihon shūgaku ryokō kyōkai 2002: 110).

Table 4.2 The aims of school excursions of senior high schools

	National school %	Public school %	Private school %	All %
To widen education by studying geography, history, politics, economics and the like directly	50.0	40.1	36.6	37.5
To investigate local culture, people and living things	33.3	40.8	36.6	39.1
To deepen the understanding of daily experiences of life in a farming, mountain or fishing village	0	0.9	1.8	1.2
To understand internationalization and international friends	83.3	10.4	23.6	13.5
To learn skiing, mountain climbing or similar sports	0	22.6	11.6	18.3
To raise awareness of the greatness and beauty of nature	66.7	45.9	46.0	45.4
To get desirable experience concerning the customs of group life and public morals	33.3	64.3	61.2	61.2
To deepen mutually the human relations of teacher and student, and student and student	50.0	62.8	48.9	57.9
To form enjoyable memories of school life	33.3	43.2	50.4	45.3
Other reason	16.7	12.5	8.0	11.4

Table 4.3 The purposes of school excursions of junior high schools

	National school %	Public school %	Private school %	Average %
To study history (historical landmarks, fine arts, literature, etc.)	20.8	22.5	25.2	22.7
To study geography (nature, civilization, geological features, etc.)	13.2	7.1	11.1	7.6
To study social science (industry, factory, study by observation, etc.)	11.3	9.7	6.4	9.5
To become familiar with nature, to train the body	6.6	3.8	9.8	4.3
To practise group life (training in human relations)	27.4	30.9	23.9	30.4
To form good memories of school life	11.3	19.9	12.4	19.2
Other reason	9.4	6.0	11.1	6.4

As Table 4.3 shows, the main purposes for the junior high school excursion were: to study subjects directly (39.8 per cent), to practise group life and human relations (30.4 per cent), to form memories (19.2 per cent), to become familiar with nature and other reasons (10.7 per cent). The aims of the junior high school excursions were (Nihon shūgaku ryokō kyōkai 2002: 110): to practise group life (80.5 per cent), to study history (60.1 per cent), to form good memories of school life (50.8 per cent) and to study social science (25.2 per cent).

The aims of the elementary high school excursions were shown in the study of Japan School Tours Association (Nihon shūgaku ryokō kyōkai 2002: 110).

As Table 4.4 shows, the most popular purpose of the elementary school excursion is related directly to studies (30.8 per cent). Other significant categories are: to get desirable experience concerning the customs of group life and public morals (24.6 per cent), to form good memories (16.0 per cent), to study, experience and raise awareness of nature (13.0 per cent), and to deepen mutually the human relations of teacher and student, and student and student (10.2 per cent).

The aims of the school excursion show that the interest in the traditional Japan is very central, although the main emphasis of the aims seems to be lifestyle (*seikatsu*), with study in the sense of studying history and so on slightly decreasing (Nihon shūgaku ryokō kyōkai 2002: 111). However, the interest in history and tradition is still very important, and this is also confirmed by the list of most popular destinations of school excursions (Nihon shūugaku ryokō kyōkai 2002: 115):

Table 4.4 The purposes of school excursions of elementary schools

	National school %	Public school %	Private school %	Average %
To widen education by studying geography, history, cultural properties and the like on-site	21.5	24.2	21.7	23.9
To widen education by studying politics, economics, industry and the like directly in important places	8.5	7.0	4.9	6.9
To raise awareness of the greatness and beauty of nature	11.5	8.3	14.9	9.0
To study and experience nature in a way which is not possible in classroom study	5.4	3.5	7.7	4.0
To deepen the understanding of daily experiences of life in a farming, mountain or fishing village	0.0	0.4	1.4	0.5
To get desirable experience concerning the customs of group life and public morals	20.8	25.2	20.0	24.6
To become aware of health and safety and improve and train the mind and body	3.1	2.4	2.0	2.4
To deepen mutually the human relations of teacher and student, and student and student	10.0	10.3	8.9	10.2
To form good memories	9.5	16.4	14.3	16.0
Other reason	7.7	2.2	4.3	2.5

Senior high schools
1 Tokyo Disneyland
2 Kiyomizudera temple, Kyoto
3 Haus den Bosch, Kyūshū
4 Tokyo metropolitan area
5 Shuri castle, Okinawa
6 Himeyuri tower, Okinawa
7 Hōryūji temple, Nara
8 Yakushi temple, Nara
9 Nara park
9 Dazaifu tenmangū shrine, Kyūshū
11 Gyokusendō cave, Okinawa
12 Tōnan shokubutsurakuen, Southeast botanical gardens, Okinawa
13 Heiwa kōen peace park, Nagasaki
14 Manzamō Manza beach (cliffs), Okinawa
14 Kokusai doori, International street, Okinawa

16 Genbaku shiryōkan, Nagasaki Atomic Bomb Museum
17 Tōdaiji temple, Nara
18 Shuri castle park, Okinawa
19 Abuchiragama cave, Okinawa
19 Mabuni no oka, Mabuni hill, Okinawa

The destinations of senior high schools have changed their characteristics within the past 10–20 years, as the destination choice is influenced by how far away it is. Many students in Saitama prefecture high schools also argue that common destinations such as Nara or Kyoto are familiar, since they have already visited them during elementary and junior high school excursions.

The results for senior high schools can be compared to the most popular destinations of junior high school and elementary school excursions (Nihon shūgaku ryokō kyōkai 2002: 113–14):

Junior high schools
1   Tokyo city
2   Tokyo Disneyland
3   Tōdaiji temple, Nara
4   Kiyomizudera temple, Kyoto
5   Tokyo metropolitan area
6   Hōryūji temple, Nara
7   National diet, Tokyo
8   Nara park
9   Kinkakuji temple, Kyoto
10 Yakushi temple, Nara
11 Sanjūsankendō temple, Kyoto
12 Asakusa Nakamise (street), Asakusaji (Sensōji) temple, Tokyo
13 Ginkakuji temple, Kyoto
14 Nijō castle, Kyoto
15 Nagasaki city
16 Tokyo tower
17 Yokohama city
18 Kaiyūkan, the Osaka aquarium
19 Genbaku shiryōkan, Nagasaki Atomic Bomb Museum
20 Space world, Kyūshū

Elementary schools
1   Kinkakuji temple, Kyoto
2   Tōdaiji temple, Nara
3   Kiyomizudera temple, Kyoto
4   Hōryūji temple, Nara
5   Tōei uzumasa eigamura, Movie village, Kyoto
6   Nijō castle, Kyoto
7   Hiroshima heiwa kinen kōen, Hiroshima memorial peace park

8 Nara park
9 Nikkō Tōshōgū, Mausoleum of shōgun Tokugawa Ieyasu
10 National diet, Tokyo
11 Heiwa kōen peace park, Nagasaki
12 Kegon taki, Kegon falls, Nikkō
13 Hiroshima heiwa kinen shiryōkan, Hiroshima peace memorial museum
14 Genbaku shiryōkan, Nagasaki Atomic Bomb Museum
15 Osaka castle
16 Tokyo tower
17 Itsukushima shrine, near Hiroshima
18 Miyajima island, near Hiroshima
19 Kamakura daibutsu, Great Buddha
20 Kasuga taisha shrine, Nara

The most popular destinations of all schools confirm that the historical Japan is a central destination of school excursions. The aims prompt the same conclusion. The statistics of aims and destination choices show that the meaning of history and social customs is a central aspect in school excursions. During the past ten years Hokkaidō and Okinawa have become popular destinations of senior high school excursions. In 2001 the most popular destinations were (Nihon shūgaku ryokō kyōkai 2002: 115):

1 Hokkaidō (23.7 per cent)
2 Kyoto (18.4 per cent)
3 Okinawa (16.1 per cent)
4 Nagano (11.0 per cent)
5 Nagasaki (8.2 per cent)
6 Tokyo (7.2 per cent)
7 Kumamoto (2.2 per cent)
8 Chiba (2.0 per cent)
9 Hiroshima (1.9 per cent)
10 Nara (1.7 per cent)

These statistics show that, although changes have occurred, the 'traditional' destinations such as Kyoto are still very popular.

Example case of school excursion

In Japan it is a popular custom for students of senior high schools to keep diaries during school excursions, and after the excursion the short accounts of the excursion are published as a book. In this chapter the meaning of tradition will be studied through a sample of these diaries. Besides these diaries, before the school excursion teachers publish a booklet or small book for students. This booklet is full of very detailed information about the school excursion, including for example maps, instructions about behaviour, timetables, names of room-mates, etc. This booklet outlines in detail the structure of the school excursion.

The following is a sample of aims from one booklet (Saitama ken 1986b: 8):

1   We will experience the knowledge gained in school at the actual site and cultivate a wide knowledge and abundant sentiments.
2   We will experience group life, recognize the viewpoint of the individual and learn individuality, cooperation and feelings of responsibility.
3   More than sharing daily life by teachers and students, enjoyable daily life will consist of a deepening appreciated friendship and understanding between teachers and students.

In this example case of a school excursion the number of participants was 17 teachers and 370 students (eight classes). In 2001 the average number of participants (students) was as follows (Nihon shūgaku ryokō kyōkai 2002: 98):

- Senior high school 255.1 (number of students per teacher 19.8) – national 161.3 (16.1), public 226.4 (19.2), private 286.1 (21.3)
- Junior high school 119.7 (number of students per teacher 14.7) – national 150.7 (17.7), public 117.8 (14.4), private 126.4 (18.7)
- Elementary school 56.4 (numbers of students per teacher 12.2) – national 105.4 (15.4), public 52.2 (11.8), private 80.8 (14.0)

The usual custom is for 6–12 students to be accommodated in one room. The timetable of school excursions is very carefully planned. The attractions are decided well in advance according to the aims of the school excursion.

Here is an example of one senior high school timetable which has the common structure of all school excursions:

Day 1:
5.10–7.10   By train to Tokyo station
8.12–13.29   Tokyo–Hiroshima by *shinkansen* train
             By bus to the harbour for the Miyajima boat
14.21–14.45 By boat to Miyajima
14.45–16.00 Study trip in Miyajima
16.00–16.35 Boat trip
16.35–17.40 By bus to Kikkawa Kankō Hotel in Hiroshima
(Check bathing time. Each class 20 minutes, e.g. 19.20–19.40.)

Day 2:
8.00–8.20   By bus to peace park, *Heiwa kinen kōen*
8.50   Photography
             Monument inspection

9.30   Visit to museum
                Study tour in Hiroshima in separate groups
12.30   Lunch at Hiroshima railway station
14.24–15.17   By *shinkansen* train to Shinkurashiki
15.40–16.40   By bus to Washūyama Kaden Hotel
(Check bathing time. Two classes 30 minutes.)

Day 3:
8.00–9.00   By bus to Kurashiki
9.10–10.30   Study tour in Kurashiki including visit to Ohara art museum
                Separate groups
10.30–13.00   By bus to Himeji castle
13.00–14.30   Photography
                Study tour in Himeji castle in separate groups
14.30–17.30   By bus to Arashiyama Hotel in Kyoto
(Check bathing time. Boys: two classes 20 minutes. Girls: each class 20 minutes.)

Day 4:
8.00–16.00   Study tour in Kyoto in separate groups
For example, Class 1 Group 4:
9.00–10.00   Nijō castle
10.00–11.00   Kiyomizudera temple
11.00–12.00   Sanjūsangendō temple
12.00–13.00   Nishi and Higashi Honganji temples
14.00–15.00   Shijō Ōmiya station
15.00–16.00   Eigamura movie village
18.00–18.40   By bus to Shinkyōgoku
18.40–20.20   Free time
20.20–21.00   By bus to hotel

Day 5:
8.00–12.40   Study tour in Kyoto in separate classes
                Check your class's route from the guidebook
For example, Class 1 (Byōdōin course):
8.00–9.15   By bus to Byōdōin temple
9.15–10.00   Visit to Byōdōin temple
10.00–10.15   By bus to Sanbōin temple
10.15–11.45   Visit to Sanbōin and Daigoji temples
11.45–12.30   By bus to Kyoto station
13.14–16.04   By *shinkansen* train to Tokyo
17.07–18.33   By train to home

This timetable and school excursions in general reflect many aspects of tradition of Japanese domestic tourism. School excursions are directed to historical places where traditional concepts or patterns of Japanese culture can be viewed. In the above timetable students visited for example the Hiei mountain temples in Kyoto, where they got to know Buddhist traditions. As the destinations of school excursions have increased, invented traditions are also considered as suitable for school excursions. The pattern of school excursions as such, I would argue, include many features of tradition of Japanese domestic tourism, including many patterns which are not questioned but considered apparently as the natural way of doing things, such as visits to many famous and culturally important places, buying presents, travelling in big groups and having tour guides and teachers as mediators. These patterns seem to have a very normative character, which can be noted in the similarity of destinations, the similarity of aims and purposes, and group sizes.

Conclusion

In Japan, tourism is a visible and noticeable phenomenon in many contexts. An interesting point in the Japanese case is the fact that tourism is not a recent or modern phenomenon, but travelling on a large scale was popularized in the Tokugawa period and the models for travelling during that time had obvious influences from earlier periods. For this reason contemporary Japanese tourism has many patterns which remind one of the earlier patterns, although the meaning of the trip has changed over all these years.

I argue that these patterns have a similar content to the traditional patterns. Travel is directed to culturally appreciated places (*meisho*), and this includes the notion of formulaic truth. The trip involves ritual-like behaviour, such as taking pictures of *meisho*, visiting shrines and temples and buying amulets, *omamori* or *ofuda*. The moral character of travel offers ontological security for the people. The tour guide is nowadays a kind of custodian or licensed speaker, whose role is that of mediator. Travel in general is very normative, and it still has a moral content, which is characterized by a formal or literal way of repeating touristic behaviour, as the aims of school excursions show. Although travel as such is not necessarily described as invariant, many places or attractions are. Many traditions in tourism have been delocalized, and they have been reconnected to the territorial boundaries of the nation state. Finally in many cases the aspects or content of travel are attention demanding compared to ordinary action or discourses.

Although the attractions often, although not always, represent invented tradition, traditional patterns are mediated during tourist trips in the behaviour of tourists. As cultural patterns give meaning to social and psychological reality, during school excursions young Japanese 'learn' and are taught to experience the 'correct' or 'natural' unquestioned behaviour of a Japanese tourist. Although there are many changes occurring in the resorts of school excursions, for example in the form of overseas travel, the tradition-like patterns still seem to exist. However, as one of the main points in this chapter it is important to emphasize that, as culture changes all the time, traditions also change, and this applies also to touristic traditions. Traditions are processes which are shaped all the time and, as they are considered to be contextual, the change of their meanings can be seen as a natural phenomenon. However, the patterns may remain the same or alike, as in the case of travelling patterns noted. Japanese domestic tourism or particularly the school excursion, *shūgaku ryokō*, seems to support the idea of the processual and contextual nature of tradition.

Notes

1 The term *nihonjinron* literally means theories or discussions about the Japanese. The term refers to a genre of texts that focus on issues of Japanese national and cultural identity.
2 *Furusato* means literally old village, but its closer English equivalents are native place, heritage and home.
3 Shils (1981: 19) claims that many modern thinkers of that time such as Tönnies, Simmel, Spengler, etc. implied, in a wide variety of ways, that 'before the coming of the ruinous modern society, the human race had lived in a condition of unbroken traditionality'.
4 These include cultural products and symbols such as pottery and porcelain, lacquer ware, paintings, woodblock prints, calligraphy, dolls, folding fans, flower arrangements, the tea ceremony, dance, music played on Japanese instruments, theatrical arts such as *nō, bunraku* and *kabuki*, lyric poetry such as *tanka* and *haiku*, etc. In these simple examples, please note that there are products and action as tradition.
5 Please note that these are examples of what tradition is supposed to include. These are not necessarily the notion of the writers, but may be examples they have presented as irrelevant.
6 In Japan as well as in other parts of the world one of the basic critiques of modernity is that modern commerce and consumerism have triggered a deep sense of unease about potential erosion of traditional culture and identity (see examples in Slater 1997: 64–8). The sustained energy that Japanese academics, journalists and business elites have brought to encountering the dilemmas of modernity is enormous (see studies of *nihonjinron*, e.g. Miyoshi 1991; Befu 1984; Yoshino 1992).
7 This reminds one of Claude Lévi-Strauss's notion of bricolage. In this context bricolage can be understood as producing new meanings in the meaning system so that former strata or familiar meanings will be connected to objects which are reorganized and placed in new environments.
8 These phrases recited in a certain place are even today used as part of a tourist attraction (famous phrases, *meisho de meiku*; see for example Takaha 1999).
9 Please note also the other literature which related essentially to travelling, such as travel literature (*kikō bungaku*), travel diaries (*tabi nikki*), handbooks (*annaiki*) and travel books (*suzume mono*).

Bibliography

Adam, B. (1996). 'Detraditionalization and the certainty of uncertain futures'. In P. Heelas, L. Scott and P. Morris (eds), *Detraditionalization: Critical Reflections on Authority and Identity*. Cambridge: Blackwell, pp. 134–48.
Befu, H. (1984). 'Civilization and culture: Japan in search of identity'. In *Japanese Civilization in the Modern World: Life and Society*, Senri Ethnological Studies, 16. Osaka: National Museum of Ethnology, pp. 59–75.

Berger, P.L. and T. Luckmann (1967). *The Social Construction of Reality: A Treatise in the Sociology of Knowledge*. New York: Anchor Books/Doubleday.

Blacker, C. (1986). *The Catalpa Bow: A Study of Shamanistic Practices in Japan*. London: George Allen & Unwin.

Boyer, P. (1990). *Tradition as Truth and Communication: A Cognitive Description of Traditional Discourse*. Cambridge: Cambridge University Press.

Davis, W. (1992). *Japanese Religion and Society: Paradigms of Structure and Change*. Albany: State University of New York Press.

Foard, J.H. (1982). 'The boundaries of compassion: Buddhism and national tradition in Japanese pilgrimage'. *Journal of Asian Studies*, XLI(2) (February), pp. 231–51.

Geertz, C. (1973). *The Interpretation of Cultures: Selected Essays*. London: Fontana Press.

Giddens, A. (1994). 'Living in a post-traditional society'. In U. Beck, A. Giddens and S. Lash (eds), *Reflexive Modernization: Politics, Tradition and Aesthetics in the Modern Social Order*. Cambridge: Polity Press, pp. 56–109.

Gorai, S. (1989). *Yugyō to junrei* [Wandering and pilgrimage]. Tokyo: Kadokawa shoten.

Graburn, N. (1983). *To Pray, Pay and Play: The Cultural Structure of Japanese Domestic Tourism*. Aix-en-Provence: CIRET.

Grapard, A.G. (1992). 'The Shinto of Yoshida Kanetomo'. *Monumenta Nipponica*, 47(1) (Spring), pp. 27–58.

Hendry, J. (1993). *Wrapping Culture: Politeness, Presentation and Power in Japan and Other Societies*. Oxford: Oxford University Press.

Hobsbawm, E. (1983). 'Introduction: inventing tradition'. In E. Hobsbawm and T. Ranger (ed.), *The Invention of Tradition*. Cambridge: Cambridge University Press, pp. 1–14.

Horner, A.E. (1990). 'The assumption of tradition: creating, collecting, and conserving cultural artifacts in the Cameroon grassfields (West Africa)'. Unpublished Ph.D dissertation, Department of Anthropology, University of California, Berkeley.

Ishimori, S. (1989). 'Popularization and commercialization of tourism in early modern Japan'. In *Japanese Civilization in the Modern World*, IV: *Economic Institutions*, Senri Ethnological Studies, 26. Osaka: National Museum of Ethnology, pp. 179–94.

—— (1995). 'Tourism and religion: from the perspective of comparative civilization'. In *Japanese Civilization in the Modern World*, IX: *Tourism*, Senri Ethnological Studies, 38. Osaka: National Museum of Ethnology, pp. 11–24.

Ishimori, S. and H. Sakaue (2000). *Bijitā sangyō ni shinro o tore* [Course to visitor business]. Tokyo: B&T bukkusu. Nikkan kōgyō shinbunsha.

Ivy, M. (1995). *Discourses of the Vanishing: Modernity, Phantasm, Japan*. Chicago: University of Chicago Press.

Kajiwara, K. (1997). 'Inward-bound, outward-bound: Japanese tourism reconsidered'. In S. Yamashita, H.K. Din and J.S. Eades (eds), *Tourism and Cultural Development in Asia and Oceania*. Bangi: Penerbit Universiti Kebangsaan Malaysia, pp. 164–77.

Kanzaki, N. (1991). 'Shūdan butsuken yusan no bunkashi' [Cultural history of group pleasure trips]. In T. Umesao (ed.), *Sesō kansatsu: Asobi to shigoto no saizensen*. Tokyo: Kodansha, pp. 29–47.

—— (1995). 'A comparative analysis of the tourist industry'. In *Japanese Civilization in the Modern World*, IX: *Tourism*, Senri Ethnological Studies, 38. Osaka: National Museum of Ethnology, pp. 39–49.

—— (1997). *Omiyage: Zōtō to tabi no nihon bunka* [*Omiyage*: Japanese culture of present exchange and travel]. Tokyo: Seikyūsha.

Kasama, T. (1987). 'A century of school excursion'. *Japan Quarterly*, XXXIV(3) (July–September), pp. 287–90.

Kitagawa, J.M. (1987). *On Understanding Japanese Religion*. Princeton, NJ: Princeton University Press.

Knight, J. (1996). 'Competing hospitalities in Japanese rural tourism'. *Annals of Tourism Research*, 23(1), pp. 165–80.

Kokudo kōtsūshō (2001). *Kankō hakusho* [White paper on tourism]. Tokyo: Sōrifu.

Martinez, D.P. (1996). 'The tourist as deity: ancient continuities in modern Japan'. In T. Selwyn (ed.), *The Tourist Image: Myths and Myth Making in Tourism*. Guildford: John Wiley & Sons, pp. 163–78.

Miyoshi, M. (1991). *Off Center: Power and Culture Relations between Japan and the United States*. Cambridge, MA: Harvard University Press.

Moeran, B. (1983). 'The language of Japanese tourism'. *Annals of Tourism Research*, 10, pp. 93–108.

—— (1996). 'The Orient strikes back. advertising and imagining Japan'. *Theory, Culture and Society*, 13(3), pp. 77–112.

Moon, O. (1997). 'Marketing nature in rural Japan: Japanese images of nature – cultural perspectives'. In P. Asquith and A. Kalland (eds), *Man and Nature in Asia*. Richmond: Curzon Press, pp. 221–35.

Nihon shūgaku ryokō kyōkai (1998). *Kankō no jittai to shikō* [Facts and aims of travel]. Tokyo: Nihon kankō kyōkai.

—— (2001). *Sūji de miru kankō 2001* [Travel in figures 2001]. Tokyo: Nihon kankō kyōkai.

—— (2002). *Shūgaku ryokō no subete* [All about school excursions], vol. 21. Tokyo: Nihon shūgaku ryokō kyōkai.

Oedewald, M. (2001). 'Kulttuuristen tekijöiden merkitys matkakokemuksen määrittelijänä japanilaisten kotimaanmatkailussa' [The meaning of cultural elements in the definition of travel experience in Japanese domestic tourism]. In S. Aho, J. Saarinen and A. Honkanen (eds), *Matkailuelämykset tutkimuskohteina*. Rovaniemi: University of Lapland, pp. 51–68.

Ooms, H. (1985). *Tokugawa Ideology: Early Constructs, 1570–1680*. Princeton, NJ: Princeton University Press.

Ota, Y. (1993). 'Bunka no kyakutaika: Kankō o tooshita bunka to aidentiti no sōzō' [Objectifying culture: creation of culture and identity in tourism]. *Minzokugaku-kenkyū*, 57(4), pp. 383–406.

Robertson, J. (1995). 'Hegemonic nostalgia, tourism, and nation-making in Japan'. In *Japanese Civilization in the Modern World*, IX: *Tourism*, Senri Ethnological Studies, 38. Osaka: National Museum of Ethnology, pp. 89–103.

—— (1998). 'It takes a village: internationalization and nostalgia in postwar Japan'. In S. Vlastos (ed.), *Mirror of Modernity: Invented Traditions of Modern Japan*. Berkeley: University of California Press, pp. 110–32.

Saitama ken Hanyu dai ichi kōtō gakkō (1986a). *Machi yume* [Waited dream]. Kōnosu: Saitama ken Hanyu dai ichi kōtō gakkō shūgakuryokō iinkai.

—— (1986b). *Machi yume: Shōwa 61 nendo shūgakuryokō no shiori* [Waited dream: guide to school excursion of 1986]. Hanyu: Saitama ken Hanyu dai ichi kōtō gakkō shūgakuryokō iinkai.

Scheiner, I. (1998). 'The Japanese village: imagined, real, contested'. In S. Vlastos (ed.), *Mirror of Modernity: Invented Traditions of Modern Japan*. Berkeley: University of California Press, pp. 67–78.

Shils, E. (1981). *Tradition*. London: Faber & Faber.

Shimomura, A. (1993). 'Wagakuni ni okeru onsenchi no kūkankōsei ni kansuru kenkyū (I): Kinsei kōki kara Meijiki ni kakete no kūkankōsei' [Studies on the space composition of the hot spring resort in Japan (I): the space composition of the hot spring resort in the later Edo and Meidi era]. In *Tōkyō daigaku nōgakubu: Enshūrinhōkoku dai*, 90 gō, pp. 23–95.

Shirahata, Y. (1996). *Ryokō no susume* [Progression of tourism]. Tokyo: Chūōkōronsha.

Slater, D. (1997). *Consumer Culture and Modernity*. Cambridge: Polity Press.

Swanson, P.L. (1981). 'Shugendō and the Yoshino-Kumano pilgrimage: an example of mountain pilgrimage'. *Monumenta Nipponica*, XXXVI(1) (Spring), pp. 55–84.

Takaha, S. (1999). *Meisho de meiku* [Famous sayings/poems in famous places]. Tokyo: Shōgakukan.

Thompson, J.B. (1990). *Ideology and Modern Culture*. Stanford, CA: Stanford University Press.

—— (1996). 'Tradition and self in a mediated world'. In P. Heelas, S. Lash and P. Morris (eds), *Detraditionalization: Critical Reflections on Authority and Identity*. Cambridge: Blackwell, pp. 89–108.

Vlastos, S. (ed.) (1998). *Mirror of Modernity: Invented Traditions of Modern Japan*. Berkeley: University of California Press.

Wagner, R. (1981). *The Invention of Culture*. Chicago: University of Chicago Press.

Williams, R. (1977). *Marxism and Literature*. Oxford: Oxford University Press.

—— (1981). *Culture*. London: Fontana.

Yoshino, K. (1992). *Cultural Nationalism in Contemporary Japan: A Sociological Enquiry*. London: Routledge.

5 Fantasy travel in time and space

A new Japanese phenomenon?

Joy Hendry

Introduction

Much of the attraction of travel is to be found in the initial dreams, the consideration of possibilities, the preparations and the planning, and then, after the trip itself, in the recounting of the experience, the recording of events, and the sharing of photographs and gifts. For many people, there is probably more time spent in these activities than on the actual trip, especially if one includes the reading of books and pamphlets, watching related television programmes and films, and surfing the internet for ideas, comparative prices, and pictures of the places under review. This 'fantasy travel' is usually carried out in the comfort of one's own home, or in a cinema or travel agent, but in this chapter I invite you to consider the phenomenon of actually travelling for fantasy: put simply, a real trip, but to a fantasy location.

It may sound a little odd, at first, but this is actually not such a new or unusual thing, especially when we add the dimension of travelling through time. For example, most countries have ways of conserving aspects of their past for presentation to their citizens, often for nationalistic purposes, and travel to a big museum can take a visitor on a fantasy adventure to many different locations, distant in time and space. World fairs and exhibitions have for a good century and a half attracted travellers from a wide radius around them to make fantasy trips to the national pavilions that open up to display their highlights, and more recently the heritage phenomenon has opened the eyes of the public to increasingly elaborate fantasy excursions down the memory lanes of themselves and their ancestors. A recent development is the admission and encouragement that this can legitimately be fantasy, alongside the education, politics and raw economic rationales (Jordanova 1989: 23).

Japan's economic success of the 1980s, along with the popularity of newly constituted ideas of *reja*, or 'leisure', enabled entrepreneurs, public servants and wealthy dreamers to stretch these ideas of fantasy travel to exciting new limits, and in this chapter I would like to introduce and examine some examples. They are divided into three sections: the first presents time travel, with parallels to the first section of this book, thus including historical travel in the present; the second focuses on travel in space, or the places that made it possible for visitors to travel within Japan but imagine themselves much farther away; and the third turns to look at fantasy travels in both time and space. In all cases, we remain physically within the nation of Japan, and for the most part the visitors are Japanese, but in the penultimate section of this chapter I will seek to place the Japanese materials in a broader context, predominantly Asian.

So what am I setting out to describe here? Are the objects of our attentions museums? Well, some might be. Are they localised fairs or exhibitions? Not usually, though they could be included. Are they perhaps Japanese versions of heritage centres? They might include those as well. Are they still serious and educational, or are they purely playful? Can they actually be compared with some pre-existing phenomena, or are they something new and different? I would like to suggest that we reserve judgement about these Japanese locations until we have had a chance to examine them. They do have names, but the ways they are categorised are quite various, and I hesitate to introduce them by those categories for fear of invoking a preconception in the reader, who may hold a pre-existing idea of how such a place should be. Let us try to look at them with fresh eyes, starting with places available for travel back through time. In this chapter, I will not be considering places where one might carry out fantasy travel into the future, though such a thing would not, in fact, be outside the bounds of possibility!

Travel in time

There are quite a few possibilities for time travel in Japan, and these also seem to attract substantial visitor numbers. A phenomenon already discussed in some detail by the co-editor of this volume, Okpyo Moon (1997), is the way older parts of historical towns have been reconstructed to create a lived impression of a time of historical glory. Streets are set apart, 'offending modern facilities such as glass windows or automatic doors' are removed, local people dress in period costume and, as they go about their business, they may even exaggerate regional accents to accentuate the experience for visitors of taking a fantasy trip into the past. Moon's fieldwork was in Aizu Wakamatsu, where the successful re-creation of older parts of the town was achieved by the Aizu Retro Society, offering local people the added value of reconstituting local identity at the same time as attracting visitors to revitalise the economy.

Moon's work was set in the context of governmental support for all kinds of efforts to revitalise parts of Japan that were losing out to urbanisation (*mura-* or *machi-okoshi*) (see also Moon 2002), in particular to the out-migration of young people, and in the late 1980s it became popular to encourage and interpret travel to these places, and others, to be for reasons of nostalgia (Creighton 1997; Ivy 1995; Knight 1993; Martinez 1990; Robertson 1988). As well as the reconstruction of parts of historical towns, then, whole rural villages have been created from abandoned houses, sometimes even moved to the site from their original location so that a complete community can be presented, with names and occupations attached to the buildings to complete the fantasy experience. A good example of this phenomenon is to be found as a side-trip to another of these famous historical towns, namely Takayama, and the side-trip to Hida Folk Village. The setting for this now largely imaginary community is particularly stunning, summer and winter, for the thatched roofs of the wooden houses blend charmingly with the surrounding green hills and foliage, and the whole becomes a complete picture postcard when enveloped in a dusting of newly fallen snow.

There are now many of these reconstructed places, and local people have found features to advertise their own as something special. An early one on the island of Shikoku is accessed by a clever suspension bridge woven from local vines, which sways across a deep gorge, immediately thrusting the visitor into a spine-chilling experience, though it must have been quite mundane in the past. This *Shikoku Mura* also has a thatched theatre among its working buildings, and events here add to the fantasy element. A writer who has investigated in some detail the circumstances surrounding the decisions to reconstruct historical buildings, from farmhouses to castles, is Adolf Ehrentraut (1989, 1995), who again drew on the theme of nostalgia, but he also explains how this was positively exploited for local economic and political purposes. Like other writers, he commented on the idealisation and aestheticisation of these representations of the past, but of course these elements are perfectly attuned to the idea of creating a little piece of fantasy in attracting visitors.

More fanciful again, however, are big parks that have actually built from scratch a historical environment, perhaps drawing on the history of a local area, but taking advantage of technological wizardry to add to the excitement of the story-telling they set out to achieve. The first one I visited was in Hokkaido, near Noboribetsu, and it aimed to reproduce highlights of the Tokugawa period of power of the Daté family, a fiefdom of northern Japan, with its chief lord based in Sendai. The robed players who wandered amongst the beautiful buildings and gardens that had been laid out in the appropriate period style included characters from a television series popular at the time, several *ninja*, who also carried out a staged display at regular intervals, and even the odd pantalooned Portuguese visitor, probably in this case marking the proximity of Hakodate, an important northern port for foreign ships and site of some of the earlier foreign settlements in Japan.

In the central, heavily populated strip of Japan, a beautiful park dedicated to the warring periods of the fifteenth and sixteenth centuries features the reproduction of an entire castle, including a great hall where a cunning combination of film, standing suits of armour, quadraphonic loudspeakers, and a shuddering floor enable the visitor to experience a simulation of the feelings of actually being immersed in a battle scene. Other constructions in the same park represent huge battlements, Buddhist temples and statues, and three different kinds of theatre, again offering performances at intervals throughout the day. Of course this is idealised, then, and it is certainly aestheticised; it makes no special claims to be an 'authentic' representation, though the buildings are impressively put together, and the theatrical players take time to explain customs of the period, such as encouraging the audience to throw money at the cast – which they did in abundance when I took part in this particular piece of fantasy.

There are of course museums that represent the past in Japan, and interestingly enough they also often offer something of a fantasy experience. The Edo Museum in Tokyo, for example, displays booths that are built like the interiors of little shops, and an open-air part of the museum offers a collection of whole houses, complete with interiors furnished in the style of the period. Not far from Nagoya, there is a museum called Meiji Mura where buildings have been brought together to illustrate the way that Western styles began to modify the Japanese traditional ones, some with a proud Western front but still comfortably Japanese behind the scenes. Inside the buildings, vignettes of life in the Meiji period are enhanced with music, Western flower arrangements and facsimiles of newspapers of the time. Museums, yes, they are named as such, but an element of fantasy travel is rather encouraged inside them!

Travels in space

In this section, I would like to consider some internal Japanese tourist destinations that make possible a kind of fantasy travel that I think had only been attempted in miniature in the past. The famous Madurodam in Amsterdam is one example of such a construction, in this case a Dutch town; in Bourton-on-the-Water, in the Cotswold district of England, a miniature version of the village has been created; and in Japan, too, it is possible to make a fantasy world tour by visiting a site named Tobu World Square, where a kind of history of world architecture is presented, but again in miniature. The visitor is thus always a Gulliver, with the buildings a Lilliput, and it is not easy to imagine oneself participating in the scene. In Japan in the 1980s, however, a veritable plethora of full-size reconstructions of foreign locations made it possible to plan a whole world tour, all inside the borders of the Japanese nation!

I have written about this phenomenon already in several places (Hendry 1997a, 1997b, 2000a, 2000b, 2007), so here let me simply summarise the kinds of places that have been offered in this genre. An early example was entitled Canadian World, a pleasant piece of parkland in the heart of Hokkaido, where the scenery was already said to be somewhat European, but actually chosen to represent an area of eastern North America known as Prince Edward Island. The reason for this was a decision by the local constructors of the park to adopt a fictitious character already famous and popular in Japan, and to build the fantasy visit around her story. The character is Anne of Green Gables, and many of the sites of the adventures created for her by

Lucy Maud Montgomery were reconstructed right here in this location. At the height of its popularity, actors were even brought from Canada to play the parts of Anne and her friends, and visitors could sign up for a mini English class with her in the school (see Figure 5.1) or to take tea with her at 4 p.m.

The adoption of fictitious characters for these fantasy places has been quite a common ploy, so that Hans Christian Andersen characters and their stories are featured in the Danish-inspired Nixe Park, and those of the Brothers Grimm in the German Glücks Königreich, both still in Hokkaido. In another large park, this time in central Japan, a large place called Parque España has big statues of Don Quixote and Sancho Panza at the entrance, and depictions of them offering theatre inside, but the fantasy goes much further. Here there are four distinct areas to visit. The first is *Ciudad*, where full-size buildings, streets, plazas and statues offer an area in which to stroll and shop, for franchise outlets of stores from Spanish-speaking countries of Latin America, as well as Spain, are abundantly available. The second zone is *Campo*, where the narrow streets and whitewashed houses (see Figure 5.2) again offer outlets to buy 'local' crafts, but one can also see them being made, and sip drinks and other refreshments in neat, Spanish-seeming outdoor cafés. The third zone is *El Mar*, quite literally by the seaside, and the fourth *Fiesta*, decorated in the Gaudí style of Barcelona, but also offering rides and other kinds of play. Throughout the park are real live Spanish artists, playing music, dancing and even performing little skits of street theatre for the

Figure 5.1 Anne of Green Gables and her friends Gilbert and Diana, portrayed at Canadian World in Hokkaido.

Figure 5.2 A street in the *Campo* section of Spain Village on the Ise peninsula.

passing public to admire. A day spent here is veritably an experience to fantasise; it is clearly not Spain, for the visit requires a few hours of train travel, or a short flight at most, but it is probably the nearest thing you can get to it without actually going there!

The most famous of these fantasy locations is actually not this one, nor is it the biggest. Outdoing them all is a Dutch park again, this time named after the Queen's palace in The Hague, or Huis ten Bosch, but actually located in Kyushu, the southernmost of Japan's four main islands. Alongside the palace, reproduced with all its lovely formal gardens, many other copies of actual buildings from Holland have been built full-size here, as are houses, churches and schools from the respective countries featured in the other places. Here, however, are rows of Dutch houses of various periods, available for purchase as second homes, windmills and tulip fields, of course, and no fewer than three enormous hotels offering rooms and service to rival their originals in Holland. There is a huge World Bazaar, selling merchandise and food from almost anywhere else, and there are bicycles to rent, European-style boats and buses to board, as visitors need a little help to navigate the land that borders no fewer than six kilometres of canalway. This fantasy experience was clearly designed to last more than an hour or two.

There are several other locations that set out to represent a single country, but there are also places where a range of full-size buildings offer the chance of a wider fantasy tour, like the miniature one mentioned above. One of these is called Little World: Museum of Mankind, so clearly choosing a designation in terms of genre, but the same fantasy experience is quite easy to make here too. Some of the buildings offer suits of clothes in the style of the location of the origin of the buildings, for example so that visitors may dress up as a French peasant from Alsace, a maiden from Bavaria or an Indian gentleman and have the resultant scene recorded on film or photograph. Festivals are celebrated here too, and invitations issued to people from the chosen place to come to Japan and create the authentic flavour of the way the season is marked in their own country. Food and drink are available in various locations throughout the park, and the same international style is represented in the dishes offered. Sight, sounds, taste and touch, then, all add to the fantasy of a museum visit.

Travel in time and space

Many of the locations in Japan available for a fantasy visit of this sort in fact combine the two dimensions of time and space in the same destination. Indeed, the first foreign village to be constructed was a place called Hollanda-*mura*, probably chosen because of its proximity to Deshima, the site of the only foreign settlement in Japan during the 250 years of Tokugawa seclusion. Now it is rather small fry, though quite charming (see Figure 5.3), and in addition a handsome Dutch galleon sets out from Huis ten Bosch to take visitors to this historical version of the Dutch experience. Actually, Huis ten Bosch itself features several museums, some of which recount stories of the

Figure 5.3 One of the early depictions of a Japanese historical link at Holland Village in Kyushu.

past relationship between Japan and Holland, or the lives of Dutch people and other Europeans who came to live in Japan. Typically, life-size models of the characters are displayed in a diorama, or perhaps sitting at a table, and this fantasy piece of time travel can also be quite educational.

Another major example of the way that fantasy travel may combine time and space is to be found at the Maruyama Shakespeare Park at the southern end of the Boso peninsula. This park has reconstructed the birthplace of the English playwright, which it claims is more like the house he would have lived in than the 'real' birthplace in Stratford-upon-Avon, because of being 'unsullied by the passage of time, and its later occupants' (publicity and noticeboards, translated into English). There are life-size reproductions of various characters here, too, each apparently having been made from genuine English models, as I heard when I happened to meet one of the people who had played this role. The visitor can thus gaze upon William's father, working at his trade of making gloves, see his mother in the kitchen, or even be inspired by the man himself, as he sits nursing his young son, Hamnet, but at a window where he can wistfully peruse the road to London.

The marital bed (see Figure 5.4) is carefully furnished with sixteenth-century-style coverings, edged with Brussels lace, according to the guide, and like all the other materials imported directly from Europe. A cradle like one that might have rocked the baby bard is available for inspection, as are many other features of the home, and the whole is set in gardens characteristic of the time, offering a range of herbs for cooking and medicinal purposes (the physic garden). The site also features a reconstruction of New Place, the home that Shakespeare is reported to have built for himself in later life but that later burned down, and the home of his mother, Mary Arden, whose original does still stand in the Warwickshire countryside. There are also other features of English tradition, such as a lych-gate, a maypole, and a set of stocks, and in the spring, on Shakespeare's birthday, I understand that a festival is held that brings these features to life! A large formal garden is laid out in front of New Place, which features statues of classical characters from Rome and Greece that have influenced Shakespeare's plays, and inside the buildings visitors can see representations and explanations of other possible influences on his life.

To support the evidence of this fantasy argument, I add material from a couple of informal interviews I carried out during visits to this park. The first was actually in a train travelling in the direction of the place, when I noticed a fellow passenger carefully examining the brochures, so I broached a conversation with him. He was a retired gentleman, life-long lover of Shakespeare and all things English, it seemed, and he told me that he had been looking forward to this visit for some time. It had been a kind of dream for him, since he was probably too old now to travel to England itself, so he was relishing the idea of spending the day enjoying all the materials that had been brought together to create a near-English experience.

In fact, the original park had also been built as a kind of dream, again by a

Figure 5.4 An imagined reproduction of the marital bed of William Shakespeare and his wife at the Shakespeare Park in Maruyama, Chiba prefecture.

life-long lover of Shakespeare, it was explained to me by one of the local publicists, this time a philanthropist with wealth to invest, who had helped encourage the local council to choose this way of revitalising the area, as described earlier in the chapter. Fields of the herb rosemary had been planted at first, creating a pleasant area for walking and breathing the aroma, accompanied by a soft rendering of music that had been selected to enhance the experience. The whole park had been designed to appeal to all five senses, he continued. The 'physic garden' is another example of the appeal to smell, perhaps as well as feel, and the visual is clear in the buildings and other constructions. Mary Arden's house is furnished inside as a café serving herbal teas and cakes to add the element of taste, and it offers for sale dried flowers and English corn dollies, each of which have quite a distinctive feel to them. Finally, I was introduced to a local Shakespearean scholar, who took me into the reconstructed Renaissance theatre that formed part of New Place, on normal days adding cinema to the fantasy experience, on high days and holidays extracts from the Shakespearean plays that inspired the whole venture.

Analysis of genre

What, then, have we here? Now we have presented examples of the phenomenon under consideration, let us attempt some kind of classification. It was mentioned at the outset that the places we have considered call themselves by various titles, and the press has picked up on others, so let's start out with a consideration of the possibilities. Museums have been mentioned throughout, and some of the places are described as foreign or historical 'villages', using the Japanese term *mura*, but a third form of classification, particularly used in the press and other popular analyses, is to call these places *tēma pāku*, a literal translation of 'theme park'. Now this last term is linguistically quite accurate, for all the places described have adopted themes to develop, but my chief concern with this appellation is that it evokes more negative images in the minds of those familiar with the genre in English-speaking countries than the places themselves deserve.

The reason that this term has been adopted within the Japanese context is not hard to discern, because most of the places in question were designed, built and opened in the leisure boom (*rejā būmu*) that followed the outstanding success of Tokyo Disneyland, a franchised version of the American outlets of the same name. This was clearly a 'theme park' in American parlance, and it was also full of fantasy, so it is not a difficult leap of association to make. However, visitors to the parks in Japan and America have been shown to hold different understandings of the use of the term and the purpose of such a location, so that, in a nutshell, a theme park in America (and even more so in the UK) is largely a place for thrilling rides, whereas in Japan the idea of taking a fantasy visit to America seemed to predominate (see, for example, Brannen 1992; Notoji 1990; Van Maanen 1992; all summarised in Hendry 2000a, Ch. 3). Thus the *gaikoku mura*, or 'foreign villages', simply offered a range of other possible countries about which to fantasise.

One big difference in the way that the parks are constructed struck me from the start of my research. In Britain and the United States, foreign themes may be chosen for theme parks, but little care is taken to represent them with any kind of accuracy, and a 'samurai woman' I saw in a park in the UK sported a bare midriff which would be entirely inappropriate for female attire in Japan. I suspect that the influence for that idea came from somewhere much more Middle Eastern, and even then hardly a woman of military class! In Busch Gardens, in the States, a representation of Big Ben, a famous London landmark, was blatantly located at Banbury Cross, a situation actually 80 miles north-west of London, and several other geographical gaffes were quite unashamedly portrayed (see Hendry 2000a: 78–81 for further detail).

In the Japanese so-called theme parks, however, buildings are copied as far as possible to replicate original models, employees are actually transported from the countries to be represented, first to construct the buildings and their surroundings, and then to demonstrate local crafts, present artistic accomplishments and generally add an air of authenticity to the place. Glücks Königreich in Hokkaido, for example, boasts cobble-stoned streets, built by German craftsmen with cobble stones from Germany; the construction of the Shakespearean park involved architects, designers and craftsmen from England, one of them chair of the Shakespeare trust in Stratford-on-Avon. Huis ten Bosch used so many Dutch red bricks in its construction that the quantity outstripped that of any other export enterprise for a whole year (Robertson 1997). And each of these parks invites European artists to visit, in Glücks Königreich to play classical music and demonstrate ballroom dancing, in the Shakespearean park to recite the words of the bard, and in Huis ten Bosch, students of Leiden University, who have their Japanese campus in the queen's palace, are paid to walk around in clogs and Dutch traditional clothes (if they are blond enough)!

The most immediate response of most of the early researchers who encountered these parks was to cast them in a post-modern idiom. They were clustered together, even described as 'European villages' (Kelsky), and they were seen as simulations (after Baudrillard 1983) or Disneyesque versions of hyperreality (after Eco 1987). Tokyo Disneyland was certainly an influential precursor to the phenomenon, but after some examination of the literature on Disney (e.g. Fjellman 1992; Hunt and Frankenberg 1990; Mills 1990; Moore 1980; Raz 1999) I decided that this approach is at best misguided, at worst horribly ethnocentric. Disneyland is just one of the *gaikoku mura* – an American one – which 'represents the best that America has to offer' (Akiba Toshiharu, quoted in Brannen 1992: 216). Canada is hardly 'European' either, though I suppose it may appear so from the United States of America!

I found it more rewarding to compare the parks with museums, a word that, after all, was sometimes used in their titles. There are several reasons for this. First, the purpose of a museum is not universally agreed, despite heavy European influence, and the preservation and display of original objects are not always given top priority. Indeed, in many parts of the world, including Japan, constructing a replica of an object is thought both to make a more effective display and better to preserve the earlier form. Consider the museum at the Ise Shrine, for example, and the Ethnographic Museum at Senri Park in Osaka, where many of the Japanese objects are specially created for display. A precious object of ancient origin is valued, to be sure, but it might well be thought preferable to keep it wrapped up than on view in a glass case.

The second reason why I feel justified in making a comparison with museums is that, even in Europe, the character of these establishments is changing. The former emphasis on observation and learning, largely aimed at an intellectual and social elite, is giving way to ideas of interaction, experience and entertainment, very often designed to popularise the activity and raise funds through entrance fees (e.g. Macdonald 1996). In this respect, our

Japanese parks are literally streets ahead of Europe, attracting much more popular support than the glass cases which some of them may also own and offer. Wherever they are found, museums have been described as turning culture into an object, as classifying it and materialising it. To quote the anthropologist Sharon Macdonald and other authors in her book *Theorizing Museums*, 'They have played a role not just in displaying the world, but in structuring a (modern) way of seeing and comprehending the world "as if it were an exhibit" ' (1996: 7).

Japanese 'theme parks' play just such a role. There is little government intervention, of course, and the relative absence of scholars removes them from the charge of imposing an elite world view on the apparently ignorant public, as many museums are said to do. Museums in the West developed in the wake of exploration and imperialist expansion (cf. Prösler 1996), so perhaps these parks may be seen as a type of world appropriation of a different order (cf. Hendry 1997b), or they could be seen as a simple expression of 'internationalisation'. In fact it may be rather appropriate to be a little fanciful in considering the meaning of these theme park/museums. In a recent book entitled *The New Museology*, which sets out to examine the nature and purpose of museums in a changing world, we are soon reminded by one author that 'Feelings about the antiquity, the authenticity, the beauty, the craftsmanship, the poignancy of objects are the stepping-stones towards fantasies' (Jordanova 1989: 23). Clearly the older, more staid variety of glass showcase museum requires more fantasy in the observer than a theme park, and in a country where 'Architecture is one of the most inspired and inspiring manifestations of [its] civilization' (Coaldrake 1996: xix) what could be more appropriate than creating parks full of buildings to gaze upon?

Look to Asia

In fact the Japanese case is not so unusual when it is examined in the context of other Asian countries, for there are several examples of parks where buildings have been carefully constructed to portray a particular theme, often enough also associated with identity. The first such park I came across was in South Korea, a pleasing place within easy reach of the capital city known as the Korean Folk Village. Unusually, it is both a popular destination for outings and a site of scholarly research. Here over a hundred buildings have been preserved, conserved and reconstructed, to show how life was lived in the long Choson period (1392–1910), preceding Japanese occupation and South Korea's entry into the industrialised world. There are demonstrations of traditional crafts, such as silk production, fan making and pottery throwing, examples of beautiful celadon vases and other exquisite materials for sale, and many houses are open to illustrate the layout of everyday life in pre-modern Korea. There is a scholar's house, and a farmer's house, and some have games laid out as well as the work of the family day. There are also illustrations of ritual and ceremony, as it was practised at the time and continues to be practised, and these displays vary appropriately with the season. This was my first exposure to such a combination of research and commercial 'entertainment', and it was the place I found with the most academic emphasis, but it is by no means exclusive to Korea.

Another example is to be found in Thailand, again a site within a day's outing from the capital, and, although it is quite extensive, a quick tour could be made in a morning or an afternoon. This park contains a mixture of full-size buildings that have been brought for preservation to *Muang Boran*, or the Ancient City, old buildings that have been copied there, and some others that are reconstructions in sizes reduced from their original models. They represent several periods in Thai architectural history, rather than the way of life of any particular period, though there is also a floating market and a small village area. There are also temples, palaces and other larger public buildings. This park was the dream child of a philanthropist who wanted to conserve some of the many building styles that the country has spawned over the years, and its open, grassy surroundings provide a pleasant backdrop to the collection.

In Indonesia, an even bigger establishment offers a space for each of the nation's provinces to construct some of its own representative buildings, along with displays of local material culture, and even sometimes food and souvenirs. Some of the houses within the provinces of Indonesia are particularly spectacular, so that the visitor is spoilt for choice, and this park took me three days to visit properly. It also contains several national museums around the side, including individual ones devoted to flora, fauna and even stamps and telecommunications, and it has a huge open space for parades and other big national events. Taman Mini Indonesia Indah was apparently built according to the whim of Madame Soeharto (Pemberton 1994: 201; Stanley 1998: 58), but supported as a project to stand for the national motto of Unity in Diversity. The park is popular with local people as well as foreign visitors, and on Sunday mornings the roads around it become quite clogged up as people make their way there to visit their own provincial area, or perhaps to watch a play in one of the many theatres offering a great variety of programmes.

Parks comparable to this one are to be found in Malaysia and Singapore, the former called Mini Malaysia, the latter the Asian Cultural Village (see Figure 5.5), and both, like Taman Mini, present the variety of cultural difference to be found in their sites of location, within the context of a national history. Singapore also has a park that shows the history of the island and its various colonial occupants in a series of dioramas, and there is another park that offers each of the ASEAN countries space to build a typical dwelling. Actually these parks have lost some of their sparkle recently, and other attractions, or educational opportunities, have perhaps displaced them in a local popular view. However, they certainly offer a series of basic construction models for Japan's range of fantasy travel possibilities, and broaden the comparative base from that of European museums and American theme parks.

Figure 5.5 Entrance to the Sentosa Asian Village, Singapore.

The nearest comparison to some of the Japanese reproductions of foreign countries is to be found in China, however, where a huge park was built in Shenzhen, the area of mainland China closest to Hong Kong, which was developed as a special economic zone before the handover of Hong Kong from Britain back to the Chinese in 1999. Actually there are three parks, two of which represent Chinese peoples and places: one named Splendid China reproduces many of the famous sites of the Chinese nation in miniature form, and the other contains a selection of houses and people from 31 of the 56 designated Chinese 'nationalities', or minority peoples. The third park is named Window of the World, and features sites from almost every corner of the earth, reproduced in a variety of different sizes, so that a very small version of London's Buckingham Palace is dwarfed by a half-size version of the ancient English standing stones known as Stonehenge at its side. A repro-duction of Himeji castle is also rather small, but a Japanese tea house has been built at normal size so that it can be entered and examined. Perhaps the most extraordinary constructions are reduced versions of Niagara Falls and the Grand Canyon, reduced but still big enough to dwarf the visitors and make quite an impression of size.

Conclusion

There are several precedents for the material manifestations that form the focus of Japanese fantasy travel, then, but none quite as fanciful, and none quite as concerned to fulfil internal intentions of authenticity. The names chosen to depict them in international terms are rarely quite accurate, for these are places that have an attraction all of their own, and there is something very Japanese about them. The reasons for this are not easy to discern, but in the context of this volume I think we can claim to have found an interesting modern version of the *tabi*, taking full advantage of up-to-date technology and the economic benefits that accrued during Japan's global commercial success.

Bibliography

Baudrillard, J. (1983). *Simulacra and Simulations*, trans. Paul Foss, Paul Patton and Philip Beitchman. New York: Semiotext(e).

Brannen, M.Y. (1992). ' "Bwana Mickey": constructing cultural consumption at Tokyo Disneyland'. In J. Tobin (ed.), *Remade in Japan*. New Haven, CT, and London: Yale University Press, pp. 216–34.

Coaldrake, W.H. (1996). *Architecture and Authority in Japan*. London: Routledge.

Creighton, M.R. (1997). 'Consuming rural Japan: the marketing of tradition in the Japanese travel industry'. *Ethnology*, 36(3), pp. 239–54.

Eco, U. (1987). *Travels in Hyperreality*. London: Picador.

Ehrentraut, A. (1989). 'The visual definition of heritage: the restoration of domestic rural architecture in Japan'. *Visual Anthropology*, 2, pp. 135–61.

—— (1995). 'Cultural nationalism, corporate interests and the production of architectural heritage in Japan'. *Canadian (CRSA/RCSA)*, 32(2), pp. 215–42.

Fjellman, S.M. (1992). *Vinyl Leaves: Walt Disney World and America*. Boulder, CO, San Francisco and Oxford: Westview Press.

Hendry, J. (1997a). 'Who is representing whom? Gardens, theme-parks and the anthropologist in Japan'. In A. James, J. Hockey and A. Dawson (eds), *After Writing Culture: Epistemology and Praxis in Contemporary Anthropology*. London: Routledge.

—— (1997b). 'The whole world as heritage? Foreign country theme parks in Japan'. In W. Nuryanti (ed.), *Tourism and Heritage Management*. Yogyakarta, Indonesia: Gadjah Mada University Press.

—— (2000a). *The Orient Strikes Back: A Global View of Cultural Display*. Oxford: Berg.

—— (2000b). 'Foreign country parks: a new theme or an old Japanese pattern?'. *Social Science of Japan Journal*, 3(2), pp. 207–20.

—— (2007). 'New gods, old pilgrimages: a whistle-stop tour of Japanese international theme parks'. In M.D. Rodriguez del Alisal, P. Ackermann and D.P. Martinez (eds), *Inspired Journeys: Pilgrimage, Travels and Encounters of Identity in Japanese Culture*. London and New York: Routledge Curzon.

Hunt, P. and R. Frankenberg (1990). 'It's a small world: Disneyland, the family and the multiple re-representations of American childhood'. In A. James and A. Prout (eds), *Constructing and Reconstructing Childhood*. London: Falmer, pp. 99–117.

Ivy, M. (1995). *Discourses of the Vanishing: Modernity, Phantasm, Japan*. Chicago: University of Chicago Press.

Jordanova, L. (1989). 'Objects of knowledge: a historical perspective on museums'. In P. Vergo (ed.), *The New Museology*. London: Reaktion Books.

Knight, J. (1993). 'Rural *kokusaika*: foreign motifs and village revival in Japan'. *Japan Forum*, 5(2), pp. 203–16.

Macdonald, S. (1996). 'Introduction'. In S. Macdonald and G. Fyfe (eds), *Theorizing Museums*. Oxford: Blackwell, pp. 1–18.

Martinez, D.P. (1990). 'Tourism and the *ama*: the search for a real Japan'. In E. Ben-Ari, B. Moeran and J. Valentine (eds), *Unwrapping Japan: Society and Culture in Anthropological Perspective*. Honolulu: Hawaii University Press, pp. 97–116.

Mills, S.F. (1990). 'Disney and the promotion of synthetic worlds'. *American Studies International*, 28(2), pp. 67–79.

Moon, O. (1997). 'Tourism and cultural development: Japanese and Korean contexts'. In Y. Shinji, K.H. Din and J.S. Eades (eds), *Tourism and Cultural Development in Asia and Oceania*, Bangi: Penerbit Universiti Kebansang Malaysia, pp. 178–93.

—— (2002). 'The countryside reinvented for urban tourists: rural transformation in the Japanese *muraokoshi* movement'. In J. Hendry and M. Raveri (eds), *Japan at Play: The Ludic and the Logic of Power*. London and New York: Routledge, pp. 228–44.

Moore, A. (1980). 'Walt Disney World: bounded ritual space and the playful pilgrimage center'. *Anthropological Quarterly*, 53(4), pp. 207–18.

Notoji, M. (1990). *Dizunirando to iu Seichii*. Tokyo: Iwanami Shoten.

Pemberton, J. (1994). 'Recollections from "beautiful Indonesia" (somewhere beyond the postmodern)'. *Public Culture*, 6, pp. 241–62.

Prösler, M. (1996). 'Museums and globalization'. In S. Macdonald and G. Fyfe (eds), *Theorizing Museums*. Oxford: Blackwell, pp. 21–44.

Raz, A. (1999). *Riding the Black Ship: Japan and Tokyo Disneyland*. Cambridge, MA, and London: Harvard University Press.

Robertson, J. (1988). '*Furusato* Japan: the culture and politics of nostalgia'. *Politics, Culture and Society*, 1(4), pp. 494–518.

—— (1997). Internationalization and nostalgia: a critical interpretation'. In S. Vlastos (ed.), *Mirror of Modernity: Invented Traditions in Modern Japan*. Berkeley: University of California Press.

Stanley, N. (1998). *Being Ourselves for You: The Global Display of Cultures*. London: Middlesex University Press.

Tema-paaku to yûenji: zenkoku 50 no kairakudo rankingu [Ranking parks and playgrounds] (1995). Special section of a tourism magazine, title misplaced.

Van Maanen, J. (1992). 'Displacing Disney: some notes on the flow of culture'. *Qualitative Sociology*, 15(1), pp. 5–35.

Part III

Travelling the familiar overseas

6   Japanese tourists in Korea

Colonial and post-colonial encounters

Okpyo Moon

Despite the observation that a quest for authentic experience is one of the prime motives of modern travelling (MacCannell 1976: 49), created fantasy worlds seem to whet the tourist appetite as much as, or often more than, the real world does. This is the case not only with the stated fantasy world such as Disneyland or other types of theme parks but also with the supposedly authentic experience tours. Despite the ostensible emphasis upon tradition and the forgotten past in popular *furusato* tourism (nostalgia-seeking tourism visiting an old home town), for instance, what is actually sought after and visited is more often a 'recreated past' rather than the real historical past (Ivy 1995; Creighton 1997). Similarly, as Graburn (2002) has pointed out, the ubiquitous foreign village theme parks (*gaikoku mura*; see also Hendry, Chapter 5 in this volume) that are said to be visited by more than 20 million Japanese people every year present a kind of 'constructed' or 'sanitized' foreignness rid of dangers and fears of actually visiting a country overseas. Whether it is the nature, history or foreignness, what is commonly found in these phenomena is an attempt to 'mark off, contain, and . . . "tame" a section of the wilder [that is, the uncontrollable] terrain . . . for the purpose of tourism' (Hendry 2000: 3).

In 2000, more than 17 million Japanese people travelled abroad, which is about 150 times the number in 1964, when the limitation upon overseas travel was officially removed. Both the strength of the Japanese yen and the quest for global participation explain this continuous growth. If Okinawa appeared as a pseudo-foreign land at an initial stage of Japanese overseas travelling, their chief destinations are now extending to most European countries in addition to the United States and many former Japanese colonies and battlefields in East and South-East Asia (Kageaki 1997; Yamashita, Chapter 7 in this volume). The tendency to fantasize can be noted in Japanese international tourism as well. According to Merry I. White (Chapter 9 in this volume), the recently popularized tourism to Italy satisfies some Japanese, especially female tourists', imagination of the uncontaminated past and of the human touch of the rural life that is believed to have disappeared in Japan in the process of rapid urbanization and consequent depopulation of the villages. These tours are typically organized, conducted and mediated by Japanese expatriates settled in Italy and offer expected repertoire:

The thousands of Japanese who visit Venice every spring (particularly in the first two weeks of May) do not come to a city unprepared for them . . . and because they come in such large numbers to such a very small space they become contained, essentialized and catered to in precisely the terms they themselves expect. . . . Venetians are proud of their unique cuisine and see themselves as a special people apart, more cosmopolitan than Romans, in fact, but they are quite glad to serve up 'Italy' to these customers hungry for the tastes the 'Italy *buumu*' in Japan has created.

(White, Chapter 9 in this volume)

Here again, therefore, it is more of an imagined world than the real that is sought after and experienced. If, as White suggests, 'externalized nostalgia' constitutes an important part of the popular Japanese tourism to Italy, one wonders why they do not visit other Asian countries such as Korea where they would probably find a past that is much closer to their own. Korea shares the tradition of irrigated paddy cultivation and family farm structure that are perhaps the most similar to the Japanese. Common sense dictates, therefore, that, if Japanese tourists are truly looking for their forgotten past, Korea must be the place to visit rather than Italy.

Yet, although it has occupied a significant position in the history of Japanese overseas travelling, tourism to Korea has been notably concentrated upon urban centres. Although colonial Korea was often depicted and represented in the language of pre-modern rurality or femininity (Kim Sŏngnye 1990), there is little sign that Japanese people who actually visited the country were ever attracted to rural villages, even during the colonial period (1910–45) when Korea became one of the major destinations for Japanese international tourism. During the post-war years, Japanese tourism to Korea has seen a great expansion, especially since the 1970s after the relationship between the two countries was normalized in 1965. But this tendency of urban focus has persisted. What Japanese tourists primarily pursued in Korea has remained the familiar and the ordinary, such as karaoke bars, drinking places, pachinko parlours, public baths, hot springs, etc. that can be easily found in the entertainment sectors in any Japanese cities, rather than otherness and change, another important motive that is said to make people travel (Moon 2002). Why, then, within the semiotic world of the Japanese tourist gaze, does Italy stand for rurality and the forgotten past while Korea stands for urban pleasure? Does the colonial legacy have anything to do with this search for the familiarity and relative ease and competence that accompany these tours? How do Japanese tourist expectations and experiences in Korea differ from those they encounter in other countries? These are the questions of some comparative interest that I will try to address in this chapter.

Japanese tourism in Korea: a historical perspective

As the nearest foreign country, Korea has remained one of the most popular destinations of Japanese overseas tourism, next only to the United States and China. In 2005, it is reported that more than 2.4 million Japanese people travelled to Korea, a number that constitutes about 14 per cent of the 17.4 million Japanese who went abroad and about a half of all the foreign tourists received by Korea that year (Nihon Kokudō Kōtsūshō 2006: 21–3). While the history of Japanese tourism to Korea goes back to the colonial period that started at the beginning of the twentieth century, the social composition of Japanese tourists visiting the country has undergone several transformations over the past hundred years or so.

Colonial period (1910–45)

Soon after the Japanese annexation of Korea in 1910, the Japan Travel Bureau (JTB) opened its branch office in Kyŏngsŏng (present-day Seoul, or Keijō in Japanese rendering) and started a modern tourist business with the help of Japanese railway companies promoting the sales of rail passes that connected the colonial Korea and Manchuria (Shirahata 1990: 448; Chōsen Shōdokufu Tetsudōkyoku 1928; Yano 1936). It was apparently an important part of the colonial policy to encourage Japanese people to travel to the newly acquired colonies and feel the glory of the expanding Japanese empire. Those who visited these areas included not only tourists coming directly from Japan but also government officials, soldiers, merchants, reporters, scholars, writers, painters and other colonial settlers. A large number of guidebooks and postcards were printed and distributed for these people, and facilities such as hotels, inns, restaurants and various kinds of pleasure centres began to appear in the major tourist spots in Korea in order to cater for Japanese tourists.

The Diamond Mountains (Kŭmkangsan), which are located in present-day North Korea and are becoming a central place for North–South dialogue, were one of the most popular tourist destinations among the Japanese visiting the colony in these early years. As early as 1921, a well-known Korean writer, Yi Kwang-su, deplored the fact that Koreans had to borrow the words of foreigners, Japanese, German or English writers, in order to learn about and appreciate the beauties of these historically significant mountains (Yi Kwang-su 1924). In the 1920s, there was already a regular train service connecting Kyŏngsŏng to the Diamond Mountains, and the JTB published numerous guidebooks for those who wish to travel to this area. Apart from the Diamond Mountains, however, other destinations were mostly large cities such as Kyŏngsŏng, Pyŏngyang, Pusan, Taegu, Kyŏngju[1] and so forth.

One package advertised in *Tour of Korea* (*Chōsen no Kankō*) published in 1939 clearly shows these preferences (Imai 1939: 26–7). The details of the ten-day itinerary of a return trip from Tokyo to Korea in this package were as follows:

First day: departure from Tokyo and train journey to Shimonoseki (22 hours)

Second day: change to the connecting boat to Pusan at Shimonoseki

Third day: a train journey to Kyŏngsŏng from Pusan

Fourth day: tour in Kyŏngsŏng

Fifth day: tour in Kyŏngsŏng and a short visit to Inchŏn

Sixth day: from Kyŏngsŏng to Pyŏngyang, tour in Pyŏngyang and to Shinŭiju

Seventh day: from Shinŭiju to Taegu (14 hours)

Eighth day: from Taegu to Kyŏngju, tour in Kyŏngju and to Pusan and to Shimonoseki

Ninth day: train journey from Shimonoseki to Tokyo (22 hours)

Tenth day: arrival at Tokyo and return home

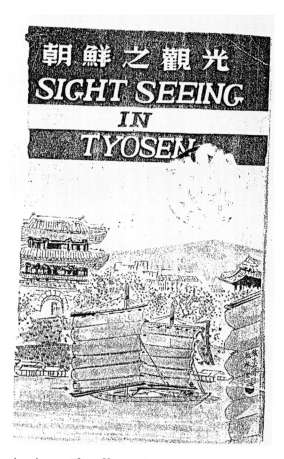

Figure 6.1 An advertisement for a Korean tour.

Source: Imai (1939).

The trip was organized around major cities in Korea, with emphasis on the capital, Kyŏngsŏng. In Kyŏngsŏng itself, the major focus was on propagandizing the features of the colonial governance. So the first-day tour included the *Chōsenjingū* (Chosŏn Shinto Shrine newly built by the colonial government on the South Mountain at a place where the National Shamanic Temple of the Chosŏn Dynasty formerly stood), the newly opened Science Centre, the *Hakubunji* (a Buddhist temple built to commemorate Itō Hirobumi),[2] Ch'anggyŏng Garden (former Ch'anggyŏng palace turned into a park with a zoo, modelled on the Ueno Park),[3] the Kyŏngsŏng stadium, and sightseeing at Honmachi-dōri (present-day Myŏngdong) and Chongno at night, etc. The second-day tour included the Commerce and Industry Promotion Centre, Kyŏngbok Palace, the Colonial Government Building, Pagoda Park and so forth.

While actual places visited by Japanese travellers concentrated on urban centres and newly constructed modern colonial facilities, many of the postcards printed and circulated during the Japanese colonial period emphasized images of pre-modern exoticism. For instance, most of the tourist postcards of the time depicted Korea with images of rural rather than urban, female rather than male, elderly people or children rather than lively young men, passive and static rather than active and moving, traditional and past-oriented rather than progressive and modern (Kwŏn Haeng-ga 2002). The continuous reproduction and wide distribution of these images helped Japanese travellers to perceive colonial Korea as something to be conquered, enlightened, modernized, desired and consumed.

The representation of colonial Korea mainly with images of folkloric rural character and femininity can be observed not only in commercialized postcards and advertisements but also in scholarly representations, art works and so forth. According to a Korean art historian, Kim Youngna, there were four major criteria of the Korea Art Exhibition (*Chōsenbijutsuten*) inaugurated in 1922 by the colonial government: 'rural colour', 'local colour', 'Korean colour' and 'something that is unique to the Korean peninsula' (*hantōsei*), and only those works that satisfied these criteria in the eyes of mostly Japanese examiners were recognized, selected and exhibited. Even in the depiction of rural life, what was preferred and selected was leisurely and pastoral landscapes appealing to the nostalgia of the modernized or modernizing Japanese rather than realistic paintings that conveyed the hardship of the life of Korean peasants of the time (Kim Youngna 2002: 298–9).

In other words, various media including scholarly and journalistic writings, art works, postcards and other types of commercial advertisement available at the time participated in the construction and dissemination of images of colonial Korea as backward, underdeveloped, pre-industrial, feminine, static and passive, close to nature, etc. and provided Japanese travellers to Korea with a basis for forming a specific kind of 'tourist gaze' (Urry 1990). It is not very difficult to imagine, therefore, that the pre-conceived images thus acquired led many Japanese travellers to accept the inevitability of colonial rule and beneficial features of colonial administration. It may also be said that the promotion of tourism during this period focusing on urban centres and developed areas in the conquered area served well as a means of effective political propaganda supporting the legitimacy of colonial domination.

Post-war years: the 1960s and 1970s

It was only after the normalization of the Korea–Japan relationship in 1965 that Japanese tourism to Korea was once again revitalized. Tourism was an important part of development strategies for many Third World countries that were attempting an economic take-off in the 1960s and 1970s, and Korea was no exception. Soon after the UN declaration of the Year of World Tourism in 1967, the Korean government adopted a policy of promoting the tourist industry and started various measures to lure the Japanese, who had been long-time guests of the country since the colonial period. It was also around this time that Japanese international tourism began to increase rapidly after the official elimination of the regulations regarding overseas travelling in 1964.

The number of Japanese visiting Korea had seen an unprecedented increase in the 1970s. Official statistics show that only 1,864 Japanese travelled to Korea in 1964, just before the liberalization of overseas travelling, but it increased to about 45,000 in 1970 and again to more than 411,000 in 1973. In 1979, the number reached over 526,000, and more than 90 per cent of them were reported to be male travellers. This extreme male concentration is notable when compared with travellers to other countries. For instance, although it is true that overseas travelling had remained as a male area especially at an initial stage, only 50–60 per cent of those who travelled to the United States and West European countries in the 1970s were reported to be male travellers (Muroi and Sasaki 1997: 185).

The earliest flock of Japanese tourists into Korea was middle-aged men who often combined sex tourism with business transactions. In many Japanese companies, the employees were treated with a yearly trip abroad in recognition of their loyal service and contribution to the company, and the destination of such trips was invariably one of the Asian countries such as Thailand, the Philippines, Taiwan or Korea. Also, with increasing economic transactions with Japan after the normalization of the relationship in 1965, it came to constitute a routine service for many Korean businessmen to treat their potential Japanese investors and business partners with various kinds of female services and entertainment. Even apart from these business-related trips, Japanese tour companies organized many male-only packages visiting one of the Asian countries.

Since the early 1970s, however, these practices, commonly known as *kisaeng* (female entertainers) parties or *kisaeng* tourism in Korea, came under severe attack from women's groups in Japan and abroad. In 1972, for instance, the Korean Christian Women's Association officially raised criticism against *kisaeng* tourism (Han'guk kyohoe yŏsŏng yŏnhaphoe 1983). In 1973, student demonstrations were reported at Kimpo airport protesting against Japanese men entering the country for the purpose of *kisaeng* tourism, and again in 1974 Japanese women's groups organized demonstrations at Haneda airport in order to stop the boarding of Japanese sex tourists (Muroi and Sasaki 1997: 188). Also, within Japan, men who wished to visit Korea came to be seen with suspicion, especially by their wives, as it was believed that they primarily went there to 'buy women'. The Korean government itself also discouraged the practice, as it was seen as a national disgrace. Perhaps as a result of the protests and criticisms, Japanese sex tourism to Korea, at least in an overt form, notably decreased toward the late 1970s, although it remained a controversial social issue in the Philippines and Thailand well into the 1980s.

Japanese sex tourism in Asia is closely linked to the pre-war history of colonial domination. In his study of colonial postcards, Kwŏn (2002) shows that one of the most prevalent images of Korea depicted was that of *kisaeng*, female entertainers, and that they were prime attractions for many Japanese tourists during the colonial period. While, in traditional Korea, most of the *kisaeng* were *yegi* (artistic entertainers), who need to be distinguished from prostitutes, the distinction became blurred, as the colonial government did not recognize it and abolished the institution of *yegi* (Son Chŏng-mok 1996; Yamashita Young-ae 1997).[4] A report written in the early 1930s described the experiences of Japanese travellers in Kyŏngsŏng as follows:

> The *yojŏng* [*ryōtei* in Japanese, a special type of restaurant where *kisaeng* entertainment was provided] and *kisaeng* in Kyŏngsŏng never comes under the scrutiny of the disciplinary measures of the police. There are altogether some 80 *yojŏng* of various classes in Hoehyŏndong and Namsandong [newly created Japanese quarters] alone, the first-class ones boasting magnificent buildings and gardens. These *yojŏng* are lighted until late at night, where men are overwhelmed with passion and money is wasted lavishly. The Land of Confucian Gentlemen in the East is now filled with the pleasures of women and drinking both day and night. Men of Showa Japan must be the children born with the blessings of Bacchus.[5]

It clearly shows that the colony was perceived and consumed as an object of desire. In the years following the Japanese annexation, large cities in Korea including Kyŏngsŏng, the places most frequently visited by the Japanese, saw a rapid increase in prostitution and entertainment quarters such as *yojŏng* (Mok Suhyŏn 2003). An apparent continuity can be observed between the pre-war and the post-war Japanese perception of Korea and in the ways in which tourism was later promoted in Korea. The tourist posters printed and distributed by the Korean government in the 1970s, for instance, invariably depicted women in Korean traditional dress either dancing or playing musical instruments such as *kayagŭm* (12-stringed Korean harp) (Kwŏn Hyŏkhee

2003: 202). The continuity with *kisaeng* images in the postcards of the colonial period cannot be missed.

The use of young female images in visual representation of a country and tourism promotion is not limited to Korea but is widely found in Asian countries such as Singapore, Thailand, the Philippines, Hong Kong, etc. These images can be contrasted with other popular tourist images: Big Ben, Westminster Abbey or the Tower of London for the United Kingdom, the Eiffel Tower, Louvre Museum, cafés or excellent wines for France, modern high-rise buildings in Manhattan, New York, or magnificent natural scenery like the Grand Canyon or Niagara Falls for the United States. In comparison, most tourist images produced and distributed by Asian countries have in them prominently shot beautiful young women, with sexual implications, even when they feature historical buildings such as temples or palaces.

Figure 6.2 A tourist poster of the 1970s.

Source: Korea Tourist Bureau.

Hall, in his analysis of the connection between Australian sex tourism and prostitution in Asian countries, points out that the relationship between those who sell sex and those who buy it in the context of tourism closely reflects the already existing relationship of dependency between advanced countries and South-East Asian countries (Hall 1992: 74). In other words, it can be said that the nature of the Korean host/Japanese guest relationship in the context of tourism had not changed much from the colonial period at least until the 1970s. Japanese tourists visiting Korea remained mostly male, and their demand and gaze shaped and conditioned the tourist infrastructure rebuilt in Korea in post-normalization years.

In addition to those who visited Korea directly or indirectly for sexual adventures, there was another type of Japanese tourists whom I may term 'returnees'. After the opening of Korea in the late nineteenth century, some Japanese and Chinese began to migrate to Korea, and after the annexation in 1910 the number of immigrants from Japan rapidly increased. Many of them came nearly empty handed and built their fortune taking advantage of the privileges given to the colonial settlers in terms of land rights and commercial and business rights (Chŏn U-yŏng 2003). They raised families and sent their children to schools in Korea. When Japan declared defeat in 1945, most of them had to return to Japan, again empty handed, leaving most of the properties they had acquired and enjoyed in the colony. These people, called *hiki-agesha* in Japan, had to face hardship and disdain from their neighbours and relatives, as they were considered as an extra burden in the post-war devastation. For many of them, especially for those who were born and raised in the colony, Korea was home as well as a symbol of the good old days that they missed.

After the normalization in 1965, many of them visited Korea in search of their old homes, and it is in this regard that they may be understood as 'returnees'. Mr C. (born in 1930), a Korean who went to a Japanese secondary school in Kyŏngsŏng in the late 1930s, recalls (in an interview) the time when several of his Japanese classmates came back to Korea in the early 1970s for the first time since the liberation in 1945, as follows:

> They came out watchful and guarded. I went to the Kimpo airport to meet them, as they had contacted me before they came. One of them asked me with a slightly frightened expression, 'Will it be all right?' They told me that they had wanted to come for a long time. But, since they were a bit worried, they decided to come as a group after looking for their classmates all over the country. Before they came, they were warned that they might meet with rough experiences, and were given some instructions regarding how to behave. Reassuring them that they were quite safe, I brought them to the city centre. But, worries, fears and awkwardness at the first encounter disappeared soon and we were right back to the school years. Stories about the teachers, about the girls they liked, about the houses and streets they lived in, stories about the

hardship they had to endure when they went back to Japan, etc.: there were so many stories to tell and questions to ask between us.

These nostalgia-seeking returnees were also mostly male, as many women still worried about safety.[6] Many of them also became repeaters, i.e. those who visited the same place again and again, as in the case of the classmates of Mr C. To them, Korea was a most familiar place where they could meet old friends and converse with them freely in the Japanese language, and a place that was full of good memories and nostalgia. In short, Korea was not really a foreign country but rather a familiar old place where they could be perhaps more relaxed than in Japan. Some of them started business on the basis of old connections and turned themselves from frightened former colonizers into benefactors of the struggling Korean economy with powerful investment potential.

It may be misleading and perhaps unfair to describe all the Japanese tourists who visited Korea in the 1970s and 1980s simply as sex tourists or returnees. In fact, as many returning colonial settlers soon became business contractors, the distinction between nostalgia-seeking returnees and business people was not always clear cut. And there were also other types of travellers, especially with the increasing exchange relationships between the two countries. As sex tourism became much more hidden after the series of protests, and as it no longer constituted a part of the prevalent business pattern, new destinations began to be developed to attract Japanese tourists. One example is Cheju Island, located off the southern coast of the Korean peninsula.[7] Even in such new resorts, however, it was not the culture, history or real life of the people that was given attention either by the tourists from Japan or by the tourist developers in Korea. The focus was still mainly on recreation and pleasure activities such as golf, shooting, hunting, casinos, karaoke and so forth.

Nash maintains that metropolitan centres have varying degrees of control over the nature of tourism and its development in foreign regions, and it is this power over touristic and related development abroad that makes a metropolitan centre imperialistic and tourism a form of imperialism (Nash 1989: 39). While such a hypothesis leaves little room to consider the role of the natives, at least until the 1970s the control exercised by Japan seems to have remained significant. As much as the economic ties being established between Japan and Korea after the normalization of diplomatic relations, tourism provided an important mechanism by which the unequal and gendered character of the Japanese guest/Korean host relationship was reproduced and intensified.

Diversification of Japanese tourists entering Korea

If the male-centred *kisaeng* tourism was the most common and perhaps the most widely publicized pattern during the 1960s and 1970s, tourism greatly diversified during the 1980s and 1990s. Since the 1990s, for instance, many Japanese high schools have been sending their students abroad for a yearly excursion. The overseas destinations include Korea, China, Hawaii, the United States, Australia, etc., and Korea, being the nearest foreign country, has become the most frequently visited one for this purpose (Shirahata 1996: 135). What is most notable, however, is the increase in female tourists. Table 6.1 shows a significant increase of Japanese tourists visiting Korea in the latter half of the 1990s, especially among women. Between 1994 and 2000, the number of female tourists more than doubled, and the increase was particularly notable in the age groups 10–19 and 20–29.[8]

Part of the background to these new trends was the change in the Japanese domestic situation. With the gradual decline of sex tourism in the face of persistent criticism and controversy in Asian countries,[9] Japanese tour companies turned their eyes to the young 'office ladies' with relatively abundant usable income and free time. Throughout the period of the bubble economy of the 1980s, numerous innovative packages were designed with this particular group as the major target. 'Spend the New Year in Paris and buy brand name jeans!' or 'Enjoy the taste of an old home having home-made pasta in an Italian village!' were some of the examples. These young women generally preferred Europe, North America and Oceania to Asian countries. Some visited Hong Kong, but Korea remained for them a 'frightening [*kowai*], gloomy [*kurai*] and boring [*tsumaranai*]' place as a tourist destination.

In the post-bubble economy of the 1990s, however, there was a significant change in the Japanese travel pattern, the general direction of which is indicated in the following statements of the 2001 tourist white paper:

> As in the recent trend in domestic tourism, 'near [*chikai*], short [*mijikai*] and cheap [*yasui*]' trips are popular in international tourism as well. . . . Travel to Asian regions has been increasing, and travel to Korea has continually increased since 1997. Good exchange rates, the existence of cheap packages, shopping potential, the availability of local airport connections, and the possibility of light-hearted weekend trips in small groups make travelling to Asian countries popular [among the Japanese].
> (Nihon Kokudō Kōtsūshō 2001: 29)

Table 6.1 The number of Japanese tourists to Korea by age group (thousands)

	0–9		10–19		20–29		30–39		40–49		50–59		60+		Total	
	M	*F*	*M*	*F*	*M*	*F*	*M*	*F*	*M*	*F*	*M*	*F*	*M*	*F*	*M*	*F*
1994	12	11	42	39	121	130	180	74	295	78	206	64	109	45	965	441
2000	26	26	53	68	176	347	270	161	314	132	353	159	196	106	1,388	999

Source: Nihon Kokudō Kōtsūshō (2001).

Note: M = male, F = female.

The fact that it was cheaper to visit Korea than to visit one of the domestic resorts was another attraction. Japanese tour companies were actively engaged in developing new images for Korea and, after the joint holding of the 2002 FIFA World Cup game was decided in the mid-1990s, Japanese major media also joined in this construction of new images. Korea-related articles or programmes notably increased in newspapers and magazines and on TV channels, and became much more rich and diverse in their contents.

These efforts apparently bore fruit and helped to change the nature of the 'tourist gaze' with regard to this former colony. The Japanese visiting Korea continuously increased in the 1990s, and their sexual and age composition was greatly diversified. One Japanese writer described the changing situation as follows in a travel magazine:

> Trips to Korea had once been so notorious for the *kisaeng* tour of Japanese men. Things have changed drastically, however, and the streets in Seoul are now seeing an extraordinary boom with young and middle-aged women crossing over from Japan. Within Korea itself, efforts are being made to upgrade and redecorate the *esute* centres, shopping malls and duty-free shops, with young [Japanese] women who are believed to have abundant usable income as their major target. . . . Especially those who have been to Korea before are more attracted to visit the land again to enjoy superb and authentic Korean dishes at a reasonable price. These new trends are setting alight the 24-hour discount shops at the famous Eastgate and Southgate markets, the old *hanjŭngmak* saunas where one used to sit covered with straw mats, and more recently the lively student streets of Shinchon and the surrounding areas. In contrast, Japanese men's travel to Korea seems to have remained old-fashioned, without any noble ideas.
>
> (Kiriyama 2001: 132–3)

If existing images affect tourism, tourism also changes the images. Until the 1980s, to many Japanese, especially young people who did not have first-hand experience, Korea was a country that is 'poor, unfriendly, hostile to the Emperor system and antagonistic to the Japanese'. It was also a dangerous place that was constantly on the verge of war or full of extremely violent demonstrations. The place was therefore of little interest, and few young people wished to know about it let alone travel there.

Into the 1990s, however, at least for some, its image has changed to a place where people are kind, men are gentle, foods are good, and women are pretty. If Korean women were depicted and consumed as objects of desire by Japanese men in the past, fair-skinned pretty Korean women are now becoming one of the major attractions for many young female tourists. It is often believed and advertised as such that 'spicy Korean food, especially *kimchi*, is good for skincare' or that the 'unique bathing style such as *hanjŭngmak* is effective', etc. (Kuroda 2002). Korea has thus become a place that they can

Figure 6.3 A magazine cover advertising shopping in Seoul.

Source: Kōbunsha Jōsei Books (2001).

visit light-heartedly and have fun and a relaxing time with good food and reliable skincare services.

Hirata (2005: 51) argues that tourism plays a significant role in changing the perception and understanding of other cultures and that this is particularly so in the case of young Japanese women visiting Korea in the late 1990s and early 2000s. It is not clear, however, to what extent such a claim can be applied to the new types of female tourism from Japan in the 1990s and 2000s. Perhaps a closer examination of the nature of the actual encounter is needed.

Esute *tourism of young Japanese women*

What I have termed *esute* tourism here designates travelling for various kinds of cosmetic and healthcare experiences, which became popular among Japanese young women in the 1990s. A typical *esute* tour package may include one or more visits to an *esute* centre, shopping and Korean banquets. Some sightseeing in the city and a visit to traditional marketplaces may be added to a longer version. The courses at the *esute* centre usually consist of a traditional steam bath or modern sauna followed by optional services of body scrubbing, oil or milk massage, foot massage, finger pressure therapy, nail art, and other kinds of Korean medicinal treatment. More sophisticated courses may include in addition the removing of facial hair (*ubugenuki*),[10] plaster packs, mugwort fumigation (*yomogi musi*) and so forth (Kuroda 2002).

It is said that there are some 80 to 100 *esute* centres within Seoul that cater for Japanese tourist needs. What is available as *esute* services these days is not merely modern innovations or something invented exclusively for tourists. Traditionally, there were Korean-style steam baths known as *hanjŭngmak*. It is a construction built in the shape of dome with stones or mud bricks. Historical records of *hanjŭngmak* as a kind of medicinal treatment appear from the period of King Sejong in the fifteenth century. Sweating and keeping the body warm have always been considered good for health in Korean medicine, and these steam bath places were found in the old town of Seoul at least until the 1980s. These were not places that people went to for washing, but for rest and rehabilitation. Many of the medicinal treatments found in modern *esute* centres, such as cupping, herbal fumigation, finger pressure therapy, etc., were all part of these traditional saunas (see Figure 6.4).

Cheap *sentō*-type public baths were introduced by the Japanese during the colonial period, replacing most traditional-style *hanjŭngmak* in big cities. Since around the 1980s, however, some of the public bath owners have begun to introduce more elaborate and innovative steam bath parlours known as *chimjilbang*. These steam bath parlours, combining public baths, massage services, etc. and a huge resting floor with TV screens and restaurants, have become extremely popular among the urban residents and emerged as a major pastime place for many middle-class families in Seoul and other big cities in the 1990s. The tourist places known as *esute* centres may be considered as an adoptive form of these new types of pastime places of urban Koreans. While the traditional steam bath kilns were rapidly disappearing and being replaced by public baths with modern sauna facilities in Seoul, some *esute* centres reconstructed them in order to enhance the exotic quality of their services. This new type of *esute* centres with a reconstructed old-style

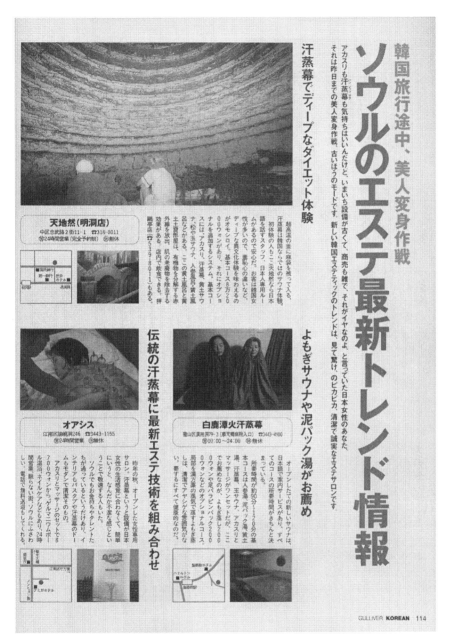

Figure 6.4 New trends in *esute* tours.

Source: Gulliver Travel Books (2001: 114).

sauna and elaborate cosmetic and healthcare services has become increasingly popular among young female tourists from Japan since the early 1990s.

As indicated above, this phenomenon may be partly explained by factors of economic concern and convenience, as it is said that the prices in Seoul are about half those of similar kinds of services in Tokyo. However, economy alone cannot explain it, as some of the *esute* centres in the more fashionable quarters of Seoul such as south of the River Han area are almost as expensive as the ones found in Japanese major cities. Other important motivations than the practical concerns of inexpensiveness and convenience may be an increasing reliability and the possibility of 'getting away'. Although similar services have become available within Japan in recent years, it is thought that Korea is the place where *esute* services originated and where one may expect better, more authentic versions of them. At a relatively cheap price, people can get away, relax and refresh themselves as much as they please in addition to treating themselves with the most exquisite services in ways that are perhaps never possible within Japan.

Moreover, to visit a place like an *esute* centre, one may also need a familiarity with public bath culture which the Japanese share with the Koreans apparently as part of the colonial legacy. In order to enjoy the services provided by the *esute* centres, one has to expose one's whole body to strangers' hands and this may not be possible unless there is a considerable degree of faith in the quality of the services provided as well as their harmlessness, if not effectiveness. This is especially so because, as we have seen above, *esute* services often involve a wide range of Korean medicinal therapies that are alien to many Japanese young people (Kuroda 2002). The fact that people often become bolder and more explorative away from home may help them experiment with these experiences; as a Japanese saying goes, *tabi no haji wa kakisute* ('Shame while travelling is to be thrown away!'). In the past, this saying has often been quoted as a cultural element that encourages the behaviour of male Japanese tourists exploring for sexual experiences. In a different way, the same may also apply to young female travellers in quest of bold, relaxing and satisfying experiences in *esute* tours.

Also, as in the case of sex tourism of Japanese males to other Asian countries, there exists a clear hierarchy in the host/guest relationship of female *esute* tourism in which the hosts, the less affluent ex-colonial subjects, appear as providers of the most intimate body care services, and the guests, the affluent Japanese female tourists, as service takers who have an obvious purchasing power. The two different kinds of travellers also share an apparent lack of interest in anything cultural or historical, or in encountering the real people at their destination.

Korea, as an ex-colony where Japanese tourists can easily go around within a carefully protected 'bubble' with the help of well-trained tour guides fluent in the Japanese language, is for them perhaps too familiar to be a foreign country (Moon 2002).[11] Although most Koreans born in the latter half of the twentieth century have not had a colonial education and are thus unable to speak Japanese, Korean society has developed, because of the historical importance of the Japanese in its tourist industry, an extremely specialized kind of infrastructure catering for Japanese needs and tastes. For instance, Korea is perhaps the only country in the world that offers college degree courses specializing in 'Tourism and Japanese studies', in which students are taught Japanese language, culture and a basic knowledge of the tourism industry to become specialized tour guides.

It is true that *esute* packages may include some sightseeing, a visit to traditional open markets, or perhaps a visit to a nearby pottery town. As mentioned earlier, however, its main part usually consists, as one tourist puts it, of 'going to *esute* every day for different kinds of services, eating delicious food, and doing shopping'. '*Esute*, gourmet and shopping' are indeed the three key words that appear in most tourist pamphlets promoting this particular type of tourism. Even when cultural interests are expressed, they seem to remain within the realm of popular ethnic elements such as Korean food, Korean costume, Korean pottery, markets, etc.

> It is '*yakiniku* [Korean barbecue beef], *esute* and *kimchi* [Korean pickled cabbage]' that come to my mind when I hear about travel to Korea. Things like *esute* are an interesting and wonderful experience of another culture [*ibunka taiken*] that one cannot get in Japan. I also like going to Southgate [Namdaemun] or Eastgate [Tongdaemun] market because there I meet turbulent and boisterous disorderliness that is hardly seen in Japan nowadays. I want to experience bargaining and negotiating the prices with merchants in the market, a thing that is not possible in places like department stores, of which there are plenty in Japan and where everything is clean, rational and modern. In Japan, there is hardly any place where one can have such an experience.
> (Female Japanese college student in her twenties, in an interview)

The statement expresses a kind of nostalgia. But, if the nostalgia of the older generation such as that of the returnee tourists mentioned above is about missing something they have experienced before, the nostalgia expressed here is an imagined one without a specific past to remember (Tanaka 1994). It is not particularly to experience or to learn about anything Korean when young people of modernized Japan want to go to a bustling marketplace and to bargain and haggle. The point, it seems, is more about getting away from Japan, where everything is regulated, ordered, disciplined and ruled by rationality. They pursue something different, perhaps something not yet fully modernized. But, certainly, Korean open markets are not the only places where they can get such an experience. Any Asian country might offer similar experiences, and in this regard, as one Japanese sociologist puts it in an interview, 'they are consuming "things Asian" [*ajiatekina mono*] rather than anything specifically Korean' (Kobayashi Kazumi, personal communication). They happened to come to Korea as the country is near and most easily accessible and not because they particularly care about Korean culture, history and people.

Korean wave (hallyu) tourism of middle-aged women

The change from male sex tourism to female *esute* tourism is often understood as signifying a positive development of the Korea/Japan relationship. It means at least that the image of Korea has changed from a generally negative one to a safe, reliable and bright one, of somewhere even young women may wish to travel. In this regard, the fact that Korea has become one of the popular destinations of young female Japanese travellers may itself be considered as a meaningful improvement. As shown above, however, a significant continuity can also be noted between the two types of tourism, especially in the general lack of interest in things cultural or historical, as well as in the basic nature of the host/guest encounter in which the former meet the latter as providers of intimate physical services.

On the other hand, what has recently become known as *hallyu* tourism seems to indicate a possibility of an encounter of a different kind. *Hallyu* or 'Korean wave' is a term that came into use in the late 1990s and early 2000s in East and South-East Asian countries to designate the rising popularity of some Korean mass cultural products. In Japan, it is believed to have started around 2003 with the broadcasting of a Korean TV drama titled *Fuyu no Sonata* ('Winter Sonata', *Fuyusona* for short) by NHK Satellite. Some enthusiastic fans started visiting Korea to see the actual places where the particular drama or film they liked had been shot and to meet, if possible, the actors and actresses concerned. It is difficult to estimate what the exact scale is of this so-called *hallyu* tourism, as it is not separately calculated. But it is generally believed that much of the recent increase in the number of Japanese tourists entering Korea can be attributed to this new phenomenon.

The main actors in this new type of tourism are typically middle-aged women among whom Korean dramas have gained most fans in Japan. In that this is perhaps the most conservative segment of the population with the least interest in travelling to an Asian country like Korea, the simple fact that they have come to have enough interest to make them actually visit the place is considered an important departure from past practices. What is more important is that their motivations for travel and their encounter with Korea are believed to be very different both from those of *kisaeng* tourism or the nostalgia-seeking returnee tourism of Japanese men in the 1960s and the 1970s and also from those of the more recent *esute* tourism of young women.

Hirata, who studied *hallyu* tourists from Japan, argues that, unlike their pleasure-seeking male predecessors, these women are not 'imperialistic' in their attitudes towards Korea. In other words, their travelling is not based on the belief that Japan and its culture are superior to Korea, a belief originating from the history of colonial domination. For these women, it is argued, travelling to Korea is meant to be a critique of Japanese modernity and a desire for self-reform (Hirata 2005; Kim 2005). What they seek and find in Korea and in its dramas is not Japan's past but a different kind of modernity from what Japan has created.

They may appear nostalgic in that many of them are said to be attracted to Korean dramas, as those dramas show things that Japan has lost, such as genuine love, warmth of human relationships, and respect for elders, etc. (Ham and Hŏ 2005). But nostalgia here needs to be distinguished from colonialist appropriation in which Korea is represented as underdeveloped, rural, folkloric or the traditional Other (Tanaka 1994). It is also different from the kind of longing for what Japan once owned and dominated as found among the returnee tourists described above. It is not a yearning and curiosity for things 'Asian' either, that is, for the things that are not fully modern yet. It represents a desire for things that are as much urban, sophisticated and modern but different from what can be found in Japan today. What is pursued and consumed in this context may be, as Iwabuchi (2002) puts it, an interest in an alternative modernity, that is, in a real otherness.

What should also be noted of these *hallyu* tourists is that they often adventure beyond the major cities that have been the final destination of most Japanese tourists visiting Korea in the past, and go into smaller cities and even to rural areas in pursuit of direct contact with people and their everyday life. Some of them are not satisfied with seeing the studios and the places where particular dramas are filmed but want to know more about the actual lives of the people. So some of them go to the ordinary residential quarters of a city or a town where a particular star they adore was born, brought up, went to school, shopped and ate. Not only that, some of them simply want to know more about the country itself where the stars come from. So they start learning the language, culture, history and so forth.

It seems therefore that tourism originally induced by consumption of mass cultural products is leading to a genuine interest in people and culture. It is true that not all Korean drama fans become *hallyu* tourists, and perhaps only a small segment of them adventure beyond fan meetings or drama location places. But, at the same time, it cannot be denied that it is a new development that indicates an encounter that is very different from the ones that have been discussed above.

Other types to be considered

There is always a danger of an excessive simplification in any attempt of clear-cut typologies and classifications. There are certainly other types of Japanese tourists visiting Korea than those discussed here. One example may be what I may call 'history tourists', whose pursuits are quite distinct from and contrasting to those of pleasure-seeking recreation tourists or those of nostalgia tourists looking for Imperial Japan's glorious and proud past. It is rather a critical self-reflection of the past of the things that have occurred in this former colony. This type of history tourism is found mostly among the

Figure 6.5 A *hallyu* tour package poster.

more educated intellectuals like teachers or citizen movement leaders who lean more toward the left rather than the right wing in terms of political ideology. They are the people who are most consciously aware of the history of colonial violence and tend to seek repentance by visiting the related historical sites:

> Recently, I had a chance to show around a group of Japanese visitors whom I had known before. They wanted to see an overview of Seoul as a post-colonial city. So I took them to Namsan Tower and explained about important buildings and facilities at the observation platform on top of the tower. Afterwards they visited the History Museum, National Museum and Folklore Museum. As some of them insisted that they must see the potteries [*yakimono*], as they were in Korea, I took them to Insadong, where there are some shops that sell potteries. But none of them wanted to go shopping in markets or to visit karaoke bars.
>
> (A Japanese professor of Korean studies, in an interview)

These people show a kind of moral obligation that, as Japanese tourists visiting Korea, they are obliged to see at least some of the remains of the colonial period. So they visit museums, palaces and also the place where the colonial government building used to stand.[12] Although the building itself was demolished, the fact that it was there is important and that they have been there is meaningful. In this sense, this type of history tourism displays the character of a pilgrimage or salvation tour. Among the 'pilgrim places' frequented by these tourists are Pagoda Park, where the March First Independence Movement started in 1919, the Westgate Prison, where many of the independence movement leaders were jailed, tortured and executed during the colonial period, and the Independence Memorial Hall in Chŏn'an, about 60 miles south of Seoul.

This type of history tourism is rarely found among women or among young people.[13] It has already been said that there is in general little interest in things cultural or historical among middle-aged women. If there is any, it is more in arts and crafts such as wrapping cloth (*furosiki*), embroidery, calligraphy, pottery and so forth (Moon 1997). History-conscious tourism is rarely found among this group. Also, among a younger generation, perhaps in the age groups thirties and forties, there are some who are explicitly critical of this kind of history-conscious tourists. They believe that Korea as a country is not a particularly attractive place as a tourist destination. It is a place where the weight of colonial history is too overwhelming and where people are forced to think that Japanese people are bad. It is therefore not a place that one might wish to visit for pleasure, relaxation and fun. They do not necessarily think of the historical pilgrimage trips of some of their elders in a positive way either. To them, visiting specifically colonial remains like Pagoda Park, Westgate Prison or Independence Hall is an excessive act that may amount to hypocrisy (from an interview).

Conclusion

It is not the main purpose of this chapter to cover exhaustively all types of Japanese tourism since the colonial period. What is intended is to consider how the nature of the tourist encounter between Japanese guests and Korean hosts has been transformed. Japanese tourism to Korea has seen a considerable growth over the past decades, especially since the mid-1960s, with a concomitant diversification of its content. As indicated above, however, an increase in the volume of tourism itself does not always bring about an enhancement of mutual understanding. To the extent that it remains as pleasure-seeking recreation tourism within urban centres with only limited contact with the people and culture concerned, an increase in the volume of tourism may instead lead to a further alienation between the hosts and guests. In the eyes of many Korean people who are not directly involved in tourist businesses, Japanese tourists are people who mostly keep to themselves and flock around in groups to pleasure quarters, casinos, shopping centres, *esute* centres, etc. without much contact with or interest in ordinary people. In many respects, therefore, Japanese tourism to Korea may be seen as representing the typical features of what Dennison Nash called 'tourism as a form of imperialism' (Nash 1989): firstly, in that it is a movement of people from a metropolitan centre to a periphery, to a former colony; secondly, in that it transforms the infrastructure of the host society in a significant way; and, thirdly, in that it strengthens the hierarchical relationships already existing between the host and guest societies.

On the other hand, there also seem to be many areas of Japanese tourism to Korea that cannot be fully understood and explained by this perspective. For instance, there are clear differences in the ways in which the host society is represented, imagined, appropriated and consumed. If a simplified typology is once again attempted, it may be said that the representation of the destination and its people to Japanese tourists has changed from the 'colonial Other' of the imperialist tourists to the 'Asian Other' of young Japanese tourists and to a 'real Other' or an alternative self of the most recent *hallyu* tourists, with accompanying changes in the nature of the tourist encounter. And, in this regard, it cannot be said that tourism merely reproduces the existing hierarchy nor always strengthens it.

Notes

1 Kyŏngju at the time may not be considered a large city. But, as the former capital of the Shilla Kingdom with numerous Buddhist temples, stone towers and statues, and also because it is located on the way from Pusan to Kyŏngsŏng, the town had often been included as a brief stop for Japanese tourists travelling by this route.

2 Itō Hirobumi was the Japanese premier at the time of colonization, who was later assassinated by a Korean Independence Movement leader, An Chung Kŭn.

3 The reconstruction of the palace started in 1984 when the zoo was removed and all the cherry blossom trees were cut. Most of the former palace buildings are now reconstructed.

4 Yamashita (1997) shows how two colonial government measures, the regulatory decree concerning *kisaeng* and the enforcement of a *kisaeng* union, worked in such a way as to dissolve the tradition of *yegi* in Korea.

5 The quotation was originally from an article titled 'The scene of the erotic streets of Kyŏngsŏng' (*Keijō no ero-gai hūkei*) printed in a journal, *Korea and Manchuria* (*Chōsen oyobi Manshū*) (April 1934), and is cited here from Son Chŏng-mok (1996: 464).

6 Hawaii, the United States and Europe were more popular destinations for women than Asia. Even nowadays when, with an overall increase of overseas tourism, the number of women visiting Asian countries has seen some growth, it constitutes less than 50 per cent.

7 With beautiful tropical scenery, numerous botanic gardens and many local specialities of seafood dishes, in addition to superb hotels, sports facilities and convenient airline services, Cheju Island has attracted many Japanese tourists over the past few decades, although the Chinese have outnumbered the Japanese in recent years. In the Golden Week of 2002 alone, it is reported that nearly 10,000 Japanese visited the island.

8 In the age group 20–29, 121,000 men (48.2 per cent) and 130,000 women (51.8 per cent) visited Korea in 1994. But, in 2000, the numbers increased to 176,000 men (33.6 per cent) and 347,000 women (66.4 per cent) respectively.

9 It was reported that Japanese sex tourism became an issue at the 1983 ASEAN meeting held in Malaysia.

10 To remove facial hair (*ubuge* in Japanese) using silk thread is supposed to be good for a better make-up effect. This practice is found in other parts of East Asia as well. In China, for instance, it is known as *kai lien* (opening of the face). Girls before marriage are often described as 'hairy peaches' and are made full-fledged women by being given this treatment on the eve of their wedding day.

11 The term 'bubble' is used here in a sense of 'environmental bubble', meaning 'strictly circumscribed world created for tourists in which they are insulated and are protected from harsh reality' (Urry 1990: 7).

12 The early Meiji stone architecture was pulled down and demolished in 1995 under Kim Yŏngsam's regime as part of the 'Recovering History Campaign' (*Rekisi wo tatenaosu undō*). The top part of the building is now exhibited at the Independence Memorial Hall in Chŏn'an.

13 According to a survey by the Korea Tourist Bureau, the places visited by tourists vary greatly by age groups. For instance, among the age group 60 or over, 60–70 per cent visit museums or palaces, while it is only about 20–30 per cent among those in their twenties (Han'guk kwangwang kongsa 2003).

References

Chŏn U. (2003). 'Iljeha sŏul namch'on sangga ŭi hyŏngsŏng kwa pyŏnch'ŏn' [The formation and change of the commercial district at Namch'on, Seoul]. In K. Kiho *et al.*, *Namch'on, Seoul: Time, Place and People*. Seoul: Seoul Studies Centre, City University of Seoul.

Chōsen Shōdokufu Tetsudōkyoku (ed.) (1928). *Chōsen no fūko* [Scenery of Korea]. Keijō: Chōsen Shōdokufu Tetsudōkyoku.

Creighton, M. (1997). 'Consuming rural Japan: the marketing of tradition and nostalgia in the Japanese travel industry'. *Ethnology*, 36(3), pp. 239–54.

Graburn, N.H.H. (2002). 'When is domestic tourism international? Multiculturalism and tourism in Japan'. Paper presented at the International Academy for the Study of Tourism (IAST), Macao.

Gulliver Travel Books (2001). *Kankoku no tatsujin* [Expert on Korea], 4. Tokyo: Magazinhausu.

Hall, C.M. (1992). 'Sex tourism in South-East Asia'. In D. Harrison (ed.), *Tourism and the Less Developed Countries*. London: Belhaven.

Ham, H. and H. Insun (2005). *Kyŏul yŏn'ga wa nabi hwantaji* [Winter Sonata and Butterfly Fantasy]. Seoul: Ch'aeksesang.

Han'guk kwangwang kongsa [Korea Tourist Bureau] (2003). *2002nyŏn Ilbon'in kwangwangkaek siltae chosa* [Survey of Japanese tourists of 2002]. Seoul: Han'guk kwangwang kongsa.

Han'guk kyohoe yŏsŏng yŏnhaphoe [Korean Christian Women's Association] (1983). *Kisaeng kwangwang* [*Kisaeng* tourism]. Seoul: Han'guk kyohoe yŏsŏng yŏnhaphoe.

Hendry, J. (2000). *The Orient Strikes Back: A Global View of Cultural Display.* Oxford: Berg.

Hirata, Y. (2005). *Han'guk ŭl sobi hanŭn ilbon: hallyu, yŏsŏng, dŭrama* [Japan consuming Korea: *hallyu*, women and drama]. Seoul: Ch'aeksesang.

Imai, H. (1939). *Chōsen no Kankō* [Tour of Korea]. Keijō: Chōsen no Kankōsha.

Ivy, M. (1995). *Discourses of the Vanishing: Modernity, Phantasm, Japan.* Chicago: University of Chicago Press.

Iwabuchi, K. (2002). *Recentering Globalization: Popular Culture and Japanese Transnationalism.* Durham, NC, and London: Duke University Press.

Kageaki, K. (1997). 'Inward-bound, outward-bound: Japanese tourism re-considered'. In Y. Shinji, K.H. Din and J.S. Eades (eds), *Tourism and Cultural Development in Asia and Oceania*. Bangi: Penerbit Universiti Kebangsaan Malaysia.

Kim S. (1990). 'Musok chŏntong ŭi tamnon bunsŏk: haeche wa chŏnmang' [An analysis of discourses of shamanic tradition: deconstruction and prospects]. *Hankuk munhwa illyuhak* [Korean cultural anthropology], 22, pp. 211–43.

Kim Ŭ. (2005). 'Ch'okukkajŏk munhwa hyŏnsang ŭrosŏ ŭi kyŏul yŏnga wa saeroun munhwasuyong' [Reception of Winter Sonata as a new type of transnational cultural phenomenon]. In *Kyŏul yŏnga: Ch'unch'ŏn kwa hanil munhwa kyoryu* [Winter Sonata: Ch'unch'ŏn and cultural exchanges between Japan and Korea]. Proceedings of Hallyu Ch'unch'ŏn Forum. Ch'unch'ŏn: Kangwon University.

Kim Y. (2002). 'Yi Insŏng ŭi hyangtosaek: minjokjuŭi wa sikminjuŭi' [Local colour of Yi Insŏng: nationalism and colonialism]. In K. Youngna (ed.), *Hanguk kŭndae misul kwa sigak munhwa* [Korean modern art and visual culture]. Seoul: Chohyŏng kyoyuk.

Kiriyama, H. (2001). 'Nihonjin no kankoku ryokō saigō rupō' [Reportage reconsidering Japanese tour to Korea]. In Gariba-toraberubutku [Gulliver travel book], *Kankoku no tatsujin* [Expert on Korea], 4. Tokyo: Magazinhausu.

Kōbunsha Jōsei Books (2001). *Kankoku souru no toku brando hatken* [Discovering of best brands in Seoul, Korea]. Tokyo: Kōbunsha.

Kuroda, F. (2002). *Souru no tatsujin* [An expert of Seoul], new edn. Tokyo: Amyūzubutkusu.

Kwŏn, H. (2002). 'Ilje sidae kwan'gwang yôpsô wa kisaeng imiji' [Images of *kisaeng* in the tourist postcards of the Japanese colonial period]. In K. Youngna (ed.), *Hanguk kŭndae misul kwa sigak munhwa* [Korean modern art and visual culture]. Seoul: Chohyông kyoyuk.

Kwŏn, H. (2003). 'Iljesidae sajin yŏpsŏ e natanan jaehyŏn ŭi chŏngch'ihak' [Politics of representation shown in the picture postcards of the Japanese colonial period]. *Hankuk munhwa illyuhak* [Korean cultural anthropology], 36(1), pp. 187–217.

MacCannell, D. (1976). *The Tourist: A New Theory of the Leisure Class*. New York: Schocken.

Mok, S. (2003). ' "Namch'on" munhwa: shikminji munhwa ŭi hŭnjŏk' [Culture of 'Namch'on': traces of colonial culture]. In K. Kiho (ed.), *Sŏul, Namch'on: shigan, changso, saram* [Seoul and Namch'on: time, place and people]. Seoul: Sŏulhak yŏn'guso.

Moon, O. (1997). 'Tourism and cultural development: Japanese and Korean contexts'. In Y. Shinji, K.H. Din and J.S. Eades (eds), *Tourism and Cultural Development in Asia and Oceania*. Bangi: Penerbit Universiti Kebangsaan Malaysia.

—— (2002). 'Traveling for the familiar: realities and fantasies of Japanese tourist encounters in Korea'. Paper presented at the 2002 International Meeting of Japan Anthropology Workshop (JAWS), Yale University, New Haven, CT.

Muroi, H. and N. Sasaki (1997). 'Tourism and prostitution in Japan'. In M.T. Sinclair (ed.), *Gender, Work and Tourism*. London: Routledge.

Nash, D. (1989). 'Tourism as a form of imperialism'. In V. Smith (ed.), *Hosts and Guests: The Anthropology of Tourism*, 2nd edn. Philadelphia: University of Pennsylvania Press.

Nihon Kokudō Kōtsūshō (ed.) (2001). *2001 Kankō Hyakusho Hese 13nen* [2001 tourist white papers]. Tokyo: Saimusho Insatsukyoku.

—— (2006). *2006 Kankō Hyakusho Hese 18nen* [2006 tourist white papers]. Tokyo: Saimusho Insatsukyoku.

Shirahata, Y. (1990). 'Ryokōgyo: mo hitotsu no seichō shinka' [Travel business: yet another myth of growth]. *Chūo Kōron*, January, pp. 446–51.

—— (1996). *Ryokōno susume: Showa ga unda shomin no shinbunka* [Encouraging travel: new culture of common people born during the Showa period]. Chūo Shinsho No. 1305. Tokyo: Chūokōronsha.

Son, C. (1996). *Ilje kanjŏmgi toshi sahoesang yŏn'gu* [Cities in the Japanese colonial period]. Seoul: Iljisa.

Tanaka, S. (1994). *Japan's Orient: Rendering Pasts into History*. Berkeley and Los Angeles: University of California Press.

Urry, J. (1990). *The Tourist Gaze: Leisure and Travel in Contemporary Societies*. London: Sage Publications.

Yamashita, Y. (1997). 'Shikminji kongch'ang chedo ŭi chŏn'gae' [Developments of licensed prostitution during the colonial period]. *Sahoe wa yŏksa* [Society and history], 51, pp. 143–81.

Yano, K. (1936). *Keinintsūran: Shinhan Taikeijō Annai* [*Keinintsūran*: the new edition of a guide to great Keijō]. Keijō: Keijō toshi bunka kenkyushō.

Yi, K. (1924). *Kŭmkangsan yugi* [Travel writings of Diamond Mountains]. Kyŏngsŏng: Shimunsa.

7 The Japanese encounter with the South

Japanese tourists in Palau

Shinji Yamashita

Introduction

In his book *Empty Meeting Grounds*, the American sociologist Dean MacCannell writes:

> Tourism is a primary ground for the production of new cultural forms on a global base. In the name of tourism, capital and modernized peoples have been deployed to the most remote regions of the world, farther than any army was ever sent.
>
> (MacCannell 1992: 1)

MacCannell's view is quite relevant for the study of tourism in the age of global mobility. However, as Okpyo Moon has pointed out, one must be attentive to the local situation and the particular context. By looking at Japanese tourists in Korea, Moon demonstrated that the nature of the host–guest relationship and the cultural implications of tourism, which are the central issues of the anthropological study of tourism (Smith 1989), vary depending on *who travels, and where* (Moon 1997: 178).

Focusing on Palau, a small newly independent Micronesian republic that is attempting to develop itself through tourism, this chapter examines the sociocultural implications of tourism in Palau, particularly through the lens of Japanese tourists.[1] Historically, Spanish governance of the Caroline Islands began in 1885. In 1899 Spain sold the islands to Germany, and then Palau came under German governance. Following Germany's defeat in the First World War, Japan colonized Micronesia from 1919 to 1945. After Japan's defeat in the Pacific War, the Caroline, Mariana and Marshall Islands became United Nations trust territories under US administration. In 1994 Palau became independent as a new republic. Tourism in Palau cannot be fully understood without referring to this historical background. By analysing the Japanese encounter with Palau in both historical and contemporary contexts, this chapter attempts to contribute to the study of Japanese tourism in the Pacific region, one of the most popular destinations for Japanese tourists.

The general features of tourism in Palau

Over the last 25 years in Palau, the number of tourists has steadily increased from 5,640 in 1980 to 82,397 in 2006, although there have been some ups and downs in recent years (see Table 7.1). The increase in the number of tourists is quite significant when one realizes that the annual number of tourists is now more than four times Palau's total population of about 20,000.

The focus of tourism in Palau is its world-famous coral reefs. Approximately 60 per cent of the visitors come to Palau for diving (Khaleghi 1996: 21). Palau tourism, then, can be primarily characterized as 'ecological nature tourism' (Graburn 1989: 32). In this context, the Palauan government, aware of the damage that can be caused to the fragile ecosystem by the rapidly growing number of visitors, now emphasizes ecotourism in its scheme of sustainable development. According to *Palau 2020: National Master Development Plan*,

Table 7.1 Visitor arrivals in Palau, 1980–2006

Year	Number
1980	5,640
1981	5,057
1982	5,330
1983	6,338
1984	9,014
1985	13,371
1986	9,612
1987	11,682
1988	15,975
1989	19,396
1990	23,398
1991	32,846
1992	36,117
1993	40,497
1994	44,073
1995	53,229
1996	69,330
1997	73,719
1998	64,194
1999	55,493
2000	57,732
2001	54,111
2002	58,441
2003	63,328
2004	89,161
2005	80,578
2006	82,397

Source: Palau Visitors Authority.

Note: Figures from 2003 exclude returning resident, employment and other (student).

'the low-in-number high quality–high cost establishments, in many ways, seem more suited to the ecosystem' (Palau Government 1996: 8–1). 'Ecotourism' and 'sustainable development' are, therefore, key words for Palau tourism today, and the Palau Visitors Authority (PVA), a semi-autonomous body created to promote and encourage the development and marketing of tourism as one of the primary economic sectors of the republic,[2] compiled a policy document in May 1997 entitled *Sustainable Development Policies and Action Plan*. The theme for the 1997 tourism awareness week was 'Tourism: Balancing between Nature and $ense', with '$ense' representing the economic benefits of the industry. During my field research in March 1998, the Palau Visitors Authority held a week-long workshop to further review its action plan.

Of the total of 64,194 visitors in 1998, the year of my field research, 21,571 were from Japan, 18,503 from Taiwan, and 12,487 from the United States. In 2006, the latest year for which statistical data are available, of the total of 82,397 visitors, 28,449 were from Taiwan, 26,892 from Japan, and 11,756 from Korea (see Table 7.2). Japan ranked number one as a country of origin from 1992 to 1995 and again from 1998 to 2002, while Taiwan was number one from 1996 to 1997 and from 2003 to 2006. Taiwan and Japan are thus the most important sources for Palau tourism, as the visitors from these two countries constitute about 70 per cent of the total visitors to Palau. The growth in Taiwanese tourists was facilitated by the introduction of a daily direct flight between Taiwan and Palau in 1996 (*Tia Belau*, 14–21 December 1996). Visitors from the United States, the former administering country,

Table 7.2 Visitor arrivals in Palau, 1992–2006, by major countries of residence

| Year | Nationality | | | | |
	Japan	*USA*	*Taiwan*	*Philippines*	*South Korea*
1992	17,021	8,032	2,749	4,032	n.a.
1993	18,554	7,861	4,171	3,622	n.a.
1994	17,493	9,700	6,126	3,554	1,221
1995	21,052	9,846	11,163	3,199	1,823
1996	22,619	9,955	23,309	3,838	2,074
1997	20,507	10,481	31,246	3,344	1,782
1998	21,571	12,487	18,503	3,033	545
1999	22,556	12,048	10,703	2,883	653
2000	21,682	6,441	14,149	3,981	586
2001	22,395	5,367	12,476	4,128	350
2002	23,748	4,774	15,819	3,410	497
2003	21,401	4,291	27,857	740	312
2004	23,845	5,979	42,158	860	5,673
2005	26,281	5,532	34,101	776	2,169
2006	26,892	5,922	28,449	1,430	11,756

Source: Palau Visitors Authority.

Note: Figures from 2003 exclude returning resident, employment and other (student).

have decreased in relative terms, while those from Korea increased sharply in 2006.

Japanese, Taiwanese, Americans and recently Koreans are the major visitor groups in Palau. There are differences in behaviour patterns by the nationality of the tourists. In its research, the Pacific Business Center Program noted such differences:

(1) *Purpose of Tourism*: Some 67 per cent of Japanese and 55 per cent of Americans mentioned 'diving' as the purpose of their visit, while 56 per cent of Taiwanese mentioned 'general tourism' (i.e., recreational tourism packaged by tour agents) as their main reason for coming to Palau.

(2) *Length of Stay*: 87 per cent of Taiwanese tourists stayed for a period of three to four nights, 47 per cent of the Japanese stayed between three and four nights, but 39 per cent of the Japanese stayed for five to six nights. Americans and Europeans stayed longer: an average of 7.57 nights and 8.51 nights respectively. They stayed longer because a trip to far-away Palau is seen as a once-in-a-lifetime event, while it takes only three hours by direct flight for Taiwanese and five hours for Japanese flying via Guam.

(3) *Types of Tour*: 88 per cent of Taiwanese and 85 per cent of Japanese tourists used package tours, but 64 per cent of Americans and 89 per cent of Europeans arranged their own visits.

(4) *Sources of Information*: 34 per cent of Japanese obtained information about Palau from magazines,[3] while 49 per cent of Taiwanese heard about Palau from travel agents. 32 per cent of Americans got their information from family and friends.

(5) *Age of Tourists*: 59 per cent of Japanese tourists are between 25 and 34 years old, while 72 per cent of Taiwanese tourists are between 25 and 44.

(Khaleghi 1996)

From the viewpoint of sustainable ecotourism as adopted by the Palauan government, the difference between Taiwanese mass or general (recreational) tourism and Japanese (and American) diving or ecotourism is important. Although the Taiwanese are major tourists in Palau, they are not necessarily the kind of tourists that Palau wants to receive. During my research in Palau in 1998, I often heard Palauan people complaining of the bad manners of the Taiwanese tourists who lack 'eco-consciousness' and damage the coral reefs, an important resource in Palauan ecotourism. Palau wants to host as many tourists as possible, but clearly ecotourism is a special niche in the tourist market that often produces conflicts with mass tourism.

In terms of the job market related to tourism, less than 40 per cent of the tourism sector in Palau is occupied by Palauans. The Palau Visitors Authority notes that 'there are very few incentives for Palauans to participate in this sector, because wages are low, training programs are in their infancy, and those who show initiative and entrepreneurship typically move to other countries' (PVA 1997: 15). By contrast, the Division of Labor Statistics reports that in 2005 there were 7,240 non-Palauans holding working permits. They included 4,577 from the Philippines, 1,245 from the People's Republic of China, and 366 from Bangladesh. Filipino immigrants work in the tourism sector, as well as in places such as hotels and restaurants. In my 1998 field research, all the employees at the hotel where I stayed in Koror, and almost all the waitresses and cooks at restaurants I visited, were Filipinos. The ironic result is that often it is Filipinos, not Palauans, who actually welcome the tourists when they arrive in Palau.

A decade ago, the Palau Visitors Authority argued that Palauan participation in the tourism labour force should not be allowed to fall below 50 per cent in the short term, and should be restored to 75 per cent by the year 2000 (PVA 1997: 5). Furthermore, there is the question of who gains and should gain from the tourist industry. An estimated 85 per cent of the revenues are enjoyed by foreign tour operators and suppliers, particularly Japanese and Taiwanese. The Palau Visitors Authority stressed, therefore, the need to create a tourist industry that is completely operated, maintained and controlled by Palauans at the termination of funding under the Compact of Free Association in 2009. Otherwise tourism could become a new form of economic colonialism for Palau.

Japanese tourists in Palau

In 2006 Japanese overseas travellers numbered 17.5 million.[4] Such a large number of Japanese tourists in the international tourism market is undoubtedly due to Japan's economic growth and the increased power of the Japanese yen, even though Japan has been in a long economic recession since the 1990s.[5] According to the World Tourism Organization, in 2006 Japan ranked as the fifth biggest tourism spender in the world, following Germany, the United States, the United Kingdom and France.[6]

Looking at destinations of Japanese international tourists, China became the number one destination in 2006, with 3.75 million Japanese visitors. In that same year, 3.67 million Japanese went to the United States (the number one destination until 2005).[7] This destination shift from the United States to China may reflect Japan's recent economic shift in the same direction. Following China and the United States, there were 2.3 million visitors going to Korea, 1.3 million to Thailand, 1.3 million to Hong Kong and 1.2 million to Taiwan.

Of 3.67 million visitors to the United States in 2006, 1.4 million visited Hawai'i. Furthermore, 950,000 visited Guam and 270,000 visited Saipan.[8] Visitors to Hawai'i, Guam and Saipan totalled 2.6 million. Although the number of visitors to these Pacific destinations has declined in recent years, especially after the 11 September terrorist attacks in the United States, the

Pacific region still provides one of the most popular destinations for the Japanese tourist market. Palau belongs to this Pacific tourist zone.

How, then, is the Pacific region perceived by Japanese tourists? The popular image of the Pacific for many Japanese is that of a 'southern seas paradise', with beautiful seas and sunshine, where Japanese tourists can escape their busy and stressful urban lives in Japan. In the stereotypical tourist brochures, Hawai'i is 'a paradise full of heavenly splendor', visiting Fiji is described as 'touring a small paradise', Rota is 'a supreme paradise', Tahiti is 'the last paradise', and so on (Akimichi 1997: 244). 'Paradise' is, then, the cliché used to describe the contemporary Pacific resorts, presented in the tourist brochures with pictures of luxury hotels, young women in swimming suits, tropical fruits, and tropical fish in the coral reefs. Under the heading 'entering the paradise of Micronesia', a tourist guidebook introduced Micronesia thus:

> Micronesia – it sounds relaxed: full of sunshine, coral reefs, an uninhibited island with coconut trees, an old car running on the single island road. Those who come from busy Japan are certainly fascinated by the free and easy landscapes and green surroundings. People wonder whether it is possible to stay on islands like these. It would be just like paradise listening to CD music while hearing the sounds of leaves of coconut trees trembling in the breeze.
>
> (Shimokawa 1999: 2)

Palau is such an island paradise in Micronesia. It is a new niche for those bored with the mass tourism of Hawai'i and Guam. With its transparent waters, it has become particularly popular as a diving spot. Diving has created a new category of tourism in the Japanese market since the early 1990s. Palau is now listed as a diving spot in the same way as Guam, Saipan, Rota, Pohnpei, Sebu, Sipadang, Bali, the Maldives, the Great Barrier Reef, Fiji, New Caledonia, Tahiti and the Red Sea.

Although most Japanese tourists use package tours, they do not necessarily behave as a group. Unlike the former stereotypical image of Japanese tourists marching behind the upraised flag of a tour conductor, Japanese diving tourists in Palau are very individualistic and free.[9] They use package tours only for economic reasons, to get cheap tickets. Further, most of the diving tourists are repeaters. In my field research in Palau, I came across a young woman who had visited Palau eight times in two and a half years. She explained her fascination with diving by emphasizing that she could forget everything by going beneath the beautiful sea with its coral reefs.

Apart from the divers, some Japanese tourists, mainly veterans and their families, visit Palau for memorial services. In the last stages of the Pacific War, many Japanese soldiers were killed in battles with the United States military. Some of the fiercest battles were fought in Palau in 1944, particularly at Angaur and Peleliu, where some 12,000 Japanese and 1,800 Americans

Figure 7.1 Palau, the paradise.

From Palau Visitors Authority brochure.

were killed. The first attempt to excavate the bones of the deceased Japanese soldiers in the Pacific region was made in 1953, and memorial tourism started in the 1960s as a continuation of this activity. Some Japanese Palauan associations, such as Sakura-kai and Palau-kai, helped in arranging tours. Before the diving tourists came to Palau, these memorial tourists were the major visitors from Japan. The older Japanese who visit Palau are still mainly memorial tourists, though today the excavation of bones is not allowed.

During my research in Palau I had a chance to visit Peleliu Island with a memorial tourist group from Hokkaido. On arrival at Peleliu they were welcomed by a local Japanese guide who had grown up in Palau as the child of a pioneer farmer during the Japanese colonial days and who had recently returned to Palau after his retirement. They visited the commemorative monument and prayed along to a pre-recorded Buddhist chant. Then they visited various memorial sites, such as the former army headquarters, abandoned tanks and cannons, Orange Beach (a famous war battle site) and the Peleliu Shrine.

Some tourists had lived in Palau during the Japanese colonial period. In 1941, approximately 13,000 Japanese resided in the town of Koror (Uehara 1990: 58). Some worked in the government sector and others in the commercial and agricultural sectors. On Babeldaob, the largest of the Palau islands, Japanese pioneered farming settlements such as Mizuho-mura, Asahi-mura, Yamato-mura and Shimizu-mura. Former residents make sentimental journeys to renew what Ichirō Tomiyama (1997: 199) has called 'memories of empire'. Among them are some Japanese people who returned to Palau after retirement to open restaurants or to work in the tourism sector. The Japanese guide on Peleliu Island was such a person.

Younger Japanese who come to Palau only for the diving are often unaware that Palau was once a Japanese colony. In addition, the tourist brochures and guidebooks disregard old colonial memories by describing Palau, for instance, as: 'Rock Islands on the blue seas. Flower gardens of coral reefs surrounding the Islands. Just by coming into contact with the landscape you

Figure 7.2 Memorial tourism at Peleliu.

can refresh yourself' (Japan Tourist Bureau Pocket Guide, *Saipan and Micronesia*, 1997: 7). The current Palauan emphasis on nature and marine tourism, therefore, seems to conceal the colonial history. However, to fully understand the Japanese touristic encounter with Palau, one has to review the history of Japanese colonization of the South.

Japanese colonization of the South and the formation of its popular image [10]

Japanese involvement in the Pacific began in the 1860s, although there had been prior accidental contacts between Pacific islanders and Japanese fishermen. Japanese labour emigration to Hawai'i started in 1868, the first year of the Meiji period. In 1875 Japan declared its control over the Ogasawara (Bonin) Islands. Because of increasing population and limited resources at home, the Japanese government at that time adopted a policy of overseas advancement (Akimichi 1997).

In the 1880s and 1890s, a group of ideologues advocated 'Southern advancement' or *nanshinron*. Among them was Tsunenori Suzuki, who went to the Marshall Islands in 1880, on the orders of then foreign minister Kaoru Inoue, to investigate the murder of a Japanese by the local people. In 1892 he published a book called *Nan'yō Tanken Jikki* (A record of exploration in the Southern Seas) based on this journey.[11] Shigetaka Shiga was another important figure, who wrote *Nan'yō Jijō* (Report on the Southern Seas) in 1887, after his journey to the Pacific islands and Australia. Ukichi Taguchi wrote *Nan'yō Keiryakuron* (On development in the Southern Seas) and established the trading company Nantō Shōkai in 1890. Yosaburō Takekoshi further popularized the image of the Southern regions by publishing his *Nangokuki* (On Southern countries) in 1910, based on his journey to what is now Southeast Asia – Shanghai, Hong Kong, Singapore, Java, Sumatra and French Indochina.

According to the political scientist Tōru Yano (1975), these expansionism accounts emphasized the underdeveloped, political backwardness of the Southern regions, and suggested that their development should be the task of Japan. Importantly, Shiga presented the *Nan'yō*, which literally means 'the Southern Seas', as another new world which belonged neither to the East nor to the West, the two civilized worlds known to Japan. Japan's advancement into the Southern regions can be seen as a method of establishing itself as a civilized country compared to this underdeveloped and backward region.

Colonial expansion into the South started with Taiwan in 1895, Micronesia in 1919 (Palau had been under Japanese occupation since 1914), and reached as far as Southeast Asia in 1941. This vast region of the Pacific and Southeast Asia was then called *Nan'yō* (the Southern Seas) or *Nanpō* (the Southern regions). After the Japanese occupation of Micronesia in 1919 under a League of Nations mandate, and especially after the Nan'yō Kōhatsu (Southern Seas Developing Company, established in 1920) successfully started sugar plantations in Saipan and Tinian, many Japanese people migrated to the region. The number increased every year. *Nan'yō-chō*, the Japanese colonial government of the Southern Seas, was established in Koror, Palau, in 1922. In 1933, 30,670 Japanese were residing in Micronesia (the total population was 80,884). In Tinian, for instance, of the 7,554 total residents, 5,538 were Japanese.

After 1935, as advancement into the Southern regions became part of a policy of imperial expansionism to form the *Daitōa Kyōeiken* or the Greater East Asian Co-prosperity Sphere, the Japanese population in the Pacific region increased even more. In 1936 Nan'yō Takushoku, a regional planning agency, was established under governmental control. Japanese residents increased to 77,000 in 1940 and then to 96,000 in 1942. In Palau, where *Nan'yō-chō*, the Japanese colonial government, was located, there were 13,000 Japanese by 1941. Big development companies opened branches, and a government Shintō shrine, *Nan'yō Jinja*, was established in 1940 with a ceremony in honour of Amaterasu Ōmikami, the Japanese sun deity. The Japanization of Micronesia thus proceeded.

The popular image of the South for the Japanese was formed through these historical processes. One popular image can be observed in a cartoon series for boys called *Bōken Dankichi* (The adventurous Dankichi).[12] Drawn by Keizō Shimada, this was a popular serial cartoon in *Shōnen Kurabu* (Boys' Club) magazine, from 1933 to 1939. It related the adventures of Dankichi, a heroic boy, who drifts to an island called Banjintō (Savage Island) somewhere in the tropical South after falling asleep on his fishing boat. He later becomes the king of this savage island of cannibals with the assistance of Karikō, a clever mouse. Dankichi is drawn with white skin, a grass skirt, and a crown on his head, while his followers in the South are dark skinned and called *kuronbō* ('black boy'). These black people have numbers on the front of their bodies and look like the stereotypical image of Africans. Animals like lions, elephants and giraffes live on Dankichi's island, although the island was modelled after the *Nan'yō*, then Japanese Micronesia.[13] Interestingly, Dankichi always wears a watch on his wrist and shoes on his feet, symbolizing his membership in the civilized world (Kawamura 1993: 110).

Another example is a popular song called *Shūchō no Musume* (Daughter of a chief) composed and written by Ichimatsu Ishida. The song became a great hit in 1930 on the radio and on disk. The lyrics go like this:

> My sweetheart is the daughter of a village chief
> She's pretty dark, but in the South Seas, she's a beauty
> In the Marshall Islands, below the equator
> She dances slowly in the shade of the palm trees
> (Translated by Mark R. Peattie 1988: 216)

According to Peattie, Micronesia was seen:

> as a distant paradise, conceived as being literally in the South Pacific, and

inhabited by primitive peoples not much different than 'savages' any-where – naked, ignorant, sensuous, and dark skinned. . . . After arriving in Micronesia, most colonists, who usually settled in one of the large Japanese communities in the islands, had little opportunity to alter this stereotype, since they made scant effort to break out of their colonial boundaries.

(Peattie 1988: 216–17)

Further, Peattie observes that there was a distinct difference between Western and Japanese residential areas in the colonial landscapes. In the latter, he writes, one could not find the colonial luxuries found in the Western colonies, partly because Japanese colonial society did not have well-defined classes and partly because the Japanese did not like to display wealth and privilege to others. In other words, there was no distinct social and economic elite in Japanese colonial society (Peattie 1996: 275). Japanese migrants to the Southern Seas mostly came from the poorer classes and regions of Japan, especially from Okinawa,[14] and Koreans were included as well.

However, a colonial social hierarchy did, of course, exist. At the top were Japanese who came from mainland Japan, with Okinawans in the middle and Koreans below them. At the bottom were the islanders, who were classified as *tōmin*. As Tomiyama (1997) explains, the *tōmin* were repre-sented and designated as 'backward' and 'lazy' and, therefore, needed to be 'treated' and 'developed'. This colonialist view of the Southern islanders, together with the popular ideas examined earlier, could be regarded as a Japanese kind of orientalism.[15] Japan needed the primitive and backward South in order to feel advanced and civilized. The literary critic Minato Kawamura writes:

The national motto of *datsua nyūō* [dissociating from Asia, joining with the West], modern Japan's long-cherished wish, was achieved not only by modernizing, civilizing and Westernizing itself but also by seeing other Asian and Pacific regions as primitive and backward. In other words, Japan's civilization and enlightenment entailed regarding the Asia and Pacific regions which shared the same cultural roots as relatively primitive and savage.

(Kawamura 1993: 120)

In this way the dual processes of 'orientalizing' Asian and Pacific regions and 'de-orientalizing' Japan itself proceeded simultaneously. The Japanese stance towards the South is thus ambiguous in terms of cultural distance: it is sometimes assumed to be 'far', a remote primitive place, and sometimes 'near', the cradle of Japanese people who share the same racial and cultural traits.[16]

Hisakatsu Hijikata and the storyboard

An important figure who contributed greatly to the formation of the 'tourist culture' in Palau today was Hisakatsu Hijikata, an artist who resided in Palau during the Japanese colonial period. As an ardent admirer of Gauguin as well as a man with interests in primitive cultures through his reading of books on ethnology and archaeology, Hijikata had a strong interest in the South (Hijikata 1991: 190–1). In 1929 he left Tokyo for Palau, following a long-cherished desire. After arriving in Palau, he soon started to teach wood carving to the islanders at the *kōgakkō* or public schools and at a handicraft school for local carpenters, as a part-time employee at the *Nan'yō-chō*. He became particularly interested in the *bai* (traditional meeting house), which had coloured storyboards on which various pictures of gods, humans, birds, fish and plants were carved. In his teaching, therefore, Hijikata encouraged his pupils to learn about and make storyboards.

As James Nason has discussed, this made Palau a major exception in the general decline of traditional craft production in Micronesia. The storyboards were small rectangular wooden boards on which various motifs from the stories were carved and painted. They were called *itabori* in Japanese and bought by Japanese residents in Palau and occasional tourists from Japan. According to Nason, new motifs were introduced for a variety of other wood carvings, such as naturalistic rooster-shaped bowls, and some support was provided for the making of jewellery from shell and turtle shell (Nason 1984: 434). The new handicrafts that were invented during the Japanese colonial days play an important role in Palau tourism today.[17]

Further, according to Earl Wesley Jernigan (1973: 168), in the 1960s (during the American occupation) rapid changes were observed in storyboard styles. They were seen in the works of Ngiraibuuch, Osiik, Sbal and Bernardino Rduloal. Of these storyboard carvers, Ngiraibuuch, Osiik and Sbal were pupils of Hijikata in their teens in the 1930s. Jernigan (1973: 266) points out that one of the most important differences between the traditional narrative style and the modern storyboard style was the representation of spatial depth in the latter. This was the result of learning about Western perspective through having been taught to draw by Japanese artists during the Japanese colonial period.

Another interesting figure was Baris Sylvester, a Palauan who began to concentrate on storyboard making during his time in jail. Jernigan writes:

> Baris' work is popular with many Americans, perhaps because it has a rustic appearance and conveys a strong sense of carved wood. It looks 'primitive' in the same sense that the work of the American painter Grandma Moses looks primitive and almost 'baroque' crowding of his compositions gives the entire surface of the board an active and rich texture. Many tourists who are unfamiliar with the arts of Palau perceive

Baris' work as more authentic or traditional, though in fact the reverse is true.

(Jernigan 1973: 248–50)

Under the influence of Baris, the jail became one of the most active centres of storyboard making in Palau. Tourists could go to the jail to order and buy storyboards from jail carvers. Even now, storyboards are still made in jail, though not sold there any more. In this way, the jail style originated by Baris now forms the mainstream of the storyboards for tourists. Further, according to Margo Vitarelli, an American artist born and raised in Palau, the number of stories depicted on the storyboards has declined compared with former times. Only a few famous stories of breadfruit and turtles, which are easily understandable to tourists, are now included. The storyboards thus have become tourist art.

The tourist encounter

One of the main tasks of the anthropology of tourism is to observe and analyse the interaction of tourists and the host society (Smith 1989). What happens, then, in the tourist encounter between Japan and Palau?

Given the colonial connection, one might assume that Japanese tourism in Palau would have a unique character. A direct example is memorial tourism.

Figure 7.3 Storyboard in the style of Baris.

For tourists of this kind, Palau is a place of colonial memories and particularly of the wartime experience. The beautiful Palauan seas may remind them of the bloody battle that turned the beach orange (the famous Orange Beach on Peleliu). But this type of tourism has become less and less significant, as the people concerned are getting older and dying. It is estimated that memorial tourism now constitutes less than 5 per cent of total tourism in Palau. The younger Japanese tourists are rarely interested in colonial history.

However, the stereotypical Japanese perception of the South in colonial days continues to be reproduced today, even in post-colonial tourist brochures and guidebooks. These emphasize free and easy relaxation, the opposite to the busy and highly developed urban life in Japan, using words such as *nonki* (easy), *nonbiri* (unhurriedly) and *kiraku* (optimistic). In the tourist guidebook for Micronesia mentioned earlier, typical tourist behaviour is depicted:

> Stay at a hotel located at the island whose main street is just 30 minutes' walk long. Snorkelling and diving on an inhabited island during the daytime, and listening to the mysterious folk tales of the island under a lamp at night. Meet the chiefs of the island taking them gifts from Japan. These chiefs who govern the island can speak Japanese very well and are friendly. Drinking Budweiser together, we think about the harsh reality of the island. But looking up to the sky with thousands of stars, *nonki* [easy and comfortable] is the word which fits the island. Relaxing after arriving on the islands, one can imagine living in Micronesia someday. Yes, this is a real way of life. The chiefs and villagers we met in the islands and the Japanese who moved to Micronesia taught it to us. As you see, Micronesia was a paradise.
>
> (Shimokawa 1999: 2)

For most Japanese, the South is regarded as a place which is in some ways 'underdeveloped' and therefore 'easygoing', though not in a negative sense. It is often viewed as a place that makes travellers feel a degree of familiarity and even nostalgia, as described in the following passage from *Tio in the Southern Islands*, a novel written by Natsuki Ikezawa, a contemporary Japanese novelist:

> 'Why do I love this place so much?' Tom [a Japanese tourist to the island] said as if he was asking himself. Then, Tomoko, his girlfriend, responded: 'Such places exist – places that make you feel as if you have lived just to visit them, even through you are seeing them for the first time. Places where you discover another self. This is the place for you. A quiet sun-lit island in the middle of the Southern Seas. Easygoing people surrounded by beautiful seas and coconut trees. And kind island boys.'
>
> (Ikezawa 1996: 144)

The South is a place that makes you feel as if you have lived. It is a place where you discover another self. For many Japanese the South is not necessarily seen as a far, exotic place. Examining the tourism in Bali, Indonesia, Misa Matsuda suggests that Japanese tourism in Bali should be analysed from the perspective not only of exoticism but also of nostalgia (Matsuda 1989: 43–5). To Westerners, Balinese culture with its *barong* dance (lion dance), Hindu temples and rice terraces may look exotic, but to the Japanese the *barong* dance is reminiscent of the Japanese lion dance, the Hindu temples may remind them of Buddhist ones in Kyoto and Nara, and rice terraces are quite normal in Japanese rural areas. As I have discussed elsewhere (Yamashita 2003: Chapter 7), Bali reminds Japanese tourists of landscapes that have vanished in present-day urban Japan. Nostalgia is, then, an important factor for the Japanese in relation to Bali. A Japanese tourist brochure even describes Bali as a 'second homeland'. This may be the case for the Pacific as well.

Just as, culturally, the contribution of the Japanese artist Hisakatsu Hijikata led to the 'invention' of the storyboard, which has become a major Palauan handicraft sold to tourists, tourism may lead to the self-consciousness of a host people. In the Pacific region, Jocelyn Linnekin (1997) has examined cultural identity in relation to tourism by taking examples from Hawai'i and Samoa. According to her, identity merchandise became popular in Hawai'i in the 1990s. The state and the tourist industry were hoping to attract a better class of tourist and revamp Hawai'i's image by offering a more 'authentic' and higher-quality tourist experience. Plastic *hula* skirts were out; respectful performances of ancient (*kahiko*) hula were in.[18] In Samoa, cultural tourism now takes the form of guided visits to rural villages, and the public market in Apia offers craft items to tourists, such as miniature kava bowls and outrigger canoes, coconut-leaf fans, shell necklaces and woven pandanus-leaf handbags.

In Palau extensive use is made of cultural symbols such as the *bai*, the traditional meeting house in Palauan culture. Government buildings, hotels and even discotheques are built in the traditional style of *bai*. *Bai* motifs are drawn on licence plates, stamps and T-shirts. Storyboard motifs appear on government buildings, in art works for sale at the airport, and on postcards. Furthermore, the Palau Visitors Authority has proposed that there is a need for an increased contribution from Palauan culture and heritage to tourism programmes and facilities. The islands possess many unique cultural features, such as the Yapese money quarry and the stone monoliths, although there has been relatively little development of these resources that could be components of either cultural-based tourism or ecotourism (PVA 1997: 44). The development plan for Babeldaob, the largest of the Palau islands, is at issue in this regard. The Division of Cultural Affairs has been making a list of the cultural and historical sites that have the greatest potential for attracting tourists.

The Palau Senior Citizen Center plays an important role in the preservation

Figure 7.4 Palau on T-shirts.

of the cultural heritage. Run by senior citizens over 55 years old, many of whom are *konketsu* (born of a Japanese father and a Palauan mother), the centre has been concerned with preserving cultural heritage by producing handicrafts and occasionally performing traditional dances. It runs a souvenir shop to sell its products. During my field research in March 1998, the centre and the Palau Visitors Authority hosted an experimental 'dinner show', offering 'a night of traditional fun and fare' to tourists. The dinner consisted of not only Palauan food but also Japanese food such as *sashimi* and *sushi*, and the entertainment included old Japanese popular songs as well.

Lastly, I should note a recent phase of Japanese overseas tourism development. With the coming of an accelerated ageing society in contemporary Japan,[19] 'long-stay' – the Japanese version of international retirement migration in which retired elderly people have been moving to foreign places in search of meaningful lives after retirement – has been coming to the fore in the Japanese overseas tourism market. If one recalls that 6.2 million people aged over 50 travelled overseas in 2006, this is a quite marketable field, especially as the 7-million-strong baby-boomer generation called *dankai-no-sedai* (the 'lump generation' of those who were born between 1947 and 1949) began to retire in 2007. In this respect, Guam, Saipan, Rota and Palau may become increasingly popular as the nearest tropical islands to Japan where one can make oneself understood in the Japanese language.

Conclusion

This chapter has examined the Japanese encounter with Palau from historical as well as contemporary perspectives. In the history of Japan's Southern advance, the South was discovered as a new world for the Japanese that belonged to neither the East nor the West. It was a backward, under-developed area, the development of which was the task of Japan. In this colonialist scheme, a great number of Japanese people migrated to the South. Palau was the centre of this Southern expansion, because *Nan'yō-chō* was located at Koror. Now, in the post-colonial age, the Japanese visit Palau as tourists rather than as migrants. Although some memorial tourists renew their memories of colonial days, a majority of the tourists today are the young divers who often do not know the colonial history. For them, the South is an easygoing and relaxing place where the workaholic Japanese can take their minds off work in a timeless 'paradise' and refresh themselves. In 'long-stay' tourism, it could become a similar paradise for elderly Japanese retirees. We may see here a post-colonial version of 'Japanese orientalism' emerging in the form of a tourism in which Palau is seen as an easygoing, nostalgic and comfortable place, the world Japan has lost in the process of development.

As for ecotourism, the new focus of Palau tourism, we should note that it is based upon a subtle balance, not only between nature and people, but also between development and sustainability. According to the report of CoPop-Chi, the Palau National Committee on Population and Children (1997: 2), Palau may have 6,000 hotel rooms by the year 2010 and be hosting 400,000 or more visitors annually. Further, the report estimated that the total population in the year 2010 could be as high as 46,000 persons, with two-thirds of them being non-Palauan.[20] The most critical problem of tourism in Palau today is, then, the question of where the breaking point lies in the ecological balance between the people, the land and the sea. Although I am not in a position to answer this question, what is clear is that, if the balance is not achieved, Palau will be unable to sustain either tourism or the nation itself. The sustainability of Palau and Palauan tourism depends on this delicate ecological balance.

At this point, ecotourism becomes the 'ideological framing' discussed by MacCannell, as quoted at the beginning of this paper. He wrote: 'Tourism is not just an aggregate of mere commercial activities; it is also an ideological framing of history, nature, and tradition; a framing that has the power to reshape culture and nature to its own needs' (MacCannell 1992: 1). The Palauan coral reefs are not simply nature itself, but nature ideologically framed by tourism. 'Nature' here has become a symbolic resource within which the Palauan government, tourist agents and tourists search for meaning and value. In this sense, ecotourism is a cultural production in which nature is 'staged', especially for a certain type of middle-class tourists from the rich

North to which Japan belongs (Ikeda 1996; Mowforth and Munt 1998: 131). It could thus also be a strong symbolic weapon for Palau to use in the contemporary politics of global environmentalism.

Notes

1 This chapter was originally published in the journal *Contemporary Pacific*, volume 12, number 2, Fall 2000, pp. 437–63, by the University of Hawai'i Press. Some minor revisions and data updating are made for the current publication. The fieldwork on which this chapter is based was carried out in March 1998 as a part of the 'Moving Cultures' project organized by the School of Humanities, Asian, and Pacific Studies, the University of Hawai'i at Mano, and funded by the Ford Foundation. I am also grateful to the Palau Visitors Authority, Japan Office, and Professor Hisashi Endo of Kyoto Bunkyo University for their offering the recent data on Palau tourism.

2 Economically, the contribution of the tourism sector to Palau's gross domestic product in 1996 was estimated to be as high as $12 million, which was around 11 per cent of the total (Palau Government 1996: 8-2).

3 Several diving magazines are published monthly in Japan. *Marine Diving*, published since 1968, has played an important role in promoting diving tourism in Japan.

4 Regarding Japanese tourism statistics, see the Japan National Tourist Organization website: http://www.jnto.go.jp.

5 However, the Japanese outbound rate of the total population (14 per cent) is still low as compared with other East Asian countries such as Taiwan (38 per cent) and Korea (22 per cent). The Japanese government has pledged to increase Japanese outbound tourists to 20 million by 2010. See the Ministry of Land, Infrastructure and Transport Japan website: http://www.mlit.go.jp.

6 World Tourism Organization website: http://unwto.org/facts/eng/highlights.htm.

7 In 2006, Japanese visitors to China increased by 10.5 per cent, while visitors to the United States, the number one destination in 2005, went down by 5.4 per cent as compared to the previous year. Visitors to China increased from 2.2 million in 1999 to 3.75 million in 2004, while the number of tourists to the United States decreased from 5 million in 1999 to 3.67 million in 2006. Japan National Tourist Organization website: http://www.jnto.go.jp.

8 Japan National Tourist Organization website: http://www.jnto.go.jp.

9 In Japan, tourism tended to become more individualistic in the 1990s, especially among the younger generation. For example, the Jal Pak tours (Japan Airlines group package tours) have been replaced by I'll tours (Japan Airlines individual package tours), which emphasize the idea of 'I will choose'.

10 A slightly different version of this section appears in my article on the history of Japanese anthropology (Yamashita 2004).

11 Jun Takayama (1995) has examined the book in detail and has pointed out that parts of it were plagiarized from the Western literature, though the book is narrated as if these were Suzuki's own observations.

12 Minato Kawamura (1993) has discussed this as well.

13 John Russel (1991: 11) sees the black 'primitives' drawn in *Bōken Dankichi* as originating in Western images of black people. The cannibal image of the Pacific can be traced back to Tsunenori Suzuki's *Nan'yō Tanken Jikki*, which describes the peoples of the South Seas as primitive and very brutal, who practice cannibalism just like beasts. However, this image, as noted before, may also be of Western origin if one considers Suzuki's plagiarism.

14 Between 50 and 60 per cent of the Japanese in the *Nan'yō* were from Okinawa, and the people from Okinawa were contemptuously referred to as 'Japan Kanaka' (Tomiyama 1997: 215).

15 Kang Sang-Jung (1996: 86) has defined 'Japanese orientalism' as being motivated by a desire to avoid Western imperialistic violence and to use Japan's own hegemonic power in the Asian and Pacific regions. He examined Japanese orientalism based on his study of Japanese colonial policy and *tōyō shigaku*, the Japanese historical science of the Orient. On *tōyō shigaku*, see the book by Stefan Tanaka (1993) which inspired Kang Sang-Jung's discussion.

16 Ichirō Tomiyama quotes the words of Rokurō Takano, a doctor and chief of the Prevention Agency in the Ministry of Health and Welfare, who wrote in 1942: 'The Japanese race is actually well suited for life in the South Seas as the Europeans clearly are not. . . . Physically and temperamentally, we are a South Sea people' (Tomiyama 1997: 208).

17 This sort of 'invention of tradition' in the colonialist and tourist eyes is reminiscent of the situation in Bali, Indonesia. In Bali, traditional culture and, particularly, performing arts such as dances were elaborated and refined in the 1930s under the Western 'tourist gaze'. The now famous *kecak* dance is a good example of this. Now it has become 'symbolic capital', exploitable for profit by being appropriated by the Balinese people within the economy of tourist development (Picard 1990, 1995: 55; Yamashita 2003: 33–8).

18 In the same article Linnekin (1997: 228) notes that, today, *kahiko* is celebrated as an 'authentic' tradition revived, even though most of the dances performed have been only recently created. In other words, 'authenticity' is produced in the touristic context.

19 It is estimated that the percentage of the population over 65 years old will increase to 29 per cent by 2025 and to 40 per cent by 2055, compared to 20 per cent in 2006. See the Cabinet Office of Japan website: http://www8.cao.go.jp/kourei/whitepaper/w-2005/gaiyou/17indexg.html.

20 However, fortunately or unfortunately, in 2007 it seems that the changes are proceeding much more slowly than expected.

References

Akimichi, T. (1997). 'Japanese views on Oceania: modernist images of paradise'. In K. Yoshida and J. Mack (eds), *Image of Other Cultures*. Osaka: NHK Service Centre.

CoPopChi, Palau National Committee on Population and Children (1997). *Population and Development: Toward Palau National Policy for Sustainable Human Development*. Koror: CoPopChi.

Graburn, N. (1989). 'Tourism: the sacred journey'. In V. Smith (ed.), *Hosts and Guests: The Anthropology of Tourism*, 2nd edn. Philadelphia: University of Pennsylvania Press.

Hijikata, H. (1991). *Hijikata Hisakatsu Chosakushū* [Hijikata Hisakatsu collected works], vol. 6. Tokyo: San'ichi shobō.

Ikeda, M. (1996). 'Kosutarika no Eko-tsūrizumu' [Eco-tourism in Costa Rica]. In *Idō no Minzokushi* [The ethnography of global mobility], Iwanami Kōza Bunkajinruigaku [Iwanami Series of Cultural Anthropology], vol. 7. Tokyo: Iwanami shoten.

Ikezawa, N. (1996). *Minami no Shima no Tio* [Tio in the Southern islands]. Tokyo: Bungeishunjū.

Jernigan, E.W. (1973). '*Lochukle*: a Palauan art tradition'. Ph.D dissertation, Department of Anthropology, University of Arizona, Tucson.

Kang, S.-J. (1996). *Orientarizumu no Kanata e* [Beyond orientalism]. Tokyo: Iwanami shoten.

Kawamura, M. (1993). 'Taishū Orientarizumu to Ajia Ninshiki' [Popular orientalism and Japanese perception of Asia]. In *Bunka no nakano Shokuminchi* [Colonies in culture], Iwanami Kōza Kindai Nihon to Shokuminchi [Iwanami series of modern Japan and colonies), vol. 7. Tokyo: Iwanami shoten.

Khaleghi, H. (1996). *An Analysis of Tourism in Palau*. Report prepared for Mary Ann Delmel, Managing Director, Palau Visitors Authority. Koror: Pacific Business Center Program.

Linnekin, J. (1997). 'Consuming cultures: tourism and the commoditization of cultural identity in the island Pacific'. In M. Picard and R. E. Wood (eds), *Tourism, Ethnicity, and the State in Asia and Pacific Societies*. Honolulu: University of Hawai'i Press.

MacCannell, D. (1992). *Empty Meeting Grounds: The Tourist Papers*. London and New York: Routledge.

Matsuda, M. (1989). 'Japanese tourists and Indonesia: images of self and other in the age of *kokusaika* (internationalization)'. MA thesis, Asian Studies, Australian National University, Canberra.

Moon, O. (1997). 'Tourism and cultural development: Japanese and Korean contexts'. In S. Yamashita, K.H. Din and J. Eades (eds), *Tourism and Cultural Development in Asia and Oceania*. Bangi: Penerbit Universiti Kebangsaan Malaysia.

Mowforth, M. and I. Munt (1998). *Tourism and Sustainability: New Tourism in the Third World*. London and New York: Routledge.

Nason, J.D. (1984). 'Tourism, handicrafts and ethnic identity in Micronesia'. *Annals of Tourism Research*, 11, pp. 421–49.

Palau Government (1996). *Palau 2020: National Master Development Plan*, Revised draft final report. Koror: Palau Government.

Palau Visitors Authority (PVA) (1997). *Sustainable Development Policies and Action Plan: Palau*. Koror: Palau Visitors Authority.

Peattie, M.R. (1988). *Nan'yō: The Rise and Fall of the Japanese in Micronesia, 1885–1945*. Honolulu: University of Hawai'i Press.

—— (1996). *Shokuminchi* [Colonies], trans. Toyomi Asano. Tokyo: Yomiurishinbunsha.

Picard, M. (1990). ' "Cultural tourism" in Bali: cultural performances as tourist attraction'. *Indonesia*, 49, pp. 37–74.

—— (1995). 'Cultural heritage and tourist capital: cultural tourism in Bali'. In M.-F. Lanfant, J.B. Allcock and E.M. Burner (eds), *International Tourism: Identity and Change*. London: Sage Publications.

Russel, J. (1991). 'Race and reflexivity: the black other in contemporary Japanese mass culture'. *Cultural Anthropology*, 6, pp. 3–25.

Shimokawa, Y. (ed.) (1999). *Sukininachatta Mikronesia* [I love Micronesia]. Tokyo: Futabasha.

Smith, V. (ed.) (1989). *Hosts and Guests: The Anthropology of Tourism*, 2nd edn. Philadelphia: University of Pennsylvania Press.

Takayama, J. (1995). *Nankai no Daitankenka Suzuki Tsunenori: Sono Kyozō to Jitsuzō* [Suzuki Tsunenori: between truth and fiction]. Tokyo: San'ichi shobō.

Tanaka, S. (1993). *Japan's Orient: Reading Pasts into History*. Berkeley: University of California Press.

Tomiyama, I. (1997). 'Colonialism and the science of the tropical zone'. In T. Barlow (ed.), *Formation of Colonial Modernity in East Asia*. Durham, NC: Duke University Press.

Uehara, S. (1990). *Umino Rakuen Palao* [Palau: a marine paradise]. Tokyo: Aminosan.

Yamashita, S. (2003). *Bali and Beyond: Explorations in the Anthropology of Tourism*, trans. Jerry Eades. New York and Oxford: Berghahn Books.

—— (2004). 'Constructing selves and others in Japanese anthropology: the case of Micronesia and Southeast Asian studies'. In S. Yamashita, J. Bosco and J.S. Eades (eds), *The Making of Anthropology in East and Southeast Asia*. New York and Oxford: Berghahn Books.

Yano, T. (1975). *'Nanshin' no Keifu* [History of Japanese 'advancement to the South'). Tokyo: Chūōkōronsha.

8 The search for the real thing
Japanese tourism to Britain

Bronwen Surman

Introduction

The Japanese are prolific travellers and have been for centuries. Today Japanese tourists are important players in the business of global tourism, and an understanding of their destination decision-making process is invaluable in understanding certain trends in tourist activity. Travelling at home or abroad is something so many nationalities enjoy. There are of course peculiar habits and stereotypes for all, but Japanese tourists, like most, are in search of a pleasurable experience, encompassing the unusual and alternative while remaining predominantly within their comfort zone.

This chapter examines the nature of Japanese outbound tourism to Britain and what has influenced destination choice within Britain. A search for the 'real thing', 'authenticity' and 'nostalgia' are prevalent in the language and themes underlying destination choice.

Whilst living in Japan I was struck by the number of travel and travel-related television programmes, and it seemed to me that television might be the single greatest influence on the travel decision-making process. However, a pilot questionnaire which focused on 'Why Britain?' indicated a predominance of alternative influences or stimuli, including youth culture, school and famous literary figures. I then used a destination-specific questionnaire focused on respondents' reactions to particular destinations and their travel habits. In these interviews I sought to explore in the tourists' own words their images and expectations of Britain. Destinations were selected from around Britain, both popular sites, such as Buckingham Palace, the British Museum, Oxford and Stratford, and rest and recreational areas, such as London's Hyde Park and Green Park. I was careful to interview a diverse cross-section: families, couples and individuals in varying age ranges. Central to my research was the method of participant observation in the form of 'tailing' over two separate periods of time, being approximately two weeks in each case, two Japanese tourists, one male and one female and both in their mid-thirties. The male tourist was on his first trip outside Japan, and the female was also on her first visit to Britain; however, she had previously visited the United States and Indonesia. This was an opportunity to observe Britain with 'new eyes'.

Associations with literature can be a powerful influence over destination choice. Traditionally this has been communicated through books and authors, but more recently it is through films and their locations, and this has led to a rise in 'set-jet' tourism. Now the growth of film-based tourism is trying to offset the economic downturn that is affecting the number of Japanese tourists coming to Britain.

Japan's domestic tourist industry has a long history, and travel (both real and imaginary) has been written about in Japan since early times. 'Marvels of literature like *Manyoshu* in the eighth century, *Tosa nikki* in the tenth century, and *Okunohosomichi* in the seventeenth century were primarily based upon experiences in travel and travel narratives' (Kajiwara, in Yamashita *et al.* 1997). However, the Japanese remain habitual tourists, both at home and abroad, and tourist associations like the British Tourist Authority (BTA) are looking to find new areas to entice this important sector of the market back on to their shores.

Outbound tourism to Britain

Holiday and business constitute the main purposes of Japanese visiting the UK, and in 2005 the BTA estimated that 47 per cent of Japanese came on holiday and 27 per cent came for business (other purposes included visiting friends, study and miscellaneous). The Japanese tourist market is distinctly segmented and, with Japan having a rapidly ageing population, these segment demographics are constantly changing.

A description of the demographics of this segmented market is given by the BTA (2007a), with 25- to 34-year-olds representing the largest segment of Japanese visitors to the UK and nearly half of all visitors being aged 25–44, and the most rapid recent growth is with the 45- to 64-year-olds (British Tourist Authority, VisitBritain 2007). These are revised demographic descriptions from the late 1990s. Three key market segments are worth noting in detail: *Dankai* (literally meaning a 'clod' or groups, referring to the 'baby-boomers' born after the Second World War) aged 55–60. *Dankai* have the time and money including savings to spend on themselves and are 'leading consumerism in almost every aspect' (Dentsu Research 2004, in BTA 2007a). This generation is often interested in restarting hobbies they used to enjoy before working, and special interest travel offers them a multitude of opportunities. *Makeinu* ('office ladies') and 'mother and daughter'. *Makeinu* are the single childless women over 30 and termed the Japanese version of 'Bridget Jones'. 'Mother and daughter' is now an increasingly popular travel style. Mothers aged 45–65 are travelling with their daughters aged 20–35, as many are living at home still with disposable incomes to spare (BTA 2007a). However, Japanese Tourism Marketing (JTM) is also identifying a new group termed *Ohitorisama* (single-not-young lady), otherwise termed single career women, and research shows that there is a very visible increase in the number of Japanese tourists travelling alone from 9.7 per cent in 1997 to 13.2 per cent in 2002 to 17 per cent in 2003.

A combination of 'push' and 'pull' factors form the motivations that determine Japanese visitor choice and expectations. In essence push factors include wealth, education, confidence, word of mouth, rite of passage, travel game shows on TV and family influence. Pull factors are more destination specific and include descriptions and imagery to win over and persuade the tourist to make a choice.

Notably, childhood influences tend to be lifelong influences. Exposure to songs, TV programmes, films and literature as children often reflects our personal tastes later in life. School is often the first introduction point for many famous places, people and literary characters. Songs learnt through school, for example reading and understanding the lyrics of a song in English, are a fun and educational way to learn the language and can often lead to further interest in that language, the group, the fashion or the place from which the group has come. The Beatles are an obvious choice and have been known to be the first music with English lyrics that Japanese students have experienced. Texts and novels were frequently cited in answer to specific questioning on the decision-making process and influences on destination choice (Surman 1998). Whether textbooks or novels on a school curriculum or in a language school are English or American in origin may have a profound effect on interest and indeed destination choice in the future.

Nostalgia and authenticity

'Nostalgia' is a theme that recurs through much of my research on Japanese tourism, from the magazine articles and brochures that describe a destination to the words that describe the Japanese tourists' anticipations and motivations. This is also apparent in Japanese domestic tourism, where there is a prolific use of *furusato* in advertising and literature. The word *furusato*, literally meaning old village, evokes a myriad of feelings. It generally refers to a 'home town', the place where one is born and raised, and a quest for the 'authentic', although of course in reality one's own home town can be quite different. There is a notion that the Japanese identify with *furusato* overseas, places that portray wholesome, natural and traditional aspects of Japan.

Similarly 'authenticity', staged or otherwise, is a recurrent theme in destination choice. Places are often referred to as 'looking authentic' or having an 'authentic atmosphere', used in relation to festivals, art, dress, etc., something that is genuine, either tangible or intangible. A destination is described as an expression of (cultural) authenticity. However, 'authentic' is a word 'often used and interpreted but much contested, disputed and discussed' (Hendry 2000: 11). Authenticity and culture, literature and history have a complex relationship and are inextricably bound. Indeed, Lowenthal said, 'If the past is a foreign country, nostalgia has made it "the foreign country with the healthiest tourist trade of all" ' (1985: 4).

Boorstein (in 1964) and Bathes (in 1972) saw tourism as a frivolous, inauthentic activity of modern capitalist society (Graburn 1983a: 15), when people do not really experience 'reality' directly, but thrive on pseudo-events and inauthentic contrived attractions (Urry 1990: 7), but to others (Mac-Cannell 1989: 1) it is a central ritual in which the search for authenticity is the central motivating force, a means of restoring authenticity that is lacking in the daily lives of modern people (Smith and Nash 1991: 18).

It was without exception that the tourists I interviewed in Oxford made reference to the 'traditional' aspects of the city and its 'beautiful old buildings'. Additionally, sightings of students in their black gowns in the city of Oxford prompted several tourists to describe it as 'old-fashioned England'. In another example a respondent described England as 'eccentric' and, on further probing to understand the full meaning of this description, it seems a positive portrayal: the tourist saw it as something *kakkoi* or 'wonderful and different'.

A popular Japanese women's magazine referred to the Cotswolds in terms of 'villages the colour of honey' and 'a handmade holiday' (*tezukuri no tabi*), asserting an 'original' and 'authentic' quality 'where I found the summer holiday one can only dream about', a place to find 'delicious tea', 'secret gardens' and 'manor houses'. Naturally, host destinations have become aware of entrepreneurial possibilities and cater to the tourists' expectations – whether or not this is staged authenticity, it appears that tourists are seeking a confirmation and 'seeing with their own eyes'.

Motivations

So what are the main motivating factors in tourist destination choice within Britain itself? According to the BTA the top motivators are heritage, history, countryside, gardens, museums and galleries, theatre, literature and character, event showing, brands and the English language (BTA 2007a).

Britain and Japan share similarities, both being island nations with a long history and a monarchy. Beautiful gardens, an abundance of art and literature and of course tea are very important to each. It is perhaps many of these attributes that the Japanese themselves hold in high esteem that form part of the draw to Britain, a 'connection', a 'shared status' and what have been termed 'shared symbols' (BTA 2007a). In fact, research has shown that, when questioned on Britain as a destination, respondents repeatedly used words such as 'culture', 'traditional', 'historic' and 'famous'.

The British Council in the late 1990s had a poster campaign to promote Britain with old and new images of Britain – to be sent to classrooms in 54 countries including Japan. The impact of the classroom learnt image should not be underestimated.

Heritage and history are paramount to the tourist industry, and literary tourism is a productive and rapidly growing sector of the expanding heritage industry, evident by the many books now available on literary tours of the

UK. Literature is a means of communicating culture. It exudes an atmospheric heritage and often spurs the imagination back to childhood memories. One may only reread a passage or poem to evoke memories of nostalgia for childhood or for the feeling of wanting to visit a place. Heritage, history and the past are indeed a business, for it seems 'today a great deal of energy is dedicated into looking backwards and towards capturing a past which, in many ways, is considered superior to the chaotic present and the dreaded future' (Dann 1994: 55).

London is the most popular destination within Britain, and first-time visitors usually go to London, with perhaps day trips out of the city. Repeat visitors tend to take package tours to places like the Lake District. Many tours to Britain outside of London have a powerful literary flavour, and most include a visit to the birthplace or home of a literary figure, as in the case of William Shakespeare and Stratford-upon-Avon, or Beatrix Potter and Hill Top Farm.

Many Japanese have an enthusiasm for British books, films and characters. The Nation Brand Index research shows that visitors are interested in visiting places from films and dramas. DVD launches also have potential, as demonstrated by the Tsutaya rental shops, which have a membership of 15 per cent of the total Japanese population. Another demonstration of the power of promotion is that Korea is currently the favourite destination for Japanese women aged 30–50 owing to continued repeats of a popular TV drama called *Winter Sonata*.

The popularity and significance of literature in Japan are reiterated in research by Joy Hendry into 'going abroad at home', where the exoticism of foreign travel is brought to Japan in the reconstruction and replication of buildings, music, crafts, food, etc. in theme parks in Japan. In these *Gaikoku Mura*, 'foreign country villages', the popularity and role of literary figures are evident, including Alice's house, Gulliver and Shakespeare's plays (see Hendry, Chapter 5 in this book). Non-British examples are also prevalent. Other examples include Anne of Green Gables, exhibited in scenes at Canadian World in Hokkaido, Heidi's Cottage in the Swiss Village in the Tohoku region, the fairy tales of the Brothers Grimm and others, Don Quixote, Camelot and Hans Christian Andersen (Hendry 2000).

Examples of literary destinations in the UK

In Britain, three 'literary' destinations stand out as having had lasting relationships with Japanese tourists.

The Brontë Society, founded in 1893 to honour and nurture a worldwide interest in the Brontës' literary achievements, looks after the Brontës' home and opened the Brontë Parsonage Museum in Haworth in 1928. The introductory leaflet is translated into several different languages, and the 'Brontë Guide' is a book written half in English and half in Japanese. The museum has met many of the needs of the visiting Japanese tourist, including signposting to Top Withins, the setting and inspiration for Wuthering Heights. Every year a bouquet of flowers arrives on Charlotte Brontë's birthday from a lady in Japan, and these are put on display.

The Wordsworth Trust 'Centre for British Romanticism' is one example of a destination with long-established links with Japan, not only through the promotion of its tourist site Dove Cottage, but also through the Zen school of Buddhism. This is illustrated by the British haiku scholar and author R.H. Blyth, who devoted a chapter in his book to kinship, Wordsworth, poetry and Zen. In it he states that Zen 'looks within' and Wordsworth 'looks without'. In 1983 the official guidebook was translated into Japanese and, in 1987, 27 Japanese academics became involved with the trust, supported by both the English Literary Society of Japan and the Japan Society of English Romanticism (McCormick 1996: 50).

Peter Rabbit has proven to be a real draw to Japanese visitors. Beatrix Potter embodies gardens and nature, and the stories have simple language, all of which can be seen to appeal to Japanese girls' love of the cute or *kawairashi*. Indeed one tourist interviewed stated that she 'loved Peter Rabbit. I want to go to the Lake District even though I am in my twenties. I still love him and my niece has all the books too.'

Hill Top Farm was the home of the children's writer Beatrix Potter. It is this property in the Lake District village of Sawrey that she purchased with the royalty earnings of her first book, *The Tale of Peter Rabbit*, in 1902. The farm, cottage and gardens were later incorporated into her other stories.

The earliest translation of *The Tale of Peter Rabbit* into Japanese in 1906 was discovered by the Japanese academic Yoshihide Kawano. It is the oldest known foreign translation of a Beatrix Potter book (World of Peter Rabbit website 2007). The title was translated as 'A Fairy Tale of Mischievous Little Rabbits'. *The Tale of Benjamin Bunny*, translated as 'The Idyllic Novel of the Sequel of the Mischievous Little Rabbits', was subsequently published in the same journal, *Japan Agricultural Magazine*, though neither translation referred to Beatrix Potter as the author.

A Japanese guidebook and welcome leaflet are available at Hill Top, and the Japanese are a specific group market for them. Staff are sent on Japanese language and custom courses, and Hill Top has had Japanese volunteers in the house for the past five years. Many Japanese tourists like to buy Potter gifts and souvenirs there, sometimes buying up to 20 fridge magnets at a time, requesting separate bags for each. As a result of this demand, a limit has now been put on the number of bags given and also on the number of tours per day.

The influence of Beatrix Potter is so strong that a full-size replica of her home has been re-created in the grounds of a children's zoo in Tokyo. This attraction opened in April 2006 and holds an archive of the writer's work. It attracts approximately 50,000 visitors a year (World of Peter Rabbit website 2007). Indeed Peter Rabbit is used to advertise over 80 products in Japan, from cling film to books about the Lake District.

There is expected to be a tourism boost effect from the *Miss Potter* movie, filmed on location in the Lake District, although it is hard to predict by just how much. However, a survey by the Cumbria Tourist Board asks businesses what factors they think are affecting their business levels, and '*Miss Potter* film' has been included as an option since the film was released. In the first three months of 2007, 3.9 per cent of respondents thought that the *Miss Potter* film had positively affected their business levels, but by the third quarter of the year this figure had gone up to 19.1 per cent. A delegation including representatives from tourism businesses, the Cumbria Tourist Board and the National Trust have been on a 'mini trade mission' to Tokyo funded by the Northwest Regional Development Agency (Insider Media 2006) to build direct relationships with operators and 'spread the word about the delights of the Lake District' to key Japanese businesspeople involved in package tours and sales to England, with the intention of keeping the Lake District at the top of their itineraries (Northwest Regional Development Agency 2006).

It appears, however, that the writers and the books themselves are not enough to draw the crowds. In 2005, 16.8 million 'departures' were made by Japanese (BTA 2007a) to destinations abroad. Britain had a 2 per cent market share with 323,000 of these Japanese visits, ranking sixteenth as a country destination choice, down from 1995, which saw Britain's best ever year of visits from Japanese tourists with 619,000 visits. The Japanese desire for travelling abroad has decreased 5 per cent over the last ten years (Leisure White Paper, in BTA 2007a), and the Indian market is now worth more to the UK visitor economy than that of Japan (BTA 2007).

The current prospects for Japanese tourism in Britain in the early part of the twenty-first century do not look favourable. Tourists are being deterred by terrorist activity, especially after attacks in London and Glasgow, floods in Gloucestershire and increasing airline surcharges. Also with a weak yen against sterling the Japanese are finding Britain an expensive destination (BTA 2007a).

Film and tourism

However, the resurgence of literature through film and the draw of celebrity has the potential to counter these influences. For example, the Harry Potter films and books have been a worldwide success, and that includes in Japan. The Potter books conceptualize all that is English, boarding schools, ceremony, mystery, great buildings, sports, quintessential Britishness and thus an opportunity on which the tourist industry can capitalize, and so it has. Many films, by the nature of the landscape and architecture displayed, 'reinforce a brand for the UK as a country steeped in history', and 'British films and television programmes play a powerful role in showcasing the UK to the rest of the world and boosting tourism' (UK Film Council 2007).

Films are proving significant in the destination decision making process and those depicting the UK are apparently responsible for attracting about 1 in 10 overseas tourists, spending around £1.8 billion a year. This is estimated to be worth around £900 million to UK GDP (UK Film Council 2007).

The British Tourist Authority (BTA) Harry Potter website was the most successful campaign site launched by the BTA in 2001, with a map showing UK Potter film locations, and has been seen by the BTA as a fantastic way to promote Britain overseas. The Harry Potter films make use of locations all over Britain, including Oxford, London (e.g. King's Cross station and the zoo), Northumbria and Gloucester. This array of destinations has given rise to various Harry Potter themed tours such as 'Harry Potter's England', 'Overnight Harry Potter Special' and 'Harry Potter Theme Tour'.

The city of Oxford has played host to many film crews, with Hogwarts Hall (in Harry's school) filmed at Christ Church and the Hogwarts Infirmary at New College cloisters (Visit Oxford 2007). Also featured is the Bodleian Library, which has had increased interest from Japanese tourists, and 'hundreds of people asked about Harry Potter tours'. Christ Church has had an increase of approximately 30 per cent in interest, and the Harry Potter weeks at London Zoo have dramatically increased visitor numbers, with the half-term week of magic in October 2001 receiving 27,000 visitors whereas the usual average visitor figure for a whole month is 33,000 (Island North Film Commission 2007).

Alnwick Castle, another location for Hogwarts, saw a 120 per cent rise in visitor numbers following the release of the films. King's Cross station has erected a plaque marking platform 9¾ in response to visitor demand.

A guide on what to do and see in Gloucester has proved so popular that it has been printed in Japanese, and now the city of Gloucester is part of the 'Cotswolds Japan Partnership', which promotes the area to the Japanese market (Gloucester City Council Online 2007).

In October 2007 the BTA's VisitBritain launched a new film tourism campaign ahead of the release of the film *The Golden Age*, the sequel to the film *Elizabeth*, which follows the life of Queen Elizabeth I through a host of attractive locations. The Tourist Board expects it to draw visitors to 'iconic and heritage attractions' throughout Britain. A map of locations is available for download, and a film synopsis, a link to the trailer, six different touring itineraries, a picture gallery and inspirational information on Britain's 'golden age of now' are made available on the website.

British tourism also hopes to benefit from other films and their iconic locations, for example from 2008 there are plans to have a tour devoted to the Oxford of Philip Pullman after the release of *The Golden Compass*, the film based on Philip Pullman's book *Northern Lights*. In an Olsberg/SPI report commissioned by film and tourism bodies, stately homes, historic and religious buildings and rural or village landscapes are the locations most likely to inspire tourism (UK Film Council 2007).

The UK's first conference on film tourism, 'The London International Film Tourism Conference', was held in March 2007 in London, and a one-day international conference entitled 'Film, Television, Tourism and Regeneration' was held in Leeds in November 2007. These demonstrate that recognition of the importance of film tourism is clearly gaining momentum.

Conclusion

In conclusion, the reality of the current marketplace is such that factors such as terrorism, foot and mouth and the general economics of travel are dominating the decisions of Japanese tourists and are driving Japanese tourists to other destinations. Whether this is a long-term trend or a temporary phenomenon is yet to be seen, but history has shown that literature and the lure of its magic demonstrate its longevity beyond that of economics. Tourists continue to seek confirmation of what they already know, but as childhood influences play an important role perhaps we should also pay attention to what children are learning in schools, the curriculum, the texts used and the geographical and cultural backdrop for this material.

Britain's heritage is an influential motivator for Japanese tourists communicated through literature first experienced at school. In fact this literature, backed by the visual imagery of the blockbuster movie, has the potential to be a powerful influence on future destination choice for those Japanese travellers in search of 'the real thing'.

Bibliography

BBC News (1998). 'UK images selling Britain to the world'. Aired on 24 September, http://news.bbc.co.uk/hi/english/uk/newsid_1 71000/171818.stm.

—— (2007). 'Japanese boom from Potter movie'. Aired on 27 September, http://news.bbc.co.uk/2/hi/uk_news/england/cumbria/6965432.stm.

British Tourist Authority (1997). *Japan Market Guide 1997–98*. London: British Tourist Authority.

—— (1998). *Profile Japan 1998/99*. London: British Tourist Authority.

British Tourist Authority/English Tourist Board/Central Statistical Office (1997). *Japan: Visitor Traffic to the UK: A Market Summary: International Passenger Survey*. London: British Tourist Authority/English Tourist Board.

British Tourist Authority, VisitBritain (2007a). *Japan Full Market Profile*. London: British Tourist Authority.

—— (2007b). *New Campaign Creates the Golden Age of Set-Jetters*. London: British Tourist Authority.

Chon, K.S., T. Inagaki and T. Ohashi (2000). *Japanese Tourists: Socio-Economic Marketing and Psychological Analysis*. Binghamton, NY: Haworth Hospitality Press.

Dann, G.M.S. (1994). *The Language of Tourism: A Sociolinguistic Perspective*. Wallingford: CAB International.

Gloucester City Council Online (2007). 'Turning Japanese', http://www.gloucester.gov.uk.

Graburn, N.H.H. (1983a). 'The anthropology of tourism'. *Annals of Tourism Research*, 10, pp. 9–33.

—— (1983b). *To Pray, Pay and Play: The Cultural Structure of Japanese Domestic Tourism*. Aix-en-Provence: Centre des Etudes Touristiques.

Hendry, J. (2000). *The Orient Strikes Back*. Oxford: Berg.

Insider Media (2006). 'How Beatrix Potter opens doors in Japan', http://www.newsco.com/productsandservices/archive/nwbi/2006-06/potter.

Island North Film Commission (2007). 'Harry Potter results: discovering the magic of Britain's attractions', http://www.infilm.ca.

Lowenthal, D. (1985). *The Past Is a Foreign Country*. Cambridge: Cambridge University Press.

MacCannell, D. (1989). 'Introduction to the 1989 edition'. In D. MacCannell, *The Tourist*. London: Macmillan Press.

McCormick, T. (1996). 'Tourism and the arts: the Wordsworth Trust and Japanese visitors'. *Insights*, 7, pp. C49–62.

Moeran, B. (1983). 'The language of Japanese tourism'. *Annals of Tourism Research*, 10, pp. 93–108.

Nash, D. and V.L. Smith (1991). 'Anthropology and tourism'. *Annals of Tourism Research*, 18, pp. 12–25.

Northwest Regional Development Agency (2006). 'Tourism officials head off to Japan', http://www.nwda.co.uk.

Pearce, D.G. and R.W. Butler (eds) (1993). *Tourism Research, Critiques and Challenges*. London: Routledge.

Said, E. (1987). *Orientalism*. New York: Random House.

Surman, B.J.E. (1998). 'Japanese tourists to Britain: a quest for the real thing'. MA thesis, Oxford Brookes University, Oxford.

UK Film Council (2007). 'Stately attraction', http://www.ukfilmcouncil.org.uk/information/news.

Urry, J. (1990). *The Tourist Gaze*. London: Sage Publications.

Visit Oxford (2007). 'Film and TV locations', http://www.visitoxford.org.

White, M. (1992). *The Japanese Overseas*. Princeton, NJ: Princeton University Press.

World of Peter Rabbit website (2007). 'Discovery of the earliest translation of *The Tale of Peter Rabbit*'. Events and Press Office, http://www.peterrabbit.com.

Yamashita, S., K.H. Din and J.S. Eades (eds) (1997). *Tourism and Cultural Development in Asia and Oceania*. Bangi: Penerbit Universiti Kebangsaan Malaysia.

9   All roads lead to home

Japanese culinary tourism in Italy

Merry I. White

The study of tourism is both local and global as people leave and return to home 'villages', having experienced a range of cultural embeddedness in foreign metropolises or other cultural landscapes. What this embeddedness and its corollaries mean engages anthropologists who approach leaving home, being away and returning home as historical, economic and social settings framed by ideas of boundaries, oppositions and locations. Tourism is a useful site for such explorations of identity and material flows of culture. Japanese tourisms demonstrate the influences of domestic marketing and trend creation on the experiences, from mass tours to more recently popular individual and more 'assimilative' experiences of other cultures. In the case of culinary tourism, the movements and contexts establish and test the parameters of palatal identity. The fact that the quest for and experience of foods as destinations are so concrete and visceral helps to ground the study of 'plated' identity. The resonances in foodways for tourists, however, are as complex and layered as any transcultural exchanges or experiences.

The literature on movements of foods commonly treats 'globalizing' food, whether it is hamburgers in Beijing or a perfect curl of pickled ginger aside serried ranks of *nigiri* (hand-moulded sushi) in a *sushiya* (sushi restaurant) in New York. These foods are the products of global marketing and the construction of foods as fashions. The study of touristic dispersals and the examination of foodways as key in the marketing of tourism motivate the current inquiry in which foods and the quest for them in an 'exotic' locale may involve both resistance to, and a nostalgic engagement of, the homeland.

Looking at Japanese tourism in Italy suggests more than the experiences of leaving, visiting and returning. I will suggest that the meaning of touristic experience, as illustrated by the case of Italy for the Japanese, demonstrates as much about the social order and its discontents in Japan as it does about the embrace of Italy as an elite European culture. The preparation through the agencies of media and travel industries, the 'selling' of Italy to Japanese, includes the promise of these sometimes subversive engagements as well as the more guidebook-checking satisfactions of standardized mass tourism.[1]

Including many of the contemporary forms of tourism undertaken by Japanese travellers, Italian travel offers both the safety of cocooned 'bus' tourism and the chance for safe adventures. The insularity of stereotyped Japanese bus tourism of the last quarter of the twentieth century has been supplanted for many by a specificity (wine tours, bread-making classes, tours of shoe factories) and more personal attachment (home stays and pensiones rather than hotels) to the local environment by tourists. While magazines and television extol the virtues of independence and 'discovery' on the road, visitors, solitary or in twos and threes, may choose to carry one of the newer guidebooks, directing the independent traveller off the beaten track and on to less-known but still 'tracked' byways. In addition and crucial to both the bus and the unguided traveller are the evocations of Italy which offer both adventure and immersion in the 'foreign' and, ultimately, a yearning for the imagined Japan of home, which to some became the prime reason to travel. As one Japanese guide said, Italy has become Japan's 'offshore *furusato*' (ancestral-country home), and people find in Italy what they feel they have lost in Japan. 'Dream Italy' is on an interestingly managed border – it provides adventures for people wanting to test the boundaries of their habitual performance of culture, and it is safely ephemeral.

That it is now Italy that is 'consumed' and consumes Japanese interest is a momentary trend, but the 'consumed Italy' reveals aspects of Japanese domestic and social arrangements and Japanese management of the global. It has not always been this destination that could demonstrate a person's 'cosmopolitanism' – among other things. For several decades after the War, in a reflection of the Meiji and Taisho era borrowings from Europe, it had been France whose cultural outpourings had represented European civilization, and it was haute cuisine that demanded connoisseurship.

Haute cuisine, in the 1970s, became emblematic of elite social class and thus available to satire. In an episode in Juzo Itami's film *Tampopo*, for example, a young clerk accompanies his corporate superiors to an elegant French restaurant, clumsily carrying all of their briefcases and looking for all the world like a 'loser'. When they are all seated, the menus are passed around and the older men, befuddled by the French, wait for the most senior (as is appropriate) to choose. But this senior manager has no clue and, fearful of losing face, extemporizes – 'I'll have a simple meal, a salad, a fish and a Heineken.' The others, with various attempts to show connoisseurship and independent decision making, get in line behind him. The last and least, the young clerk, enters into meticulous detail with the waiter on his order and asks for the sommelier to consult with on the wines. His sophistication baffles the others, who are shocked at his insolence in using it. A deep knowledge of French food and wine is associated with elites, but here the joke is that the class status ladder is turned upside down.

By the mid-1980s, French restaurants had the edge in status, but by then independent, wage-earning young women had become the leading consumers of leisure in Japan. Unwilling to spend for the starched linen and the haute cuisine menus of French restaurants, young women, obeying the injunctions of women's magazines and marketing, began to go to the *kigaru de yasui* (cheap and cheerful) Italian restaurants, more relaxed and inexpensive, but still markedly European and chic. And, by the mid-1990s, Italian restaurants, cookbooks and foods had become the main objects of young women's culinary desires. These women (and their middle-aged mothers and aunts, who, with their children grown, were now free of the duties of the home) became the chief consumers of travel to Italy as well. For many, Italy was not only the paradisiacal homeland of the foods they enjoyed in Japan, but it was also an escape from the social and domestic demands on them at home. Young women who wanted to delay marriage might go to Italy for a few years of language learning and cooking school, justified as 'feminine' and suitable for marriage preparation. Older women, finding themselves at the cusp of their husbands' retirements, similarly sought respite in *onna tengoku* (women's heaven), in advance of the care of a retired and dependent spouse.

Instructed by guidebooks, magazines and a growing Japan-directed tourist industry in Italy, women came to Italy for more than checklist tourism, monuments and museums. They wanted the experience and a confirmation of the Italy they'd been taught, an Italy that might even, for some, act as a buffer between them and what seemed an all-too-predictable life. Some have stayed well beyond the appropriate age for marriage, and some have returned to Japan, creating independent careers using the culinary, linguistic and cultural skills they have obtained to prepare another generation of travellers, cooks and independent women, professionalizing their own travel experiences. The older forms of tourism have not disappeared, but choices have proliferated.

Globalizing and the new tourism in Italy

> It's so Italian! Just as I thought!
> (A middle-aged Japanese woman with a tour group at a restaurant in
> Venice, May 1999)

> La cacciucco e un coke, per favore.
> (A twenty-something Japanese woman, travelling alone, at a restaurant
> in Pisa, October 1999)

These two tourists in Italy reflect old and new trends in taste tourism and reveal diversity and change in Japan's 'globalization'. The first woman's experience is the product of what we might call the 'old tourism'; the experience of the second is a product of one of the many 'new tourisms' which, however plural, personal and 'localized', still guide the visitor to the 'right way' in foreign parts. The first woman is enjoying spaghetti with tomato sauce, an emblem of Italian cooking reinforced by marketing and media diffusion in Japan since the Second World War and culminating in the woman's need to eat this particular 'Italy' even where Italians would not, in Venice, where the food culture is very different from Japanese imaginings of Italy. The menu at this small restaurant is in Japanese, which for her confirms that she is in a place approved by travel books, magazines and the tour bus guides. Her experience conforms to a programme of 'Italy' that she and her colleagues on this trip have learned in their media- and market-directed experiences of 'global consumption' at home in Japan. But there are other Italys available beyond those of a 'standard package' Italy. The second tourist, off the paths beaten by travel agencies and other organizers of Italy for the Japanese visitor, has attempted several: but she is no less a consumer of an 'imagined' Italy than is her red-sauce-seeking compatriot. As a consumer of one of the 'new tourisms', 'experience tourism', she is in search of an imagined self-in-Italy, a knowledgeable, sophisticated woman of the world displaying her cosmopolitanism in a learned Italy, but remaining open to transformations of that self possible only through an engagement beyond the safety of what she already knows. Her guide is not a flag-carrying Japanese interpreter but a collection of books: a cookbook, a personal memoir by a Japanese expatriate in Italy, a dictionary and a copy of *Chikyu no Arukikata* (The way to walk the world), the bible of 'independent travellers' from Japan to many parts of the world. What she brings back is not armloads of *omiyage* (souvenirs) but what she may display as 'experience' or 'personal transformation' into a global person. What she has ordered in Pisa (though six miles from the coast) is a fish stew similar to a bouillabaisse in France, and ordering it in Italian with the addition of the most 'global' drink of all, Coca-Cola, marks her as a knowledgeable traveller even if the more locally appropriate drink would have been *un mezzo litro di vino bianco* (a half-litre of white wine) or, at the least, a bottle of *acqua minerale*.

The idea of seeking self-transformation, along lines construed to be appropriate to Japan and Japanese people, underlies one of the new tourisms, and this too is marketed to tourists as one of the justifications and goals of the pleasures of travel and consumption. The logic of the market for a place as much as for a fashion or other commodity moves from the singular to the multiple and diverse, from the product for local mass consumption to proliferating possibilities for 'individual globalization' in the upward trajectory of exported comestibles. We may now want to refer to 'tourists' without bias or prejudice as people engaging in the more contained, programmatic tourism of the past, and to 'travellers' as those who engage in a variety of delineated experiences more available to individuals than to groups – and perhaps, with the acknowledgement that within this term lie swamps and quicksands of confusion, to 'globalizers', those who produce those experiences for themselves and others, facilitators of 'experience tourism'. Japanese food tourism in Italy, an example of the literal ingestion of experience, demonstrates multiple, changing and individualized engagements in the world rather than the singular phenomenon that has been called 'globalization'.

The locations of 'globalization' themselves persist in diversifying, even as institutional phenomena such as laws, neo-colonial economies and military engagements seem to be attempting homogenization, or at least control of sites of resources and production against the divisive aspects of diversity.

Tourism and the industries that support it are useful 'sites' for examining changes of boundary experiences both at the microcosmic level of individual experience and at the level of larger agencies such as nations. We have seen the results of the reconfiguration of air travel in airports everywhere in the world, as American standards for security against terrorism are applied elsewhere. An airport in Dar es Salaam is as 'global' (or more so) as one in New York, in the merchandising and the mechanisms of travel: in the common culture of travel, we all show passports, we all have our bags (and now our bodies) inspected and we all have learned the signs for the WC and the way to stand in line, take our seats and buckle our seatbelts. But at the destination, tourists, even those with minimal local contact, have new culture-learning to do beyond the borders of the expected.

Tourism as a configured form of travel, a contained and predictable experience of the alien environment and culture, is not a new phenomenon, though the scale and breadth of today's tourisms exceed those of the past, whether Western or Japanese. Travel has been seen as a source of experience and transformation over time and space. There have been lists of expected sights since the days of the Roman Empire when the 'Seven Wonders of the World' were first created. Pilgrimage routes in Europe, Japan and India included known sites which were visited as sights rather than as locations for prayer, purification and sanctification. The Grand Tour was a European nineteenth-century educational rite for elite British and American young people (with proper chaperoning); travel was also prescribed for aristocratic young men whose families wanted their sons to forget an inappropriate romantic liaison or who desired that their sons build character and sow their wild oats safely (presumably anonymously) offshore.

The Japanese 'new tourisms', according to one Japanese travel agent, are now more individuated and experiential, and promise some kind of transformation – something that sticks and is not just left behind when the traveller returns home. In post-war Japan, tourism has become a common experience, all but required for middle-class people as it would have been for elites in Britain in the early twentieth century. The tourism of the 1970s and 1980s became a routinized mass experience as more people of all social classes could afford a sojourn in the US or Europe. The possibility of touring as transformative adventure was experienced only by a few marginal renegades, backpackers or *datsu-sara* (abandoning salary) second-chancers.

The popularity of the *Chikyu no Arukikata* guidebooks (nicknamed disparagingly *Chikyu no Mayoikata* – The way to get lost in the world – by Japanese guides in Italy) demonstrates an ironic contradiction: the books aim to liberate travellers from group tours into independent experiences but to guide them safely through their adventure. The places visited are the ones the bus tours visit; the restaurants often are the ones where the buses stop too. More independent and/or English-reading travellers tend to use American or Australian guidebooks such as those published by Lonely Planet, still of course presenting relatively beaten paths.

For the 'new tourists', 'Europe' is not a checklist of sites, not a ten-day tour of a day or two per country, but more specialized trips – art, *esute* ('aesthetic' body treatments), sports, automobile design, fashion – to specific places valorized and popularized in Japanese media and marketing, preparing visitors for these places with information about experiences they could (not *should*) have before returning. And, in Italy, the leading speciality tours disclose the pleasures and demands of connoisseurship in food and wine. Eating in Italy, whether it is repatriated *itameshi* (domesticated 'Italian' foods)[2] or local curiosities – *trippa* (tripe), *baccala* (salt cod) – never sampled in Japan, has become a popular reason to travel. While it is obviously a difficult experience to bring home – else why travel? – the culinary knowledge one obtains along with the bags of *funghi porcini* is seen as transformative. The new tourists bring to Italy and to their experiences of Italy-in-Japan particular modes of considering non-domestic cultural phenomena, and they also reflect particular social and economic phenomena of the moment they are in. They expect to experience, not only to visit and record the moment in photographs, and not only to mark the event by purchases of *omiyage* for others at home. All of this is expected, but it is nonetheless expected to transform the visitor.[3]

Within Japan, proliferating markets, new economic and social realities for individuals and families, and the media management of experience are all relevant to the expansion of the new tourisms and particularly to the ways in which 'Italy' has become a trend within Japan. French restaurants have morphed into Italian ones, fashions from Milan have beaten out haute couture from Paris, and travel agents compete for the huge market of especially women travelling to Italy. In August 1999, a women's theme park, Venus Fort, opened at Odaiba on Tokyo Bay featuring arcaded Italian streets, romantic cobble-stoned piazzas and even a cathedral straight out of Tuscany.[4] One performs a consumer *passeggiatta* here, not a mad dash to shop, but a stroll, as if at dusk in Rome. The (indoor) skies change, transforming from midday to a romantic sunset, as you walk the alleyways, perhaps (in an act transgressive in Japanese food etiquette) licking a *gelato* cone as you walk. The dream, as the brochures indicate, is every woman's desire to be at home and yet in Italy.

Italian travel, especially for those with interests in food and culture, has become de rigueur to satisfy a personal dream, to transform oneself for a time or perhaps permanently – and not only, as in the case of the women in the epigraphs, to confirm various trained preconceptions of the *real* Italy but also to confirm a personal and independent engagement there, whether through language study, solitary 'un-cocooned' travel, or trying foods or experiences not in the standard package. The representations of Italy in Japan are, however, sometimes exploited by those who are the objects of tourism, in this case those who present Italian foods in Italy to Japanese tourists.

Getting with the programme: red sauce for the masses

The thousands of Japanese who visit Venice every spring (particularly in the first two weeks of May) do not come to a city unprepared for them (and other tourists looking for a known Italy), and because they come in such large numbers to such a very small space they become contained, essentialized and catered to in precisely the terms they themselves expect. Venice, Rome, Florence and Milan are nearly compulsory stops for most first-time Japanese visitors, and local hotels, tourist agencies, guide services and restaurateurs are ready well before Golden Week to provide the comfort of *itameshi*.

Each winter, during the damp, cold, slow time of January and February, Venetian tourist restaurants between the Rialto and San Marco, that clogged, well-trodden path that many tourists of all nationalities never leave during their one- or two-day stay in Venice, make special accommodations for these May guests. Cooks are brought from southern Italy to Venice and prepare large quantities of their specialities, the local *sugo al pomodoro* and pasta that Japanese and others have taken for 'Italian', but that are far from the seafood, *risi e bisi, fegato alla veneziana* and other local delicacies of the northern Veneto.[5] Venetians are proud of their unique cuisine and see themselves as a special people apart, more cosmopolitan than Romans, in fact, but they are quite glad to serve up 'Italy' to these customers hungry for the tastes the 'Italy *buumu*' in Japan has created – extensions of the foods learned as 'Italian' from Americans, as well as marketed particularly for Japanese tastes in *itameshi* restaurants such as Capricciosa in Japan – and some restaurants even use the descriptions provided in *Chikyu no Arukikata* to guide their cooking of Italian foods for the Japanese visitor.

Touristic globalisms: breaking the mould or creating new ones?

We might suggest that the 'old tourism' of the Japanese, depicted as contained and protected tour groups on buses, shopping for expected *omiyage* and taking pictures of themselves in front of a predictable collection of sites visited, may represent one kind of globalization, while the 'new tourisms', plural and changing, may represent the aspects of a second – which is of course the product both of standardizing and routinizing trend creation by marketing and media, and of personal determination and the idiosyncratic mobilization of desires. Both are globalized. The first is disparaged as stuffy and *dasai* (unsophisticated) and the second glamorized as more sincere and transformative. For both, however, the evocations of the foreign involve a complicated invocation of Japan, whether as a confirmation of membership in Japanese culture directly or in a 'spun' version of an externalized nostalgia for a Japan that is said to have disappeared. In neither case, however, is 'globalization' sufficient for our understanding of the phenomenon.

If globalization is not like the Emperor's new clothes, requiring a small child to ask if it exists at all, we must ask what it is, and see if its costume provides adequate coverage. Coca-Cola and McDonald's represent post-war icons of globalization. Colonialism, imperialism, labour force movements and mass market media and communications have created the personnel, standards, goods, transport, and sense of a global 'menu' or 'recipe' that crosses borders. But the standardization of a recipe or the commonalities of a musical form do not in themselves create a wholesale transformation to what the Japanese call *mukokuseki* (no-country) or 'cultural-odour-free'[6] goods or populations. Rap music in France, Taiwan and Turkey betrays little of a common origin beyond the strong bass line.

I would suggest using 'globalizations' as shorthand (without expecting much more of it as a powerful analytic descriptor) for all the *processes* engaging peoples, practices, material cultures and ideologies with each other. These might include Appadurai's (1998) institutional and cultural 'scapes' and flows as well as the cumulative effect of the border crossers negotiating those flows. In fact, globalization as movements of peoples has itself become a commodity, with its own marketable icons. One example of this is a shop in Paris's Marais district, the old Jewish quarter, selling tchotchkes and gift items including a chessboard whose pieces are rabbis engaged in talmudic disputes: the shop's name – I am not making this up – is Diasporama.

If instead of taking as given that there is a concrete quality, substance and description called 'global' we look at it as a process and set of subjective experiences ripe for ethnographic examination – and complication – we may yet see at least a partially clothed Emperor. Noting that Japanese tourists are well prepared for at least something called 'Italian' when they arrive in Italy and noting that Italian tourist services are well prepared to give that to them is evidence of some kind of globalization, but when broken down to its components it can be seen as the result of marketing – or as the result of flows of people influenced by previous contacts, a critical mass of Italian experiences creating an audience for the Italy that they encounter and that receives them.

Yes, we can say that globalization is going on in this instance: but it defines processes and movement, not final states. It is flows and many small distinctions and transformations. It is not all headed in the same direction; the flows are from and to many centres. Saskia Sassen's *The Global City* (2001), for example, notes that there are certain shared qualities and functions among London, New York, Paris and Tokyo (so-called 'primate cities') and that these locations are both givers and receivers of flows, generating the 'global' standards (for all aspects of production and lifestyle).[7] The existence of 'global' standards, institutions and expectations doesn't make the experience of one an exact replica of another. The Bill Murray character in the film *Lost in Translation*, though seemingly desensitized by depression in a generic international hotel in Tokyo, oblivious to the 'unique' and exceptional experiences he might have (and indeed was having) in Japan, has what might be considered a universalized a-cultural existence in Japan. His companion, however, makes touristic forays into Japan, as if to illustrate that she at least can partake of the spiritual/aesthetic or simply kitschy – as in matter out of place – 'Japans' of popular conception. But for these moments, they seem to say, the film might be set anywhere.

Tourism itself, the kind undertaken to seek out the unique or special, is both evidence of marked distinctions and the device by which to channel or re-imagine or perpetuate them. In many ways it is a contradictory *counter-global* force. While it epitomizes a globalizing flow, it spotlights *differences* as a rationale for travel. Tourism depends on the attractions inherent in distinction, both 'natural' and 'imagined'. It contains also certain agreements as to what happens for and to tourists. The whole event is also contained in story-lines and imagery of a place. What has been made of Italy and its foodways, for example, for Japanese visitors by their own tourist literature and guides is a stand-in for a past Japan, a place where food, prepared by grandmother (*la cucina della nonna* in Italy), becomes emblematic of what is seen as lost in today's Japan.[8] Going to Italy as an independent traveller sets one apart as a sophisticated adventurer, even as Italy is attractive to Japanese as a displaced 'old home'. Grandmother's home cooking transformed into a red-sauce Italian pasta dish rather than the *miso shiru* of a Japanese past can provide a legitimized reason for young and older Japanese women to escape the actual kitchens of home. Making an offshore *furusato* of Italy might seem to invoke conservative values and nostalgia for an imagined past when they were intact in the home, but it can also provide the means for subversion of those values. The 'motion sickness' of a trip to one's own past is far less than the culture shock of immersion in a truly foreign land.

Notes

1   The fieldwork for this study was conducted in Bologna, Venezia, Firenze, Siena, Pisa and parts of Liguria and Toscana during October and May 1999, June 2001 and June 2002 and was further updated by visits in 2004 and 2007.

2   *Itameshi* (*Itaria no meshi*) means Italian foods as eaten in Japan. It is comparable to the transformation of Chinese foods served in ordinary *chuukaryoori* restaurants in Japan: accommodations to local tastes are performed, such as smaller portions and lighter seasoning. It is interesting to note that one chain, Capricciosa, touts its serving style as being authentically Italian: a stack of plates and bowls is put in front of one person, and if there is a woman in the party she gets them. She then serves everyone. This is a purely Japanese construction of *alla famiglia*: most Italian restaurants would not serve this way, and of course this depends on the very Japanese convention that everyone orders the same thing. Many 'italianate' dishes are prepared also for take-out from convenience stores and department stores, and several packaged mixes are available, some featuring photos of Japanese and Italian chefs sporting Italian flag colours. Italian food has taken precedence over French food recently in Japan, and Japanese French chefs are sent to Italy for retraining.

3   In Italy there are many expatriate Japanese tour guides and interpreters, as well as Japanese running cooking schools, home-stay programmes, *agriturismo* agencies and the like for Japanese visitors. The first wave of these expatriates arrived from Japan about 30 years ago, disgruntled by the failures of student activism and hoping to settle in a politically friendly environment such as communist Tuscany. They

work as guides who help 'localize' experiences for Japanese tourists in various ways, even as they themselves feel politically and culturally remote from Japan. A guide said 'I must help them see how alike Italy and Japan are, so they can relax.' One man said, 'When I go to Japan I am a visitor: I cannot "return" to Japan.' One man runs an *agriturismo* organic farm and vineyard with lodgings for Japanese groups – often farmers or residents of rural Japan – wanting an 'ecotourist' experience and home stay. He also uses the site as a work and therapy camp for troubled youth from Japan. His politics created the farm, but what the tourists come for, he says, is what they imagine Japan used to be. A Japanese guide in his fifties, taking advantage of his close ties to communist villages in the hills of Tuscany, brings random lots of Japanese tourists in busloads, whatever their actual purpose and identity, billing them as members of the Japanese Communist Party, giving mayors of these villages a chance to act as hosts to their *fratelli giapponesi* (Japanese comrades) and giving the non-Italian-speaking, unsuspecting 'communists' from Japan a gala experience of Italian hospitality.

4 See my 'La Dolce Vita – Japanese style', on Venus Fort as a perfected, feminine Italy, unpublished manuscript.

5 Tomato sauce is the universalized sine qua non of Italian food for many non-Italians, including Americans whose own popular notion of Italy came with the southern Italians who formed the first wave of immigrants to the United States. For Japanese raised in the post-war period, this same 'Italy' was introduced with the Allied Occupation, particularly by the American soldiers whose ancestors had come to the US from the Mezzogiorno, the southern, tomato-sauce-eating part of Italy. While pizza is considered in Japan to be an American *washoku* dish according to Sylvie Guichard-Anguis, pasta and other dishes are 'Italian'. For middle-aged Japanese, such as the woman in the Venetian restaurant, to eat Italian is to eat pasta with red sauce.

6 See Koichi Iwabuchi (2002).

7 Several phenomena, including the issues raised by a common currency, labour force, industrial policy, etc. among EU countries in Europe and problems affecting the management of such organizations as UNESCO in Paris, seem to indicate difficulties raised by pan-national or supra-national institutions. French cultural stipends to artists are threatened, they say, by EU regulations, as are cultural preferences for certain crops, now to be moved to more profitable zones outside France.

8 There are many points of reference for Japanese domestic ideologies in Italian food (nationalism, ruralism, cultural purity, family and mother, among others – as well as an evocation of anti-formalism, independence and youth!) as it is marketed for Japanese.

Bibliography

Appadurai, A. (1998). *Modernity at Large*. Minneapolis: University of Minnesota Press.

Befu, H. (2000). 'Thoughts on Japanese globalization'. Unpublished manuscript.

Cwiertka, Katarzyna (2000). 'Why food matters for globalization'. Unpublished manuscript.

Hannerz, U. (1992). *Cultural Complexity: Studies in the Social Organization of Meaning*. New York: Columbia University Press.

Hendry, J. (1999). 'Cultural display in museums and theme parks: a deconstruction of Western hegemony'. Paper presented at the Japan Anthropology Workshop, Osaka, Japan.

Iwabuchi, K. (2002). *Recentering Japanese Globalization: Popular Culture and Japanese Transnationalism*. Durham, NC: Duke University Press.

Martinez, D.P. (1998). *The Worlds of Japanese Popular Culture: Gender, Shifting Boundaries and Global Cultures*. Cambridge: Cambridge University Press.

Robertson, R. (1990). 'Mapping the global condition: globalization as the central concept'. In M. Featherstone (ed.), *Global Culture: Nationalism, Globalization and Modernity*. New York: Sage.

Sassen, S. (2001). *The Global City*. Princeton, NJ: Princeton University Press.

Tobin, J. (1992). *Remade in Japan: Everyday Life and Consumer Taste in a Changing Society*. New Haven, CT: Yale University Press.

Index

Note: References in *italic* are to illustrations.

.